Failed Masculinities

For Lilu and Baba, the pre- and postcolonial Indian men

Failed Masculinities
The Men in Satyajit Ray's Films

Devapriya Sanyal

EDINBURGH
University Press

Edinburgh University Press is one of the leading university presses in the UK. We publish academic books and journals in our selected subject areas across the humanities and social sciences, combining cutting-edge scholarship with high editorial and production values to produce academic works of lasting importance. For more information visit our website: edinburghuniversitypress.com

© Devapriya Sanyal, 2023, 2024

Edinburgh University Press Ltd
13 Infirmary Street, Edinburgh, EH1 1LT

First published in hardback by Edinburgh University Press 2023

Typeset in Monotype Ehrhardt by
Cheshire Typesetting Ltd, Cuddington, Cheshire

A CIP record for this book is available from the British Library

ISBN 978 1 3995 1114 8 (hardback)
ISBN 978 1 3995 1115 5 (paperback)
ISBN 978 1 3995 1116 2 (webready PDF)
ISBN 978 1 3995 1117 9 (epub)

The right of Devapriya Sanyal to be identified as author of this work has been asserted in accordance with the Copyright, Designs and Patents Act 1988 and the Copyright and Related Rights Regulations 2003 (SI No. 2498).

Contents

List of Figures	vi
Acknowledgements	viii
Introduction: Satyajit Ray's Films, his Men and the Inscription of the Nation	1
1. The Colonial and the Premodern: *Shatranj Ke Khiladi, Jalsaghar* and *Devi*	23
2. An Uncertain India: Early Nationalism in *Charulata* and *Ghare Baire*	41
3. Breaking with the Past: The Apu Trilogy	59
4. 'For all we have and are': The Post-Independence Bourgeoisie in *Kanchenjungha* and *Kapurush*	73
5. The Hollow Men: The Complacent 'Achiever' in *Nayak, Aranyer Din Ratri* and *Seemabaddha*	89
6. Trying Times: Aspiration and Failure in *Kanchenjunga, Mahanagar, Pratidwandi* and *Jana Aranya*	105
7. At Odds with the Nation: *Joy Baba Felunath, Hirak Rajar Deshe* and *Sadgati*	125
8. 'An Essay on Man': The Wise Person in *Ganashatru, Shakha Prosakha* and *Agantuk*	141
Conclusion: Moving Away from the Nation	159
Bibliography	165
Index	170

Figures

1.1	The two noblemen try various devices to keep playing their games of chess in the face of distractions	25
1.2	The clash of tradition and modernity, the old versus the new	32
2.1	Charulata eventually egged on by her brother-in-law and literary ambitions	46
2.2	Sandip and Nikhil's fight over their individual ideologies stretches to that of possessing the woman's body	51
3.1	The old and the new, the past and the present – the father and the son in *Pather Panchali*	62
3.2	Breaking with the family past of being a priest	65
3.3	Marriage as friendship and mutual respect	68
4.1	The beauty of the Himalayas with its rich flora and fauna is lost on the Ray Bahadur	80
4.2	The décor and the sartorial style of the key protagonists reveal a lot about the milieu	84
5.1	The actor who can be himself for a day	92
5.2	The game that brings them together but also divides	95
5.3	Shyamlendu revealing his most private thoughts to Tutul	97
6.1	After a few tense scenes between the couple Subrata asks Arati to resign	110
6.2	Siddhartha is unhappy with the whiff of scandal in Sutapa's conduct but stands up for her	114
6.3	Somnath, burdened by middle-class qualms, hesitates at first but he is soon overcome by Mitter's hard stance	117
7.1	The heady concoction of religion mixed with corruption and business	129
7.2	The evil king who is ultimately vanquished by the power of the good	132
7.3	The unwieldy log which refuses to yield to Dukhi's blunt axe and empty stomach	135
8.1	The two brothers, one representing corruption and greed and the other a selfless attitude to save humanity	146

8.2 The brothers at dinner with their families 148
8.3 The figure of the sage framed in a particular way that looms
large, perhaps to showcase his moral stature 152

Acknowledgements

As a first, my special thanks to my parents, without whom this writerly life wouldn't have been possible.

My deep gratitude to Gillian Leslie, my editor, for taking up the project and Sam Johnson for always answering my zillion queries regarding the publication process at EUP.

I would like to thank the anonymous peer reviewers for their extremely helpful comments which helped shape the manuscript.

My extended family, my brother, and our helper at home Anjali Mashi deserve many thanks for putting up with me in spite of the many tantrums I threw while writing this book. Simba, my beloved pup, deserves a special mention for keeping me distracted and not letting the burden of writing get to me.

Martin Shingler for guiding me to this excellent press and for his kind words, always.

I am forever beholden to M. K. Raghavendra for having taught me cinema, especially Indian cinema and how to read it politically.

Introduction
Satyajit Ray's Films, his Men and the Inscription of the Nation

Satyajit Ray: Bengali, Indian or International?

This book is about Satyajit Ray's cinema with a focus on his male characters, but the first issue to be resolved – before all others are taken up – is where he belongs as a filmmaker. The question concerns whether he was Bengali, and primarily attached to local Bengal culture since he often described himself as 'Bengali' rather than Indian; 'Indian' since he was one of independent India's most prestigious cultural exports; or 'international' because of his acceptance as auteur at the international level, unmatched by any other Indian filmmaker. This is an issue of importance not only because it has been debated, but because his cultural location as a director would also influence our reading of his films. At the international level, films from unfamiliar cultures bear the burden of representing more than the story elements, including character and the immediate milieu, while representations of dominant groups are seen as indicative of diversity.[1] It has been suggested that Ray unconsciously 'represented' a unique place – Nishchindipur – when he used the music associated with the village in *Pather Panchali* to accompany a different village in its sequel, *Aparajito*.[2] It is, of course, simplistic to read the use of the same music in this way, as implying congruity between the two spaces, but we may still say that whenever a space is photographed, it can in a sense 'represent' an abstraction as well – a village dwelling representing *the* village dwelling. In India itself early photographic portraits, it has been noted, were painted over to reintroduce decorative elements that preceded photography,[3] to turn the individual into an archetype like a landowner or a matriarch rather than merely an ordinary individual, and even spaces in this sense could become abstractions. Since the village Nishchindipur is not of great interest in the film, perhaps even Indians are justified in regarding it as an 'Indian village' despite characteristics specific to Bengal, even though cultural theorists may frown upon this.[4] Popular cinema in India has consistently represented villages as national abstractions, for instance Ramgarh in *Sholay*.

This notion of what a portrayal is 'representative' of is a complicated one and, in the largest sense, Ray was international; David Bordwell has convincingly shown[5] that along with directors like Akira Kurosawa and Ingmar Bergman, he belongs to the 'art cinema', an international category created by post-war exhibition conditions largely driven by the film festivals in which the multi-film work (like 'The Apu Trilogy') is an essential part. At the other end, his is a regional Bengali cinema, and Neepa Majumdar[6] has argued that the reception to Ray in Bengal has been influenced by his work for children and juvenile audiences, such as his detective films and children's stories as well as his work as an illustrator. She cites his humour in *Pather Panchali*, reminiscent of the magazine *Sandesh* (founded by Ray's grandfather), in which the presence of rain is announced by a drop descending on the bald head of a dozing man. In this book Ray is treated as a 'national' filmmaker, since he was important in defining the culture of a newly independent country, but this is a conscious choice, since he could be regarded differently with equal justification – although this would lead to other conclusions. At the same time, the book does not treat him as 'iconic' in relation to the nation, since his position vis-à-vis the establishment kept changing throughout his lifetime. What remained consistent, however, was Ray's commitment to a certain liberal view of what the nation should be, which he saw being abandoned by politics in the mid-part of his career.

The issue of modernity becomes important when dealing with Ray's cinema, since Nehruvian modernity is largely the context in which his films are examined in this book. In writing about Ray's engagement with modernity, Ravi Vasudevan notes that rather than playing out 'a "destinal" narrative' that provides a 'redemptive identification' with modernity for the protagonist, Ray was in a dialogue with modernity, split in the forms of subjectivity it gave rise to:

> Rather than see Ray playing out a 'destinal' narrative that provides for a redemptive and authenticating identification with modernity for the protagonist, I want to suggest that he was involved in a rather more complicated dialogue with the modern, showing it to be necessarily and irreducibly split in the forms of subjectivity it gave rise to. In a sense this is the condition of modernity, and authentication lies in the articulation of a split position which constantly gestures to some antecedent self that has been displaced and is in danger of entirely disappearing from consciousness. The force of this particular modernist move lies in the bid not only to find a form that can articulate this splitting and hold on to both parts, but in determinedly seeking out

the repressed dimensions of that former self, and laying claim, on behalf of modernity, to the ability to bring it into view.[7]

Rephrased, Apu's gaze in *Pather Panchali* is not simply a 'modern' one but one with stable cultural antecedents, a perhaps repressed side that will be revealed under scrutiny. This becomes particularly evident in the third part of The Apu Trilogy and will be examined in due course. This split between the atomised 'modern citizen' and the burden of the past he or she carries is a recurring concern in the book and the individual chapters demonstrate where this led Ray's films in his later career. Ray's preoccupation was with modernity but he was not, as has been contrarily argued, a 'modernist' with an avant-garde agenda.[8] His influences were Hollywood and Jean Renoir, which are 'classical'. The modernists and the avant-garde (like the early Bunuel and Germaine Dulac, who made *The Seashell and the Clergyman*) tried to break with past forms of expression in a way that Ray did not, although his form of filmmaking departed from cinematic practice in India. The early avant-garde filmmakers (who worked in silent cinema) were also cosmopolitan and their influence declined with the growth of the national cinemas,[9] while Ray was steeped in local culture and the aim of this book is partly to examine his involvement in the nation.

The Nation and National Cinema

'National cinema' alongside genre and auteur is a key way of categorising the cinemas of the world. It seems necessary to try and make sense of what a nation is, before going on to discuss ways of writing the 'national'. Most political scientists are agreed on two fundamental issues – first, that of all the political doctrines, the 'national' is the one that most lacks a founding father, and second, that it is notoriously difficult to define despite the fact that as a term it has such common currency. Benedict Anderson, perhaps offering the most succinct definition of the modern nation, regards it as 'an imagined political community – and imagined as both inherently limited and sovereign.'[10] Throughout history, there has been a constant interaction between social organisation and culture. By definition, culture is a term that refers both to material production (artefacts) and to symbolic production (the aesthetic). In both instances, culture functions as the record and reflection of social history and the social process. Therefore, concepts of nation and national identity are also bound up in this socio-cultural functioning.

Concepts of nation and national identity, when they are perceived in terms of socio-political processes and the cultural/cinematic articulations of these processes, inevitably mean that cinema speaks the national and the national speaks cinema. In other words, within the specific context addressed here, film functions as a cultural articulation of a nation (even if it subverts it, it still addresses/reflects it, albeit oppositionally). In so doing, film textualises the nation and subsequently constructs a series of relations around the concepts; firstly, of state and citizen, then of state, citizen and the other (such as the 'foreign'). In this way, cinema – a 'national' cinema – is inescapably 'reduced' to a series of enunciations that reverberate around two fundamental concepts: identity and difference.

Culture is made up of art, among other things. That art, however, is almost unexceptionally class-inflected within Western societies – and even in India, which is an erstwhile colony – and is predominantly middle-class in its constitution. Therefore, issues of identity in discourses will be primarily framed and focused within that particular notion of a 'national' identity. National identity and, thereby, unity will tend to mean middle-class consensus; the rest will be difference/otherness.

As one can see, the concepts of nation bring it very close to myth, since it is a mental construction that claims to be a reality. The point here is that the 'unreal' nation had to be imagined to give people a secure sense of identity. In the writing of a national cinema, therefore, there are two fundamental yet crucial axes of reflection to be considered. First, how is the 'national' enunciated? In other words, what are the texts and what meanings do they in turn mobilise? And, secondly, how does one enunciate the national or, expressed more simply, what is there, what does it mean, and how do we write its meaning? What needs to be studied is how the particular cinema contributes to the construction of the nation. Graeme Turner, whose work focused on national fictions, becomes particularly important here, since (relying on Claude Levy Strauss) he makes the point that the narratives of a country are produced by its indigenous culture, which performs a reflexive role in order to understand its own signification – in other words, 'narration is a culture's way of understanding itself'.[11]

The Creation of the National Subject by Culture

India's is a postcolonial society rather than a 'decoloniality'. Postcoloniality, it has been theorised, emerged largely in the academy. In India, modernity/ coloniality did not produce an oppositional stance in the colonised intelligentsia to begin with, as large segments of the intelligentsia, in the initial phase, accepted the superiority of Western thought in different ways. It was only with the emergence of nationalist consciousness in the latter part of the nineteenth century that an oppositional discourse began to take shape. Decoloniality produced the tradition of Frantz Fanon, C. L. R. James and Aime Cesaire[12] as radical opposition to colonialism. Satyajit Ray was a product of postcolonial society, a creation of the liberal intelligentsia that inherited power from the colonialists peacefully, although postcolonialism did make a significant contribution in terms of its re-examination of Western knowledge in its relation with the colonised world. Ray's successful adoption of Western filmmaking practice while dealing with indigenous reality is a kind of synthesis that begins with an interrogation of both the way the West represented India in cinema and the way Indian cinema represented its own reality.

The creation of the national community has, by Benedict Anderson, been traced to the advent of the novel and the newspaper,[13] and we may see the education system instituted by the British as playing a part in the creation of the 'national subject' – both education in English and in the Indian languages – and it was hence among the highly educated classes that the 'nation' was first imagined. The educated classes who imagined the nation may then be taken to be the earliest national subjects. The readers of literature – both in English and Indian languages – would be the first among them. The printing press was the key to the creation of nationalist sentiment in India under the British, through the printing of novels and newspapers in English and the Indian languages, notably in the Presidency towns. The colonialists, eager to keep in touch with the home country, imported large quantities of popular fiction. Some of the books found their way into elite Indian homes[14] from which the writerly class in India emerged. Fiction was written both in English and the local languages, but it was in Indian language literature that nationalism emerged.[15] This is something Ray takes note of in *Charulata* (1964), which portrays the period.

The national subject was hence first created by literature – more so in the local language than in English, because of the possible threat of prosecution for sedition hanging over English language writing. Expressions of nationalism are virtually absent in cinema before 1947, although theorists have seen incipient nationalism in Indian cinema even in the Phalke era.[16] Still, that is more a matter of excavating such significance through interpretation, with mythological motifs seen as incipient nationalism. Cinema – given the urban conditions of exhibition – was more visible than language literature (which often emerged from small towns), which made it vulnerable to state action before Independence. Ray's films – which appeared only in the post-Independence era – have never been described as 'nationalist', but they still had a significant role to play in national culture after Independence. Ray may have been Bengali, but 'Bengaliness' was not a cultural project the way the 'national' was, and Satyajit Ray's family had been at the periphery of nationalism since the 1920s.

Satyajit Ray as a National Filmmaker

Satyajit Ray's family, although steeped in literature, was initially not at the forefront of nationalist activity and was deeply interested in Western arts and culture; yet, from the days of the *swadeshi* movement onwards, they became sympathetic to the nationalist cause. Satyajit Ray's grandfather, Upendrakishore Ray, was politically moderate and hence loyal to the British Empire. Like other moderates of the early twentieth century, however, he participated in protests against Viceroy Lord Curzon's arbitrary division of the Bengal Presidency in 1905. Satyajit's father Sukumar Ray was outwardly apolitical, but that did not deter him from poking fun at colonialism in his early plays, and composing at least one song calling for national resurgence.

Ray, much like his father, did not show much overt interest in political nationalism during his adolescence and early working years. Ray, who worked in a British-owned advertising agency in the 1940s, got on well with his British bosses but felt it anti-national to trumpet the virtues of foreign-made soap, oil and toothpaste.

None of his attitudes towards colonialism were, of course, immediately perceptible in Ray's celebrated first film, *Pather Panchali* (1955). However, critics have seen it – along with *Aparajito* and *Apur Sansar*, the other films of The Apu Trilogy – as reflecting and complementing the optimistic Nehruvian vision of a new, progressive India. This is in spite of the fact that the films were set in the 1930s and 40s and despite the complete absence in the films of the dams, irrigation projects and machinery that characterised the high hopes of Nehru's India, and which featured prominently in such films as Mehboob Khan's *Mother India* (1957). But Nehru was a steadfast supporter of the young filmmaker and Ray, on his part, admired Nehru deeply and even contemplated making a short documentary which would help the Prime Minister raise national morale during the 1962 war with China. This mutual admiration had little to do with such typically Nehruvian projects as state socialism or industrialisation, but stemmed more from the cosmopolitan liberalism that Ray saw in Nehru and the artistic sensibility that he detected in the Prime Minister's writings.[17] Nehru had a delicate understanding of the need for social and religious liberalism in his vast and disparate society. It was his liberal, rather than his socialist, political judgement that characterised the Pandit's rule[18] and it was this liberal, Westernised Nehru that Ray chiefly admired.

With *Pather Panchali* becoming a success in the West, Satyajit Ray became a leading filmmaker of the 'Third World' in the 1950s. In various nations with a colonial legacy there arose individual 'auteurs', usually members of the postcolonial elite, who tried to create national cinemas, which despite being based on the Hollywood model in what could be described as 'realist' styles, explored social and domestic life in the Third World hitherto explored before. The filmmakers of this group (who often acknowledged the influence of Italian Neo-realism), aside from Ray, included Fernando Birri from Brazil, Leopoldo Torre Nillson from Argentina, Tomas Alea and Humberto Solas from Cuba, Antonio Eugenio from Bolivia, Youssef Chahine from Egypt and Lester Peries from Ceylon (later Sri Lanka). The cinema represented by this group of auteurs has, by and large, been most respected, partly because it strongly opposed the 'mindless escapism' of the Third World commercial cinema contemporary to it and could be judged by aesthetics familiar to the West.[19]

Ray, often described as being among the last of India's Renaissance men, because of his versatility, was also one of the last great representatives of a movement for India triggered by the coming of the British, through whom outward-looking Indians made their first contact with the Western civilisation and culture. The *bhadralok* class to which Ray belonged was a Western-educated elite whose concerns were primarily democracy, nationalism, social equality and the emancipation of women, but they were also brought up on world literature which favoured realism and mimesis.[20]

Ray was a product of this culture, with Western antecedents and audiences recognising international filmmaking practices in Ray's cinema.[21] This was perhaps the first moment when Ray got a measure of how successful he would be in translating lessons in filmmaking which he had imbibed entirely by watching Hollywood films, although Jean Renoir, with whom Ray worked on *The River* (1951), advised him not to imitate Hollywood.[22] If we were to identify what Ray did in *Pather Panchali*, it was to find the means to be true to Indian reality but in film language recognisable outside India.[23] That Ray has not had a successor of his stature recognised suggests that the film language he was employing was not 'Indian' so much as acceptable to international film practice. But on the flip side, he has not found wide acceptance within India outside the film clubs and those attuned to international cinema, and he has not been influential even among art filmmakers, as comparisons with other Indian films made in this book's chapters will show. Ravi Vasudevan's view of Ray's 'double-take' was not quite recognised by Indian audiences, although thinkers like Amartya Sen, whose field is outside cinema, have acknowledged this aspect.[24]

Jawaharlal Nehru's concept of a modern India was to use the state creatively to reconstitute Indian society, reforming it and bringing it in line with what he took to be the movement of universal history.[25] Nehru was a socialist who preferred the developmental model based on planning. By the mid-1950s Nehru achieved some actual success in putting into practice his ideas of development. The years between 1950 and 1962 were given to optimism, and Jawaharlal Nehru's foreign policy initiatives played a key role in building up the national self-esteem. Ray's own trajectory in filmmaking or choice of subject matter was in tune with this, in the sense that it tried to integrate Indian culture with the West as had hitherto not been done. One could even propose that his 'internationalist' idiom was much more suited to Nehruvian dreams of India's position in the world.

For Satyajit Ray, Italian Neo-realism, which had also been trying in its own way to participate and also recalibrate the project of nationhood after Italy's defeat in the War, proved to be a useful model and *Pather Panchali* bears influences of that – namely synthesising a language of cinema able to express exclusively what was observed in Indian reality. After 1947 the state began paying attention to cultural policy and, although Ray may not have articulated it, a careful study of his films shows that they still address the following questions that policy was taken up with:

(a) the position that the state and the cultural establishment took with regard to a form such as a national cinema in mobilising a national fantasy around Independence;
(b) positioning itself in the hierarchy of already established arts such as literature and other visual arts;
(c) their role in determining and influencing the public and public cultural policy at the same time.

That modern Indian art had undertaken such a project has been brought out by Bhaskar Sarkar, who argues for what he terms the 'construal of national culture and heritage, its discourses and practices seeking to form an aesthetic canon'.[26]

Popular Cinema and the Nation

Ray's cinema differed from popular cinema in many ways, although nationhood was already inscribed in it. Since nationhood was an existing notion even before 1947, there was a sense of shared nationhood among the educated and Ray could not but have been drawn into that like many of the other filmmakers of the Third World, but in a different idiom from that of popular cinema. What is also perhaps significant is the fact that India as a nation had never been absent in these portrayals, but rather had been represented only covertly or allegorically. In the years immediately following Independence in 1947, Indian cinema was caught up in the endeavour of nation-building, offering narratives that lay out in detail the challenges and choices facing its audiences. Popular cinema had contributed to a 'pre-national' cinema in a way, since it was already suturing differences and addressing national issues current at the time, although the nation was yet to be. For instance, the motif of the weak man and strong woman in films like Mehboob Khan's *Aurat* (1940) and P. C. Barua's *Devdas* (1935) has been attributed to a common crisis of masculinity,[27] traced to the ordering of sexualities under colonialism.[28]

Still, historical questions are not directly posed and the concerns have to be interpreted. *Mother India* may fleetingly invoke irrigation projects, but little else in its narrative addresses the 'contemporary'.[29] Ray's cinema is important both for what it says about the nation's contemporary history and for what it reveals about its past in its historical interpretation – as opposed to popular historical films like *Mughal-e-Azam* (1960), in which history is turned into a costume drama based around forbidden love. Hindustan is invoked in this film and others from before 1947, like *Humayun* (1945) – in which the loyalty of the Muslim ruler to India is affirmed – but Ray's films explicitly locate themselves at defined historical moments and engage with the issues of the times. They are not, by and large, allegorical as popular films have been. *Pather Panchali* may seem the noteworthy exception here, but that will be discussed later.

Popular cinema used melodrama as its only mode, right up to the commencement of the new millennium, in a way that Ray did not. Since there is some disagreement as to this,[30] it is necessary to define melodrama clearly. Melodrama is seen to engage in strong emotionalism, moral polarisation, extreme situations and actions, overt villains, inflated or extravagant expression, abrupt changes in fortune, dark plotting and suspense and persecution of the good, but alongside an ultimate reward for virtue.[31] None of this is true of Ray's films, but it is certainly true of popular cinema. Popular cinema uses the melodramatic element in the service of its allegorical role, as for instance, the mother in *Deewar* (1975) sanctioning the killing of her criminal son by her other son, a police officer.[32] What popular cinema appears to do with history is not to 'document' it so much as present it in the timeless language of myth, in the effort to make ongoing history understandable to tradition. Since this renders popular cinema's characters as archetypes from mythology,[33] what is proposed about Ray's films in this book cannot evidently be done with popular cinema.

Ray's films are most readily seen as adaptations of literature – usually important or contemporary novels – and, unlike much of the art cinema that followed his work, they are exercises in storytelling that draw from human experience, not explicitly taken up with 'social issues'. They mostly deal with transitions in society and important historical moments such as the decline of the landed aristocracy (*Jalsaghar*, 1958), the Bengal Renaissance (*Charulata*, 1964), the Naxalite movement (*Pratidwandi*, 1970) and the Swadeshi movement (*Ghare Baire*, 1984) to name a few, all of these being part of the historical experience or memories of the past. Most of the others – for instance *Pratidwandi* in the above – are located in the *historical present*, notable exceptions being the children's films and the detective stories, which include no such identifiable markers. Ray, as will be brought out, made extensive changes in adapting literature and the sources furnish his films with a point of focus, but the sources' authors cannot be considered co-authors of the films the way Shakespeare would be for a film adaptation of one of his great tragedies, for which faithfulness is a perennial issue. The original work here becomes more relevant for the changes Ray makes, as will become evident in the discussion of films like *Shatranj Ke Khiladi*, based on Premchand's Hindi short story.

Pather Panchali and its precursors

Bibhutibhushan Bandopadhyay's novel, as distinct from Ray's film, highlights the man-nature bond, as a way to celebrate the land and its people. In comparison, Satyajit Ray's film is a more complex take on the narrative, conveying it to some other level with a different thrust. At first glance there are no historical references in the film and Ray hardly brings in 'independent India' as a motif. But one senses that the film could not have been made before 1947 and it takes a while for us to understand why; it is as if the sense of independent nationhood is somehow inscribed in it.

The freedom afforded by the form devised by Ray to pack a simple storyline with evidence of the times through emblems pertaining to modernity, the motif of individual growth alongside the linear development of character and the angular probing of inner emotions. As an indication of its attention to classical narration, there are few Indian films from outside of Ray's own oeuvre in which the sense of a definite chartable space emerges as clearly as Harihar Ray's humble abode in *Pather Panchali*.

Ray infused the outlines of this source with more contemporary influences, essentially with less celebration than the novelist. Even as Ray retains the purity of vision of *Pather Panchali*'s author, he removes the 'sonar bangla' sheen that Bandopadhyay had interwoven into his text, replacing it with a grimmer reality, representative of what was then Bengal. Ray imbues his text with a harshness missing from the romantic Bandopadhyay's text, and this may have been interpreted politically as his 'peddling Indian poverty in the West', as opposed to focusing on India's modern aspects as represented by irrigation projects.[34] But the film is hardly a reversal of the novelist's purpose; as Chidananda Dasgupta acknowledges, 'He shares Bibhutibhushan's Hindu view of life as a continuum, a flow in which loss and gain are two sides of the same coin …'[35] The film has a metaphysics that a sole focus on 'depiction of poverty' does not take into account, and which is given a new emphasis that conveys the arrival of 'modernity'.

As already indicated, Ray became part of a fraternity of artists in Nehru's India who tried to define a national culture. The idea of artists being co-opted into the project of cultural nationhood is usually viewed with suspicion by left-wing cultural ideologues. To problematise the distrust and suspicion, the issue with 'national culture' in a country like India is that the national culture that is sought to be created and held up to the world is high culture, while the vast multitude lives at a substantially lower cultural level. Geeta Kapur, in her book *When was Modernism?*, holds up Ritwik Ghatak[36] chiefly because he was directly addressing post-Independence contradictions instead of celebrating Independence. A key issue brought up is that *Pather Panchali* is set in the colonial era, but the colonial consciousness is not addressed and the village appears to be from the historical present and a product of the consciousness created by this, rather than from the colonial past:

> The Apu trilogy is replete with symbols of colonial India in which it is temporally placed, but the colonial (like the national) consciousness is not really addressed. The village as a pristine community of precolonial India is linked directly with the sense of the historical present, Ray's own contemporary India, where the nation is the determining but invisible trajectory in the wake of which the individual can at last be valorized.[37]

It is undoubtedly true that the happenings in *Pather Panchali* are difficult to 'place' historically. In adapting a novel from 1929 in 1955, he invoked neither colonialism nor independent India. We are left reading the film as an allegory of the independent nation almost by default. Bibhutibhushan did not explicitly invoke colonialism in the novel, and Ray may have only been trying to be faithful to him, but Kapur's charges still merit scrutiny. She argues that Ray's film is actually the opposite of an allegory of

Nehru's India and even backs this up by proposing that it is an allegory by default,[38] in that it was a narrativisation of the self via the nation; reading it as allegory is reading one thing for another, which the work may or may not sustain. This allegorical interpretation of *Pather Panchali* may not be easy for the reader to grasp, but Apu, in one's reckoning, could be symbolic of the new nation when he rejects the old ways of his forefathers, namely in rejecting the path of becoming a traditional Brahmin priest, and actually making his way by getting a college education and relocating to the city to eventually become an author. This movement from village to city can also be seen as a movement towards modernity, since the city was an emblem of modernity in Nehruvian reckoning and features heavily in 1950s cinema. While Bibhutibhushan's novel is a more personal rendition of Apu's journey, in Ray's hands it tacitly becomes 'national allegory'. In fact, it would not be far-fetched to describe the film as a bildungsroman of sorts – both for Apu and the new nation.[39]

Still, it should be noted that Ray has himself never insisted that his intent in the film was allegorical, and that is entirely our reading. It is a fact that there is no portrayal of socio-economic relationships in the film and the single relationship outside the family is the one with the rich neighbour, with whom Harihar's family has no economic dependency. What we see is 'village life' through some assorted characters and landscapes in which neither colonial life nor the independent nation are implicated. 'Allegory of independence' is therefore simply the sense of an unfettered consciousness visible in the film, Apu (literally) opening his eyes to a fresh world and not one burdened by immiseration. Harihar's family is poor, but poverty owing to exploitation is hardly what the film is about. It has, rather, a metaphysics pertaining to death and renewal instead of a socially constructed universe, which is perhaps what demarcates the film from the kind of Western realism emanating from countries such as Italy.

Satyajit Ray and Literature

Since the nation was first inscribed in India's literature, Ray's films naturally drew from the writings of others. Ray was instrumental in conveying the culture of Bengal (as depicted in Bibhutibhushan's novel) in the realm of cinema. The differences between Ray's films and their literary counterparts were not merely those between the medium of the novel and that of film. The characters and even the emotions remained the same, but, to them, Ray brought in coherence and linearity and a certain sense of history. He contextualised and made concrete some of these timeless tales.

Ray's India in the film may be influenced by Bibhutibhushan, but – and this is Geeta Kapur's criticism – it still corresponds to a contemporary India of Ray's times as allegory. It is Apu's footsteps which 'mark the transition of an impoverished but literate and gracefully poised culture of perennial India'[40] towards modernity. But it may have been the last film of Ray's in which the context is not directly specified. None of his later films after The Apu Trilogy can be read as allegory in entirely the same way, since there are some historical markers, but these will be examined later in the book.

The important thing for this book, however, is the fact that Ray, throughout his career as a filmmaker, went about creating characters by adapting from literature, often from novels written after 1947. One recognises in them Indians from the post-Independence era, usually (to quote Geeta Kapur) '"self-regarding" members of the middle-class intelligentsia';[41] one can even see them as models for the kind of educated citizenry that newly independent India was producing, suggested by film critics worldwide in reviews such as that of *Aranyer Din Ratri* (1970) by Pauline Kael in the New Yorker.[42] Categorising these characters and relating them to the milieu is what this book is exploring, and the rationale is that Ray's portrayal of men paints a picture of India's trajectory from the colonial period to contemporary times. But to his study of men, Ray brought in a certain kind of detachment, a very different approach to that which he brought to his women. Since he was describing a patriarchal society, his feminine portrayals are overlaid with a sense of what is socially desirable, while his men are entirely products of detached yet incisive observation. But on closer scrutiny, the masculinity of his male characters is still problematised repeatedly.

Masculinity and its Significance

Any study of film motifs and their significance relies implicitly on prior studies of Hollywood, simply because Hollywood has been studied so extensively. Important academic studies of Hindi cinema have hence drawn on work on American melodrama and noir,[43] for instance those by Marcia Landy and Sylvia Hartley. The role played by the male characters in inscribing the nation in Hollywood films has been studied in relation to the times. Men being away during the war, for instance, created a crisis which engendered the motif of the absent father,[44] in turn causing a psychological crisis for their children, as depicted in certain films by Hitchcock (*Notorious*, *Psycho*). It should be evident from these that the importance of the male presence (or absence) does not show itself only in the machismo of popular cinema's indomitably masculine heroes, but is also manifested in the woman (like the femme fatale in noir), since masculinity itself is provoked by the woman, either onscreen or offscreen. As earlier indicated, the weak man in Indian cinema of the 1930s and 1940s manifests itself in the strong woman. It is the same in Ray's films, in that in most of them, the men – who are often wanting – reveal themselves in feminine strength.

If locating this book in the context of masculinity theory is necessary, the filmic construction of masculinity has been examined in relation to four key areas:[45] the body, as in epics and adventure films in which the male body is connotative of power and strength; in the all-action movies where there is a sexualisation of male violence; in relation to the external world, where 'proper' men exercise authority and behave courageously in adversity and sport and chivalrously towards ladies; and, lastly, in their inward selves when there is a mismatch between what men aspire to be and what they are. The resulting inadequacies are caused by the disjuncture between the demands made upon them and their incapacity to fulfil them. This last aspect is perhaps most important to us, since masculinity is there in the nature of an impossible fiction,[46] which is sometimes the sense in Ray's films.

Before we look at Ray's films, we need to consider popular cinema as a space with a much more transparent relationship with the dominant ideology. Although we find that not much work has been done on the subject of masculinity in Indian cinema, the intimate relationship between masculinity and the nation has been duly noted:

> Hindi cinema's narratives are unfailingly centered on a hero and heroine, who together constitute its fundamental templates in which masculinity is the flip side of femininity. Changes in masculinity in repose to the nation's history are discussed in popular Hindi film criticism. An aspect of constructing masculinity is the hero's role as a primary agent shaping the nation's history. Like all heroes, the Hindi film hero upholds the law; or, on occasion, he is the heroic outlaw.[47]

Examining popular Hindi cinema in terms of the four key areas discussed earlier, the male body – Dharmendra earlier and Salman Khan later – is in the service of the nation. The Salman Khan starrer *Bharat* (2019) virtually traces the protagonist's life through national history, beginning with Independence. Action films – which are increasingly patriotic like *Uri: The Surgical Strike* (2019) – use all-male action in the same way. The dastardliest villains in popular Hindi films, it should be noted, are 'national enemies' in that their primary hate objects are national emblems. In *Sholay* (1975), which has the most celebrated villain in Hindi film history,

Gabbar hates the state and its officials. The destruction of the villain is done one-on-one by an armless former policeman.

When we come to the third category, best exemplified by the leader (e.g.: *Lagaan*, 2001) or the loner who struggles against all odds (e.g. Amitabh Bachchan as the Angry Young Man in *Deewar* (1975)), we find that in the former case, the leader directs a community that can be taken to allegorise the nation, since it includes the nation's constituent categories in terms of religion and caste. In the case of the loner, he comes into conflict with the nation state that destroys him – even while doing so regretfully. In this film it is the criminal's brother, the policeman, who is responsible for his death. There is a sense of misplaced masculinity in films, cut from the mold but tinged by admiration.

As regards the last category of failed masculinity, the archetype would be the earliest *Devdas* (1935), made in the colonial era and, it can be argued, representing the colonial exchange as that between a weak son and a stern father. In the postcolonial era, the motif of weak masculinity is rare, since it would imply weak nationhood, but it has been noted in two films – Guru Dutt's *Jaal* (1952) and *Baazigar* (1993) – which have interpreted as conveying the distance of the moral state from the action.[48]

The weak state in 1980s cinema is not interpreted through the motif of failed masculinity, but through notions like vigilante justice[49] and vengeance for rape. It may be useful to here invoke a film about rape, *Insaaf Ka Tarazu* (1980), which heralded these portrayals. In the film a raped woman kills the man who raped her when he also rapes her younger sister. There is a key opening section in which a military man (played by Dharmendra, known for his portrayals of masculinity) kills a rapist in the act and then defends his action in court, saying that dishonouring a woman is akin to dishonouring the motherland. I propose that ultimately, the most masculine people represent the nation.

But the issue here is whether Ray's films can be studied using the same template as indicated above, especially through the last category. The difference is that where masculinity is weak in Ray's films, it arguably reinforces a critique of the independent nation. There is no such critique in popular films of the post-colonial era. Ray's films admit patriarchy at the outset and, after placing men in positions of control, often show them failing at the roles that they have apportioned to themselves, which provides the women with unusual roles that society itself has not traditionally given them. Since Ray's cinema is exceptional and does not readily fit masculinity theory as do the more popular/quotidian works of Indian cinema, it would be useful here to cite Noel Carroll's argument about the differences between theory and interpretation in film study:

> There are no grounds for thinking that film theory must have anything to do with film interpretation in every case. Indeed, in many cases, one would anticipate that the two activities would have to part company. Film theory speaks of the general case, whereas film interpretation deals with problematic or puzzling cases, or with the highly distinctive cases of cinematic masterworks. Film theory tracks the regularity and the norm, while film interpretation finds its natural calling in dealing with the deviation, with what violates the norm or with what exceeds it or what reimagines it. [50]

Therefore, rather than try to fit Ray's cinema – its portrayal of men and women chiefly – into the paradigm of masculinity theory, what is proposed here is to examine the films primarily, with what has just been said about the portrayals of masculinity in Indian cinema in mind. In order to be certain of this, references will be made to other kinds of cinema, in particular Hindi popular cinema, since that is also a 'national cinema' but one with very different kinds of representation. If popular film representations connote dominant attitudes, Ray's differences will mark him out as the exception.

Chapterisation

As already indicated, this book tries to look at the trajectory of Indian history by examining the construction of Satyajit Ray's masculine characters, seen in relation to the women. The book has been divided into chosen time frames, which also correspond with certain key moments in history as depicted by Ray. Needless to add, they do not reflect on the trajectory of the nation nor its teleology, but on Ray's own subjective rendering of it given his own attachment to Nehruvian ideas, of which the chapters take note.

Chapter 1: The Colonial and the Premodern: Shatranj Ke Khiladi, Jalsaghar *and* Devi

This is a chapter in which I examine Ray's portrayal of colonialism and the subjects created by it, the subjects of a colonial power which is making way for an independent nation and bestowing a new identity upon them. They are a dying breed caught between tradition and colonial modernity, as the circumstances they find themselves in are about to give way to a newer state of being. Masculinity through the overt dominance of one male viewpoint over another is a key motif.

Chapter 2: An Uncertain India: Early Nationalism in Charulata *and* Ghare Baire

I look at these figures who have interacted with the colonial power and absorbed its ways, but have also felt the stirrings of a nascent nationalism within themselves. These characters could also be reflecting on the first reformers of nineteenth-century Bengal as it tried to break free of tradition. The men are engaged in anticipating what it means to be citizens of a nation – instead of subjects of the colonial power – and how to understand nationhood. These films also speculate on the zeitgeist of nineteenth-century India. The women become more important here and the chapter reflects upon that, with regard to the meaning of weak masculinity.

Chapter 3: Breaking with the Past: The Apu Trilogy

Pather Panchali literally put India on the world map when it won several international awards and, in a way, came to depict the highest form of Indian artistic effort in cinema as acknowledged by the West. What has got less attention is that it can be read as a national allegory by portraying the maturing of a young boy from a family steeped in tradition, who awakens to modernity and embarks upon an independent path. This chapter focuses on the entire trilogy as the biography of a young man who gives up his family vocation to become a writer, and what this implies. Apu the adult becoming a writer but abandoning this upon his marriage is a motif that will be examined.

Chapter 4: 'For all we have and are': The Post-Independence Bourgeoisie in Kanchenjungha *and* Kapurush

This chapter reflects on the class of men created out of the interaction with the British in colonial times, who, in other words, represented the post-Independence bourgeoisie. They are a breed of men who are anachronistic in contemporary times because of their nostalgia for an erstwhile British state in India, which is felt by them to be superior to the India run by Indians, and still carry prestige associated with British rule in a certain class.

Chapter 5: The Hollow Men: The Complacent 'Achiever' *in* Nayak, Aranyer Din Ratri *and* Seemabaddha

Even as the 1960s and 1970s created large scale dissatisfaction, this period favoured the few, who had frequently to shed their earlier ideals.

This chapter looks at this class of men that emerged in the turbulent 70s, who share certain common characteristics in that they favour personal advancement and are willing to play the game as long as it benefits them. A feminine presence is introduced into the narrative as a way of interrogating masculinity.

Chapter 6: *Trying Times: Aspiration and Failure in* Kanchenjunga, Mahanagar, Pratidwandi *and* Jana Aranya

This chapter looks at the post-Independence male subjects in the modern Indian city, represented by Calcutta, as they negotiate their way through pitfalls and frustrations, even as the Nehruvian dreams of 'modern India' falter morally after Nehru's demise in 1964 and a new era emerges with scarce opportunities. Here again, the position of the women reflects upon the failure of masculinity. While the men are roughly contemporary to those in Chapter 5, they are regarded separately by Ray.

Chapter 7: *At Odds with the Nation:* Joy Baba Felunath, Hirak Rajar Deshe *and* Sadgati

The five-year period between 1979–1984 may be considered a period of decline for Ray within India, since he was apparently sidelined under Mrs Gandhi, perhaps for having been critical of her party. The three films examined here are among his least ambitious. He received the Dada Saheb Phalke Award – given to important film personalities – only in 1985, after Mrs Gandhi's death. What masculinity means in this context would also be significant.

Chapter 8: *'An Essay on Man': The Wise Person in* Ganashatru, Shakha Prosakha *and* Agantuk

This is the chapter in which I deal with Ray's last three films, which constitute a statement on civilisation as he saw it, much in the same vein as Rabindranath Tagore's. The wise men in them, in some way, reflect on Satyajit Ray's own self-image and are a consequence of his mythical stature. They are based on screenplays written by him and have the appearance of the testament of a sage who has counsel to offer to his fellow citizens. Ray's rise to preeminent stature within India will also become pertinent here. Ray's relationship with the nation seems to transform substantially by the end of his career.

Conclusion: Moving Away from the Nation

The Conclusion tries to plot Ray's trajectory in relation to the nation. He began as a national filmmaker but became 'universalist' like Tagore in his last films. How did this happen? Was there something in India's development that affected him?

Notes

1. Ella Shohat and Robert Stam (1994), *Unthinking Eurocentrism, Multiculturalism and the Media* (London: Routledge), 182.
2. Neepa Majumdar, 'Pather Panchali: From Realism to Melodrama,' in R. L. Rutsky and Jeffrey Geiger (eds), *Film Analysis: A Norton Reader* (New York: Norton, 2005), 513.
3. Christopher Pinney, *Camera Indica: The Social Life of Indian Photographs* (Chicago: University of Chicago Press, 1995), 149.
4. In dealing with Ray's portrayal of the sameness of rural Bengal, a critic has the following to say: 'While Western viewers might be tempted to read any Indian film as representative of all of India, urban Indian viewers (and filmmakers like Satyajit Ray) might be similarly inclined to view any filmic Indian village as representative of all of rural India.' Neepa Majumdar, 'Pather Panchali: From Realism to Melodrama,' in Rutsky and Geiger (2005), 514.
5. David Bordwell, 'The Art Cinema as a Mode of Film Practice,' in Leo Braudy and Marshall Cohen (eds), *Film Theory and Criticism: Introductory Readings*, 5th Edition (New York: Oxford University Press, 2004), 716–24.
6. Neepa Majumdar, 'Pather Panchali: From Realism to Melodrama,' in Rutsky and Geiger (2005), 516.
7. Ravi Vasudevan, *The Melodramatic Public: Film Form and Spectatorship in Indian Cinema* (Ranikhet: Permanent Black, 2010), 165. Here is Keya Ganguly on Ray: '(Ray's films), I contend, exemplify what (Raymond) Williams called the "one general property" of the avant-garde, which was, he said, to "pion[eer] new methods and purposes in writing, art and thought".'
8. Keya Ganguly, *Cinema, Emergence and the Films of Satyajit Ray* (Berkeley: University of California Press, 2010), 3. Ray did not pioneer new methods but rather brought an existing mode of filmic narration to Indian cinema. Ravi Varma also did this with Indian art when he used the European idiom of oil painting on Indian mythological subjects, but he cannot be called 'avant-garde'.
9. 'The problem of language in European film production, distribution and exhibition – resulting from the introduction of sound – was intensified by lingering nationalistic feelings that were the remnants of World War I and a precursor of World War II. Nationalism threatened the adroitness of the avant-garde's cosmopolitan networks. Due to the utopian nature of its political underpinning that did not allow for anything but a rejection

of the petty national concerns of the reigning powers, the avant-garde was unable to respond adequately to the crisis.' Marijke de Valck, *Film Festivals: From European Geopolitics to Global Cinephilia* (Amsterdam: Amsterdam University Press, 2007), 23–4.
10. Benedict Anderson, *Imagined Communities: Reflections on the Origin and Spread of Nationalism* (London: Verso, 1983), 15.
11. Graeme Turner, *National Fictions: Literature, Film and the Construction of the Australian Narrative* (London: Routledge, 1993), 12.
12. Aditya Nigam, *Decolonizing Theory: Thinking Across Traditions* (New Delhi: Bloomsbury, 2020), 2.
13. Anderson (1983), 25–6.
14. In 1863–4, the value of the imports was over 300,000 pounds. See Priya Joshi, 'Culture and Consumption: Fiction, the Reading Public and the British Novel in Colonial India', *Book History* I/1, 1998, 196–220.
15. Meenakshi Mukherjee, 'Nation, Novel, Language', in *The Perishable Empire: Essays on Indian Writing in English* (New Delhi: Oxford University Press, 2000), 17–18, 22.
16. Phalke's aim in his mythological films was apparently to introduce the traditional sacred into the space of the colonial 'modern'. Ashish Rajadhyaksha, 'The Phalke Era: Conflict of Traditional Form and Modern Technology', *Journal of Arts and Ideas* 14–15, 1987, 67.
17. Jawaharlal Nehru's writings most admired by Ray are in two books: *Glimpses of World History* and *Discovery of India*. Bert Cardullo, *Satyajit Ray: Interviews* (Jackson: University Press of Mississippi, 2007), 50.
18. C. A. Bayly, *Recovering Liberties: Indian Thought in the Age of Liberalism and Empire* (Cambridge and New York: Cambridge University Press, 2012), 343–357.
19. Roy Armes, *Third World Filmmaking and the West* (Berkeley: University Press of California, 1987), 85.
20. Mimesis is the basic theoretical principle in the creation of art, much favoured in cinema. The word derived from a Greek verb meaning 'to imitate'; the philosopher Aristotle adapted the term to fit his idea that art observes whom and what we observe in the real world. Aristotle used the term in the sense of 're-presentation' rather than copying.
21. As an example, after being screened at Cannes, Arturo Lanocito of *Corriere della Serra* wrote about *Pather Panchali*: '... the breadth of the story became large, the purity of the images corresponded to the purity of the subject. On very few occasions had we seen on the screen the novel of a childhood spent in the fields told with such felicity of expression ... we had witnessed a kind of self-revelation of Indian film art.' Marie Seton, *Portrait of a Director: Satyajit Ray* (Bloomington: Indiana University Press, 1971), 9.
22. Satyajit Ray, *My Years with Apu* (New Delhi: Penguin, 1996), 17.
23. 'It is simply that Ray learned and rigorously applied certain accepted principles of filmmaking to narrative which, till that time, seemed to resist these

principles, these modes of cinematic storytelling, so that, for a while at least, Indian cinema was perhaps integrated with world cinema through his films.' M. K. Raghavendra, *50 Indian Film Classics* (Noida: Collins, 2009), 57.

24. 'One important thing to note immediately here is that the native culture which Ray emphasizes is not some pure vision of a tradition-bound society, but the heterogeneous lives and commitments of contemporary India. The Indian who does the 'twist' is as much there as the one who chants his mantras by the Ganges.' Amartya Sen, *The Argumentative Indian: Writings on Indian History, Culture and Identity* (New York: Farrar, Straus and Giroux, 2005), 129.
25. Sunil Khilnani, *The Idea of India* (New Delhi: Penguin, 2016), 33–4.
26. Bhaskar Sarkar, *Mourning the Nation* (New Delhi: Orient Blackswan, 2008), 53.
27. M. K. Raghavendra, *Seduced by the Familiar: Narration and Meaning in Indian Popular Cinema* (New Delhi: Oxford University Press, 2008), 86–8.
28. Ashis Nandy, *The Intimate Enemy: Loss and Recovery of Self Under Colonialism* (New Delhi: Oxford University Press, 1985), 6–10.
29. The older son Ramu is shown in the garb of a statesman at the conclusion, but there is no context in the narrative pointing to him entering politics to attain such stature. Raghavendra (2008), 34.
30. For instance, Neepa Majumdar, 'Pather Panchali: From Realism to Melodrama', in Rutsky and Geiger (2005), 520. Majumdar cites Durga's death as a melodramatic moment, but it hardly fits this definition of melodrama as moral polarisation.
31. Peter Brooks, *The Melodramatic Imagination: Balzac, Henry James, Melodrama and the Mode of Excess* (New York: Columbia University Press, 1985), 11–12.
32. Madhava Prasad, *Ideology of the Hindi Film: A Historical Construction* (New Delhi: Oxford University Press, 1998), 149.
33. The angry young man played by Amitabh in *Deewar*, for instance, has been associated with Mrs Gandhi's era by theorists like Madhava Prasad, but he has also been seen as the 'good-bad hero' derived from Karna of the *Mahabharata*. Sudhir Kakar, *Intimate Relations: Exploring Indian Sexuality* (New Delhi: Penguin, 1989), 60.
34. One noted exchange was in Parliament. Nargis had become a member of the Rajya Sabha, and in 1980 denounced Ray for displaying India's poverty to the West. Report in Probe India cited by Rosie Thomas (1989), 'Sanctity and Scandal: The Mythologization of Mother India', *Quarterly Review of Film and Video* 2/3, 24.
35. Chidananda Dasgupta, *The Cinema of Satyajit Ray* (New Delhi: NBT, 2001), 44.
36. '… it is probably the refusal on Ray's part to directly address the contemporary that makes the Apu trilogy function as a national allegory. For anything more frontal would be too partisan even as it would be, paradoxically, too

divisive – like the contradiction of Indian Independence presented by Ritwik Ghatak in his three post-partition films: *Meghe Dhaka Tara, Subarnarekha, Komal Gandhar.*' Geeta Kapur, 'Sovereign Subject: Ray's Apu', in *When was Modernism? Contemporary Cultural Practice in India* (New Delhi: Manohar, 2003), 226.
37. Ibid., 205.
38. Ibid., 205.
39. Bildungsroman is a special kind of novel that focuses on the psychological and moral growth of its main character, from his or her youth to adulthood. Such a type of novel is also known as a 'coming of age novel'.
40. Stanley Kaufmann in *The New Republic*, September 1958.
41. Kapur (2003), 204.
42. 'It is the tragedy of the bright young generation who have internalized the master race (like many of the refugees from Hitler who came to America); their status identity is so British that they treat all non-Anglicized Indians as non-persons. The caste system and the British attitudes seem to have conspired to turn them into self-parodies – clowns who ape the worst snobberies of the British.' Pauline Kael, *Reeling* (Toronto: Little, Brown and Company, 1976), 142.
43. Madhava Prasad (*Ideology of the Hindi Film*) and Ravi Vasudevan (*Making Meaning in Indian Cinema*) are two well-known Indian film theorists/critics who employ this strategy.
44. Mike Chopra-Gant, *Hollywood Genres and Post-War America: Masculinity, Family and Nation in Popular Movies and Film Noir* (New York: I. B. Tauris, 2006), 66–70.
45. John Beynon, *Masculinities and Culture* (Philadelphia: Open University Press, 2002), 65–6.
46. Richard Dyer, 'Rock – The Last Guy You'd have Figured' in *The Culture of Queers* (London: Routledge, 2001), 161.
47. Jyotika Virdi, *The Cinematic ImagiNation: Indian Popular Films and Social History* (Delhi: Permanent Black, 2003), 87–8.
48. Raghavendra (2008), 132, 244.
49. Ibid., 211–17.
50. Noel Carroll, 'Prospects for Film Theory: A Personal Assessment', in David Bordwell and Noel Carroll (eds), *Post Theory: Reconstructing Film Studies* (Madison: The University of Wisconsin Press, 1996), 42–3.

CHAPTER 1

The Colonial and the Premodern: *Shatranj Ke Khiladi*, *Jalsaghar* and *Devi*

A case was made in the Introduction for Satyajit Ray as a national filmmaker, and the epithet 'national' would include his portrayal of India before it became a nation, i.e. its time under British colonisation. All three of the films discussed in this chapter are connected by the common thread in their portrayals of the decline of feudalism as a force and decaying tradition. They are all based in nineteenth-century India and as such offer us glimpses of key moments of Indian history that contribute to our sense of a nation with a historical trajectory. These films also document the struggle between tradition and modernity as the advent of the British in the country brought in its wake many new developments, the end of numerous kingdoms, the zamindari system as social organisation and the strengthening of colonialism alongside the burgeoning of the Bengal cultural Renaissance. The three films have been studied chronologically (in historical terms) so as to be able to afford a sense of the changes Ray saw as wrought in Indian society in the nineteenth century under the impact of colonial modernity.

The Incursions of Colonialism: *Shatranj Ke Khiladi* (1977)

Of the three films dealt with in this chapter, Satyajit Ray's *Shatranj Ke Khiladi* is historically placed at the earliest moment and can be used as a template to understand all three as representing, on the one hand, the clash between tradition and colonial modernity and on the other, that between two different civilisations. It presents to us, in effect, with more than the coloniser-versus-colonised theme in which colonisation is simply the betrayal of faith. In Premchand's story the political events happen offstage, as it were, and it can be seen as a critique of the self-absorbed aristocracy doing little when their land is usurped by the colonisers but getting into a murderous rage over a chess game. In Ray's film, General Outram and Nawab Wajid Ali Shah – representing the two opposing sides – are fleshed out and the film emerges as the clash of ideas bred by two different and even opposing civilisations – with neither Outram nor Wajid Ali Shah painted in absolute terms, although the British are the victors. The Nawab is a patron of music and the fine arts, by nature a poet and a connoisseur of beauty. He is unable to see or hear what his subjects are afraid of – a takeover by the British. The Munshi, a character introduced by Ray, is someone with his eyes and ears in the right place. He is the first person who talks about it to Mirza and Mir – the two chess-obsessed principal characters in the film. The British have an hour-by-hour report of the Nawab's activities – his religious life and his artistic pursuits mainly – which make him a very unfit ruler according to General Outram, the Resident in Awadh who plans to annex the kingdom.

To Outram, Wajid Ali Shah is no administrator and unfit to rule. But the details of the king's personal life too disgust him. There is in effect a double vision operating here – Outram's contempt for Wajid Ali Shah as an administrator and his disgust at him as a man, which is why the Nawab's effeminate side becomes also important in ousting him. Outram decides that the king's time is spent in flying kites, dancing the *raas*, participating in *mushairas* or spending time with his concubines, which leaves him very little time for administration.[1] Although the British desire for Awadh is not for good governance but rather access to the riches in the imperial treasury, nevertheless Outram's articulated ideas about Wajid Ali Shah being unfit to rule are not unjustified.[2]

The two noblemen, Mirza Sajjad Ali and Mir Roshan Ali, are also in the film only as extensions of the king and have eyes and ears for nothing except pleasure – although that is entirely chess. Premchand's story paints the whole Lucknow populace in hedonistic terms and the aristocrats are only symptomatic.[3] They remain oblivious to everything – the dalliances of their wives and the British taking over their state after deposing their king. Ray presents the obsessive chess-playing by the husbands alongside their wives' sexual escapades to highlight the self-absorbed conduct of the Awadhis, in that they were engaged in nothing external to them, attending solely to their own affairs. The two noblemen try various devices to keep playing their games of chess in the face of distractions, getting into a fight to the extent of even wanting to kill each other when one of them is on the verge of losing a game. But alongside this, they also refuse to take up real arms to protect or fight for their king.

The reason why the British are able to take over Lucknow and Awadh is because Outram's ideas of kingship entail the ability to keep abreast of what is happening in one's kingdom; pursuing poetry and dancing 'with bells on his feet like nautch girls' are disgusting aspects of the

Figure 1.1 The two noblemen try various devices to keep playing their games of chess in the face of distractions.

ruler, although Wajid Ali Shah's subjects are not seen to be complaining about their king. A point to be noted here, however, is that the reason for a 'complaint' here could only be that the king is seen to be inferior to another – with cultural attainment being a value. Evidently, it could not be induced by a reference to 'democratic rights' of the citizens. Britain was a different matter, since citizenship meant something different there, but Outram is not making this allowance. In the instant case the Nawab is not compared to anyone else; it is also to be noted that he was cultured and had similar 'good qualities' even if they were not those of an administrator. Akbar, for instance, is widely eulogised for patronising the 'nine gems' in his court (writers, thinkers, musicians). When Ray presents Wajid Ali Shah's subjects, kite-flying and cock-fights seem to be what preoccupy them, suggesting a people given more to distractions than to toil. But there is a sense in Ray's film that what are 'moral failings' (in the Nawab) for Outram could be virtues for the aristocrat. Overall, Ray is ambivalent about both Outram and Wajid Ali Shah,[4] the latter a bad administrator but culturally sophisticated, while the former is not inaccurate about the Nawab as an administrator, but hypocritical about the real motives of the British.

Where Premchand criticises the Nawab and dismisses his rule as being ineffective and ripe for British takeover, Ray's representation of the same happenings is more contextualised. Premchand's story is nationalistic regret of colonialism, while Ray's is a postcolonial study and a historical recreation of the essential conflict. Ray tried to examine both sides of Wajid Ali Shah when he asserted 'I think there were two aspects to Wajid Ali Shah's character, one which you could admire and one which you couldn't. I saw the King as an artist, a composer who made some contributions to the form of singing that developed in Lucknow. The fact that he was a great patron of music – that was one redeeming feature about the King.'[5] Here, as we may gather, Ray is sensitive to Wajid Ali Shah both as a man of culture and an indifferent administrator. Premchand mentions the name of the Nawab only once in his story, for he is more interested in a nationalistic take, blaming him for the victory of the British. Premchand, ironically, is closer to Ray's Outram in this perspective! He expects attitudes that could not have been held by Indian rulers in the period.

In contrast to Premchand, it is almost as if Ray is, dispassionately, drawing up the character of the Indian male under colonisation, when neither nation nor freedom meant much but personal cultural attainment did. Indian history tells us that the British made alliances with Indian kings against each other. Ray's tone is that of gentle irony, which many abroad as well as nearer to home missed. It is not overt denunciation, but if one pays close enough attention they will be able see the filmmaker trying to bring out the complexity of a tale that might have been reduced to simple binaries.[6]

This brings us to the marital problems of the two protagonists, played out comically, and both of them are sexually inadequate; their 'male' aggression is entirely on the chessboard. Premchand suggests it but Ray fleshes it out considerably. The weakness of the Indian male under colonialism was duly registered by mainstream cinema, which led to various motifs including *Devdas* and the female vigilante figure in *Hunterwali* (1935), the woman protagonist plated by Fearless Nadia (a.k.a. Mary Evans). Ray is arguably doing the same thing in the film by portraying his protagonists' sexual failings. The third kind of masculinity described in the introduction pertained to the 'leader of people' and it is a fact here that while Wajid Ali Shah is 'cultured', he is no leader of people, and that is Outram's chief complaint against him – that he is not a responsible administrator. It could be argued that Ray is breaking up the historical Nawab into two parts: his actual political trajectory, and his problematised masculinity, projected onto the two aristocrats who cannot manage their own households. The nobility not being 'masculine' here is arguably equated with India under the Company in the nineteenth century not having leaders because of their 'inwardness'.

Feudalism and the Mercantile Bourgeoisie: *Jalsaghar* (1958)

Immediately after making *Pather Panchali*, Ray turned his attention to the life of the zamindars of the nineteenth and twentieth centuries, who exerted influence on the Bengali way of life, sometimes – though not always – towards the social good. Although decadent, they exercised their wealth and power in the twin directions of social reform and patronage of the arts and culture. The decadent side is presented in popular cinema in Abrar Alvi's classic film *Sahib Bibi Aur Ghulam* (1962), but Ray's film, once again, embraces greater complexity by not authoring a lament. When Ray made *Jalsaghar*, he was perhaps the first in Indian cinema to work on the notion of a man functioning as a subject of history, and this becomes clearer if we compare it with Abrar Alvi's film, in which one does not get a sense of the past except as nostalgia. Ray's tone in the film, although elegiac, is not without irony.

By Ray's own admission, *Jalsaghar* was adapted for the screen because *Aparajito* (1956) failed at the box office. Ray felt Tarashankar Banerjee's short story had the right amount of singing, and so according to him it was poised to be a light-hearted rendition of a music-loving zamindar. However, as the music began to be composed for the film and Indian classical music came to be extensively used, Ray's treatment of the subject too underwent a significant change. It became a study of the passing of a kind of life with heavy elegiac tones – the portrayal of a dying generation of feudal landlords who were also patrons of the arts. *Jalsaghar* is dominated by the figure of Biswambhar Roy, a haughty, arrogant, music-loving scion of a decadent zamindari line. Biswambhar loves music with a deep, abiding passion and would rather spend the remnants of his coffers to sink into the strains of good music, and he holds jalsas[7] (7) in his crumbling mansion. But Ray also sees that culture has other value and this is also a way to exert his influence over his subjects through spectacle. 'Breeding' is something an aristocrat uses to wield influence over those he already has economic power over. Decadence, in this context, can be defined as breeding exceeding its economic advantages.

In Ray's film, Biswambhar's young son has taken after him, with no interest in studies except for music, and enjoys riding the elephant and his father's favorite stallion. To maintain the erstwhile splendour of his dynasty, Biswambhar wants to borrow from the bank – an application which is turned down – and he pawns his wife's jewellery to hold a splendid *upnayan* (initiation) ceremony for his son. Mahim Ganguly, a neighbour who is a rising businessman, wishes to lease a part of Biswambhar's land for his sand quarrying business, which might help save Roy's depleting treasury; but Biswambhar refuses to get into any kind of dealings with such a 'contemptible' subject. The image that Ray conjures up of Biswambhar Roy is of someone culturally proud who does not let go of any opportunity to show off his own lineage, also suggested by the line of portraits on the walls of his mansion. Mahim Ganguly, in contrast, is someone who has learned to move with the times and take advantage of the business opportunities that colonialism has brought in its wake by ingratiating himself.

Biswambhar is a sympathetic character in Ray's treatment, but what might disrupt the flow of our sympathy is his insistence on snubbing his neighbour habitually and without much justification. When Mahim Ganguly comes to invite Biswambhar on the occasion of the inauguration of his own more garish 'jalsaghar', Biswambhar lets it be known that that, unlike himself, Mahim is only a pretender to culture. But what is interesting here is the fact that Mahim Ganguly aspires to be like Biswambhar and emulate his lifestyle even though he is not of aristocratic lineage and is constantly rebuffed. It implies a more complex interpersonal relationship, especially in political terms, since it portrays the conflict between the landed aristocracy in decline and the rising mercantile class – because of the reliance of the British establishment in India on the latter class. One could read into it Ray's own sympathy for a tragic figure like Biswambhar Roy (done in by his own grandeur) since Tarashankar's story has no figure corresponding to Ganguly. Both Wajid Ali Shah (*Shatranj Ke Khiladi*) and Biswambhar Roy are men who act as patrons of fine music and art – a system that will disappear with the rise of the British in India. The success of the colonialism in India, it would seem, ended many things like patronage for the arts, which depended on the sense of personal attainment. The basic conflict seems, again, to be between cultural self-esteem and the pragmatic management of one's duties entrusted to oneself by social position.

However, Biswambhar's inability to move with the times, much like his inability to preserve his dwindling resources, bespeaks of his innate tendency to be 'inward looking', i.e. his inability to see solutions to his predicament in his outward conduct.[8] In spite of numerous warnings, from both his wife and nayeb (manager), pertaining to his cash-strapped zamindari, Biswambhar yearns only to dazzle everyone with his jalsas and refuses to have anything to do with Mahim Ganguly's business schemes, which he looks down upon. Even as Biswambhar continues to flounder (much of his land is gobbled up by the encroaching Padma, which has almost reached his doorstep), and having lost both his wife and son, his palace now blackened by age and neglect, Mahim tells the nayeb that old ways count for more. The zamindar's elephant – symbolic of aristocracy – still draws salutations from the ordinary folks, while Mahim's new car gets pelted with stones. There is no irony in Mahim Ganguly's utterances and even as he succeeds in business, he admires the ways of the declining aristocrat. There is arguably a commentary on traditional hierarchy – in that the wealthiest and most powerful in society looked up in some way to those who were poor, but with scholarship or culture.

Ray's treatment of the zamindar differs on many counts from Tarashankar's. For one, Biswambhar Roy dominates the screen right from the beginning. Played charismatically by Chabbi Biswas, a formidable actor of Bengali cinema, he not only brings alive the decadence and fading opulence of a system in decline, but expands upon human vulnerabilities too. Tarashankar Banerjee's story, which took inspiration from the actual ostentation and display of grandeur by the Nimtita zamindar Upendranarayan Choudhury, uses a highly critical tone, but the story takes on another hue when Ray adapts it. It becomes a serious study of a way of life fast disappearing under the onslaught of the modernity hastened by colonialism. The composer used by Ray was Ustad Vilayat Khan, singing and dancing sequences in the film are of a level not previously presented in Indian cinema, and this lends to Biswambhar's credibility as a patron. For Ray, Biswambhar is someone who is unable to look into the future, too engrossed in his past and obsessed with his ancestry. It is in his bid to live up to both that he loses everything – even his life. While Tarashankar's zamindar in the story has an epiphanic moment and asks for the jalsaghar to be shut forever, Ray's Biswambhar Roy refuses to redeem himself. He would rather show the 'upstart' his place even if it means holding the last grand jalsa with the last few coins left with him. In Tarashankar's story the zaminar's mistress is Krishna Bai the dancer, but Ray refuses to contaminate the zamindar's love of music with sexual overtones. He is also a competent esraj player, as he accompanies his young son, who has a musical voice. Ray's effort in making *Jalsaghar* is to recreate a passing moment; the old, although in decline, is going out in splendour, which is partly what has given it so much influence.

Through his particular portrayal of Biswambhar Roy and his times, Ray offers a commentary on the Indian mindset vis-à-vis the British, a feature the film shares with the others dealt with in this chapter. Without being overtly critical like Tarashankar, Ray maintains some distance from both his principal characters and subjects, neither of whom are lampooned.

Biswambhar has dignity and is a patron of culture, but Mahim Ganguly is a self-made man who has worked his way into his position. Their conflict is not really acknowledged by the latter, who continues to outwardly honour Biswambhar. One could see a parallel between the way Ray treats the story and his adaptation of Premchand in *Shatranj Ke Khilari*, in that he is more ambivalent towards 'decadence' than the original writers were.

The conflict between Biswambhar and Mahim can be placed alongside that between Nawab Wajid Ali Shah and General Outram, to help us gauge what Ray could be getting at. While Biswambhar, like the Nawab, is a patron of the arts even when that role destroys him, Mahim Ganguly is a product of colonial modernity and an indigenous inheritor of Outram's mantle. The difference is that where Outram was openly hostile to the cultured Nawab, wanting to have him cast out and put on a pension, Mahim admires Biswambhar and tries to emulate him, even as another side of him is being pragmatic. Ray's double vision is operating in this film as well, being admiring of the cultured individual grounded in tradition even as he sees him as incurably self-destructive. Ray may be a modernist, but he is a modernist who respects his cultural past and sees how the mercantile mindset created by the colonialists destroyed something very valuable. Or to phrase it differently, whatever aspects of culture were traditionally valued could only lead to self-destruction under modernity.

Tradition and Modernity: *Devi* (1960)

In *Devi* too, much like *Jalsaghar*, Ray's interest in the zamindari system continues. Only this time around the conflict is more overt in that colonial modernity has begun to make its presence felt and results in direct conflict within a family – a father and a son who represent opposing mindsets. *Devi*'s plot hinges around the traditional belief that woman can become an incarnation of a goddess and the conflict it creates in a society on the cusp of modernity. The female protagonist in the film is Doya, the young, guileless village daughter-in-law of a rich, orthodox zamindar family. Her father-in-law Kalikinkar Roy is an ageing, pious devotee of goddess Kali; he has a compelling vision one night (*swapnadesh*) of Doya's divine status and believes it to be the goddess's blessings upon his family. Umaprasad, Kalikinkar's younger son, is a rational person getting an English education in Calcutta, where the Brahmo Samaj established by Raja Ram Mohan Roy in 1830 has begun to make its presence felt. It advocated women's emancipation through abolition of sati, widow remarriage and education and Umaprasad has evidently fallen under its influence.

Doya is educated and so is Kalikinkar, but in an older, closed and traditional way. Kalikinkar, deeply intoxicated with religiosity and also lacking Westernised education, finds it easy to propagate the irrational thought that his daughter-in-law is a goddess incarnate. Umaprasad, however, remains sceptical and even pronounces his father insane. The father's response is to quote Sanskrit hymns from memory to prove himself right and his son wrong. Umaprasad is convinced of Doya's human status and, time and again, Ray offers us glimpses of the girl's helplessness and inability to articulate her misgivings. But she too is mired in superstition and refuses to run away with Umaprasad – fearing divine wrath will be visited upon her husband. Doya's capability to cure a sick child further establishes her divinity and Umaprasad finds himself unable to defy his father.

In the beginning, Ray establishes the atmosphere in Kalikinkar's household – having lost his wife a few years ago, he has sought solace in worship even more ardently, and the goddess Kali reigns as the supreme deity. Doya helps him with the puja preparations each day, and looks after his basic comforts and medical needs. Kalikinkar's ineffectual elder son Taraprasad lives with his wife and young son Pradyumna in the same household, and goes along with whatever his father says without questioning his dictates. The film begins with a close-up of Durga puja being celebrated with much fanfare in the Roy household, with both Kalikinkar and Taraprasad looking on with fevered eyes brimming over with devotion. Umaprasad, however, enjoys the festive moment with his wife and nephew without investing it with any special religious significance, without an inkling of what will happen.

Satyajit Ray, writing in 1982 on the film,[9] talks about the influential cult of the Mother Goddess and the impact it had upon orthodox Hindu society, Kalikinkar being a vivid example of that. Coupled with that is his important position as a zamindar – not only landowner but spiritual guide to his people – which helps to establish his word as more than that of a mere landlord. The son's helplessness in trying to have his voice heard in the face of the developing situation and rescuing his wife from impending disaster is all documented carefully, but is not without some personal investment in it on Ray's part. Ray, being a Brahmo, in which the agenda largely revolved around reforming Hinduism by getting rid of its idolatry, polytheism and other excesses, arguably sets a Brahmo-inspired agenda but via the medium of the human players in the story.

This conflict between father and son over Doya intensified by Ray in his film is missing from Prabhat Kumar Mukherjee's original story. 'The son's character is very much developed in this film according to my feelings,' Ray said of Umaprasad's character in his film, 'for dramatic reasons. I was full of sympathy for him. I believed his arguments were much stronger than the father's arguments, because of the irrationality involved.'[10] This statement then becomes significant on two counts: first, the Freudian angle that Kael[11] pointed out no longer remains pertinent, and second, even the woman's (Doya) figure becomes secondary. The clash then takes place on the basis of opposing ideas about modernity and not over the possession of the woman's body as many critics would have it. There is a great affinity for Freudian interpretations among Western critics, but that is not something Indian/Bengali audiences would respond to and Ray had to address them.

Modernity ushered in by the British is what engages Ray in the film. While Edward Said[12] noted the biases in the claims made by Western critics that it was colonisation that ushered modernity into what they deemed 'primitive civilizations' – especially Africa and India – one cannot ignore the fact that even as the Bengal Renaissance was a result of colonialism's intervention in Bengali society, it contained elements that opposed British rule.[13] The son's character conjured up by Ray touches on this notion since Umaprasad is getting an English education. Even though the milieu in which the story is set goes against the son finally – his wife is lost to him as she goes mad over the death of her nephew – the clash between civilisations emerges from the drama, as in *Shatranj Ke Khilari*. Even though some reviews criticised Ray's film as being devoid of human

Figure 1.2 The clash of tradition and modernity, the old versus the new.

drama,[14] one still senses a strong human purpose in the film. If the original short story comes across as cold and didactic, essentially denouncing the orthodox father as backward, Ray, in contrast, draws up his characters in a more dispassionate manner – although the domineering Kalikinkar is less sympathetically portrayed than either Wajid Ali Shah or Biswambhar Roy.

Doya herself is never sure who she really is; Ray's portrayal of her youth and naivety alongside her position of a daughter-in-law in an upper caste, conservative household helps convince us as to why she would listen to her father-in-law's wishes rather than follow her own weakly sceptical impulses. Kalikinkar is not like Wajid Ali Shah and Umaprasad is no Outram, but there is still a comparable conflict here between two different attitudes: the traditional one in which religious belief is overpowering and the sceptical one introduced by Western education. Still, what cannot be missed is Ray's considerably less sympathetic view of tradition here than in the other two films in the chapter. My own supposition is that it is because he is dealing directly with issues raised by the Brahmos.

Ashis Nandy has something to say about the cult of Kali and its position in the reformism of the times, especially pertaining to Raja Ram Mohan Roy and the Brahmo Samaj, doubly important here because Ray himself was a Brahmo.[15] Ram Mohan Roy tried to Christianise Hinduism and, in the process, rejected various heathen practices, of which a principal one was Kali worship because – in her worship – human sacrifices were included, along with the use of wine, criminal intercourse and licentious songs. We may assume that Umaprasad, under the influence of reformism, may have been aghast at seeing his guileless wife becoming an incarnation of Kali. *Devi* comes at a later moment in Indian history than the other two films dealt with in this chapter, but Ray is much more hostile to 'tradition' in this film. The cruel irony is that Doya, who is worshipped as a goddess, is destroyed by such worship and to make it more cruel, the goddess is all-powerful but Doya is powerless not to be the goddess.[16] But the chief observation here is that, in the other two films, tradition is represented by relatively milder aspects like music and dance and the indifference by the ruler to his administrative responsibilities. In *Devi*, it is represented by what Brahmos regarded as the bane of Hinduism – resulting in the much harsher outcome in the film. We must also factor this into Nehruvian modernity, which may be taken to be in line with Ray's own sentiments.

Conclusion: Modernity and Colonialism

It is interesting to note that the modernity which the colonisers brought in their wake was resisted by the movement it would unknowingly usher in – the Bengal Renaissance. The modern, as enunciated by Immanuel Kant,[17] begins with the enlightenment, in which man learned to arrive at conclusions in a rational manner. It consisted in rooting all knowledge, culture, morality and institutions in the freedom of the individual, rather than tradition. The Western world reached the heights of modernity in the nineteenth century, while the non-Western world reached it mainly through the painful external process of colonisation by various European powers. Experimental sciences, philosophy, art, literature, economic and political life were areas in which modernity was particularly influential. What this chapter has done is to reframe the generally accepted understandings of the relationship between colonialism and modernity and make a useful contribution to rethinking modernity in the light of experiences other than those of Western subjects, in this case India and Nehruvian modernity. Even if British colonialism planted the seeds of the modern in India, it was harvested very differently from the way the British expected it to be.

The relationship between colonialism and modernity is a contested one. An interpretation is that colonialism brought modern values and institutions to the colonised world. Historians like Niall Ferguson (2004)[18] promote the idea that Britain not only 'made' the modern world, but has no reason to apologise for the world that was made, and even Karl Marx saw colonialism as a necessary step in the development of India.[19] Others, such as William McNeill, reinforce such sentiments by suggesting that we must 'admire those who pioneered the [modern] enterprise and treat the human adventure on earth as an amazing success story, despite all the suffering entailed'.[20] Questions regarding who this 'we' are and whether 'we' must celebrate the successes (of some) despite the suffering (of others) form the nub of postcolonial and other criticisms. As Ashis Nandy[21] argues, there is continuity between not being recognised as a subject in historical narratives and subjection in the present.

The pre-colonised world is typically represented as the repository of all that is traditional and the colonised world – whether in positive or negative terms – is seen to embody (or has the potential to embody) the nascent modern. A basic assumption, as has been asserted, is that the world that 'colonialism replaced or destroyed belongs to the irretrievable past and is irrelevant for our [modern] purposes'.[22] Further, the focus in much of the standard historical and sociological literature has primarily been on the presumed unidirectional nature of the relationship whereby colonial powers take 'modernity' – as expressed in the modern institutions of the state, market economy and bureaucracy – to the colonised. The evidentiary base, together with the normative presuppositions, of such claims (and many more) have been seriously called into question by historians, sociologists, anthropologists and others over the last few decades. This has been in large part as a consequence of increasingly available research from around the globe that contests many complacent assumptions about the origin, nature and spread of what we have come to understand as modernity. There has also been significant research addressing the multitude of ways in which the modern was created in the colonial context – the work of Cohen and Dirks,[23] for example, details the invention of fingerprinting and other modes of governmentality within the colonies before being imported 'back' to the metropole.

Colonial India never found representation in cinema explicitly when India was a colony. Hindi cinema, being prolific in its output, also has the widest reach and that experience would need to be addressed by it, but cinema was dependent on cumbersome technology and exhibition arrangements precluded the possibility of escaping censorship. If one is to look at Hindi cinema of the pre-Independence era, one gets the sense that colonial India finds its representation only allegorically. M. K. Raghavendra reads *Devdas* and other films of the 1930s and 40s in the light of the colonial encounter. The motif of the weak son and authoritarian father (as in *Devdas*) allegorises the coloniser-colonised relationship, and Raghavendra goes on to see this leaving Indian cinema around 1942–1943 with the British reversals against the Japanese. The weak son asserting his independence and breaking with his authoritarian father is actually portrayed in Mehboob Khan's *Taqdeer* (1943).[24] But once India ceased to be a colony, mainstream cinema (or art cinema) did not try to re-examine the past, which is why Ray's re-examinations of the colonial past are so valuable.

In post-Independence cinema, films like *Junoon* (1978), *1942: A Love Story* (1995) and *Mangal Pandey: The Rising* (2010) insist on showing the British simply as an oppressor and the subjugated colonised already as a subjugated 'national community'. The Indian protagonists come across as 'patriotic' (when the nation had not yet been imagined) and the whole film then goes on to become a eulogy of the nation, usually referred to as 'Bharat Mata', and all Indians as her sons. In Shyam Benegal's *Junoon* (in which the masculinity of the Indians is highlighted), Sarfaraz, played by Naseeruddin Shah, is the avenging spirit on behalf of all Indians against the British residents and soldiers of a town in north India. Based on Ruskin Bond's short story 'A Flight of Pigeons', the film is set around the 1857 Sepoy Mutiny. The film also includes a love story between Javed Khan, a Pathan and member of the local landed gentry, and Ruth Labadoor, whose mother is half-Indian and her father an Englishman. Sarfaraz is a martyr and Javed Khan also dies fighting, while Ruth accepts his love and remains unwedded. The white woman Ruth's undying love for an Indian martyr becomes a token acknowledgement of India as already a 'nation', even if it is under the yoke of the British.[25] The same trope is also used in the patriotic *Lagaan* (2001), when a British woman loves an Indian man but he prefers an Indian woman, as a gesture towards 'national loyalties'.

One does not find references to the colonial period in Indian historical films except in such terms. In Mrinal Sen's *Interview* for instance, the proclivity of some of the characters to dress and conduct themselves as our British masters is seen by him as a colonial hangover. The framing sequence has a statue from the colonial period being hauled away for scrap metal, which is a way of notionally erasing the colonial past. Colonialism, therefore, is only a matter of regret and is interpreted as straightforward oppression of a people already a nation, instead of a process impacting upon a people-to-be.

However, as we examine Satyajit Ray's films in the light of the larger field of Indian cinema, one cannot help but notice the subtle and complex touches that he brings to the portrayal of the colonial relationships. In the first place, he does not see a 'nation' in India before 1947 but only nascent dialectic between the traditional and the modern, which would develop into nationalism much later. This emergent dialectic is of course embodied in the Bengal Renaissance, an interaction in which newer ways of looking and understanding the world that incorporated both what could be taken from the West and what was important to tradition found a place, but the films of Satyajit Ray that deal with this aspect of Indian history will be examined only in the next chapter.

Notes

1. Premchand's story does not provide the details of the king's life. Ray consulted Sharar Abdul Halim, *Lucknow: The Last Phase of an Oriental Culture* (New Delhi: Oxford University Press, 2000). I would propose that the personal lives of the two protagonists are brought in by Ray as a way of fleshing out Wajid Ali Shah. It is not that Wajid Ali Shah had their kind of life, but the lives of noblemen would suggest how the ruler might have lived.
2. The British had very definite ideas about kings and kingship. It was known as the divine right to rule, which meant that the king would be seen as the representative of God on Earth and which naturally endowed him with a lot of power and made him authoritarian, with little power residing with his subjects. The Godhead being masculine, the king would also naturally have to be someone who was physically powerful and masculine, exerting control. Queen Elizabeth I, as a 'virgin queen', propagates the myth of a woman ruler

surrendering her femininity. With England moving gradually into democracy, Parliament gaining power, this notion of the ruler's masculinity apparently remained.
3. Frances W. Pritchett, 'The Chess Players: From Premchand to Satyajit Ray', *Journal of South Asian Literature* 21/2, Essays on Premchand (Summer, Fall 1986), 66.
4. Ray uses irony in portraying Wajid Ali Shah, for instance in the following moments of the film: playing Krishna to the Gopis, the accompanying love song composed by Wajid Ali Shah, his celebrating Mohurrum, his reclining with his adoring concubines. Lastly, there is the sight of Wajid Ali Shah on his throne, accompanied by the voice-over: 'Nevertheless there were times when the king sat on his throne.' Darius Cooper, 'The White Man's Burdens and the Whims of the Chess-besotted Aristocrats: Colonialism in Satyajit Ray's *The Chess Players*', *Journal of South Asian Literature* 28/1/2, Miscellany (Spring, Fall 1993), 210.
5. Ray spoke to Andrew Robinson about this film, which Robinson wrote about in his book *Satyajit Ray: The Inner Eye* (New Delhi: Oxford University Press, 2004), 242–3.
6. Such a 'binary' representation in Indian cinema would naturally take a nationalist viewpoint such as the one taken today when dealing with the British, as for instance in Shashi Tharoor's *An Era of Darkness: The British Empire in India* (Delhi: Aleph, 2016), which demands British reparations to India for deeds done when no 'India' existed or was even envisaged. An instance of the difficulty is presented by the Kohinoor Diamond, which was gifted to the British in Lahore by Maharaja Ranjeet Singh's descendant. Should the diamond go to Pakistan, India or the Sikh community? Ray is aware of the problems inherent in simply castigating the British for colonialism.
7. Jalsas are musical soirees which were especially pertinent to the Bengali zamindars.
8. This behaviour is peculiar to all three protagonists in these films. By 'inward looking' I mean not the ability to introspect, but the inability to see the world for what it is, being preoccupied instead with a personal way of life. A ruler's complete immersion in culture would be an example.
9. Satyajit Ray dwelt at length on *Devi*: 'The Western critic who hopes to do a great deal of homework before he confronts the film. He must read up on the cult of the Mother Goddess ... the son's ultimate helplessness will convince him only if he is aware of the stranglehold of Hindu orthodoxy in 19th-century Bengal' as quoted in Robinson (2004), 121.
10. Ibid., p 124.
11. Pauline Kael's ideas about *Devi* involve the potential 'Freudian angle' in which she reads *Devi* as the exploitation of a young girl, with her father-in-law coveting her sexually. Pauline Kael, *I Lost it at the Movies* (New York: Bantam, 1966), 226–7.

12. Edward Said, *Orientalism: Western Conceptions of the Orient* (New York: Vintage, 1979), 3.
13. The Bengal Renaissance refers largely to the social, cultural, psychological and intellectual changes in Bengal during the nineteenth century, as a result of contact between certain sympathetic British officials and missionaries on the one hand and the Hindu intelligentsia on the other, and the arrival of the printing press facilitated it. However, it is this very interaction, along with English education, that would bring about a national consciousness on the part of the Indians and hence the protest against British rule in India in the twentieth century.
14. A review is quoted at some length in Marie Seton's book *Portrait of a Director: Satyajit Ray* (New Delhi: Penguin, 2004), 133: 'Instead of developing this story as a moving human drama, Satyajit Ray has given it a documentary treatment, taking meticulous care to capture the period and the locale in intimate details, but skipping over the dramatic moments in a calculated effort to bypass entanglements …'
15. Ashis Nandy, 'Sati: A Nineteenth Century Tale of Women, Violence and Protest', in *At the Edge of Psychology: Essays in Politics and Culture* (New Delhi: Oxford University Press, 1980), 22.
16. Nikki Guninder Kaur Singh, 'From Flesh to Stone: the Divine Metamorphosis in Satyajit Ray's *Devi*', in *Journal of South Asian Literature* 28/1/2, Miscellany (Spring, Fall 1993), 227–50.
17. Immanuel Kant's ideas on the modern included the terms of man's ability to think for himself and no longer being oppressed by institutions or irrational thoughts, and as a moment in which history moved forward rationally. <https://maritain.nd.edu/jmc/etext/mamt01.htm> (last accessed 11 January 2022).
18. Niall Ferguson, *Empire: How Britain made the Modern World* (New York: Basic Books, 2003), xxi.
19. Karl Marx, in his article 'The British Rule in India' written for the *New York Daily Tribune*, June 25, 1853 discusses at length the British rule in India <https://www.jstor.org/stable/41855631> (last accessed 2 June 2021).
20. William McNeill, *The Rise of the West: A History of the Human Community* (Chicago: University of Chicago Press, 1990), 3.
21. Ashish Nandy argues that there is continuity between not being recognised as a subject in historical narratives and subjection in the present. *The Intimate Enemy: Loss and Recovery of Self under Colonialism* (New Delhi: Oxford University Press, 2009), pp 91–2.
22. Satya P. Mohanty, *Colonialism, Modernity and Literature: A View from India* (New York and London: Palgrave Macmillan, 2011), 2.
23. Bernard S. Cohen and Nicholas Dirks, 'Beyond the Fringe: The Nation State, Colonialism, and the Technologies of Power', in *Journal of Historical Sociology*, 1/2, June 1988, 224–9.
24. M. K. Raghavendra, *Seduced by the Familiar: Narration and Meaning in Indian Popular Cinema* (New Delhi: Oxford University Press, 2008), 89.

25. Interestingly, this film comes immediately after *Shatranj Ke Khiladi*, but with a different viewpoint. It does not dwell on the complexities of the colonizer/colonised relationship and how it transformed India, but rather makes patriotic assertions – the implicit discourse being India as a national community.

CHAPTER 2

An Uncertain India: Early Nationalism in *Charulata* and *Ghare Baire*

In the previous chapter the focus was on the incursion of colonial modernity into Indian society and the advent of the modern Indian. This incursion gave rise to a socio-cultural movement in the nineteenth century, generally called the Bengal Renaissance, and consequently to a spiritual sense of a 'nation' and helped prompt the struggle for freedom, culminating in Independence, alongside the painful events of the partition. This chapter deals with the genesis of the nationalist struggle, which to my mind, began with the East-West interaction, creating a special breed of Indian men who would later take up the mantle of the freedom struggle. The two films dealt with here – *Charulata* and *Ghare Baire* – deal with these aspects and are linked by protagonists who are subjects of the British empire; the films depict important moments in the narrative of Indian history as it unfolded. Gender is an important part of the significance of these films, since both of them are about women/wives who are torn between loyalty to their husbands and extra-marital relationships. Needless to add, the extra-marital relations featured have socio-political ramifications.

In today's political India, nationalism has come to occupy a central position in the discourse around India's past. This is ironic since in the nineteenth century, Indians did not yet have a sense of what 'freedom', 'democracy' or nation or even nationalism meant. And yet in the span of less than 100 years, nationalism has come to mean so much. It has come to mean what Benedict Anderson acknowledged as 'profound emotional legacy'.[1] However, even before discussing nationalism, a definition of the nation needs to be repeated and Anderson describes it as 'an imagined political community – and imagined as both inherently limited and sovereign'.[2]

Non-Western nationalisms, according to Anderson, were entirely applications of Western models of nationhood, national identity and nationalist agitation. Before Anderson, however, Bruce McCully had asserted that nineteenth-century Indian nationalism was an 'exotic growth implanted by foreign hands and influence' and the great Indian nationalist figures of the time had invented little or nothing in the way of ideology.³ Perhaps there is some truth in what McCully said, but the fact that a land hitherto divided by language, caste, religion and cultural traditions could be made to unite into a coherent and unified nation is nonetheless deserving of inquiry especially since it was anti-British, coming out against the very agency that had ostensibly created it. English education, while it transformed India, could not have transformed the colonised into individuals capable of resisting colonialism on their own, although a dialectic was set into motion. But if colonialism only set into motion a historical process that culminated in the independent nation, those awakened must still have earlier had the seeds of an unnamed primal yearning.

As Anderson and others have argued, it was print capitalism and its associations that disseminated Western nationalist ideologies in the non-West; however, what must be acknowledged is also the fact that Indian-nationals-to-be invested in presses, worked as journalists, created civic and political associations and published and distributed their ideas in the press, or in their family newsletters or in meetings held by their associations.⁴ It resulted in the great nineteenth-century project of attempting to rid Hinduism of premodern elements and transforming it into a faith fit for modern men and women. Partha Chatterjee offered the argument that Indian nationalists of the nineteenth century, accepting their political powerlessness against the colonial state, concentrated on building up their own 'inner domain and cultural identity', and it was in the sovereign inner space in which they sought to prepare themselves for future political hegemony.⁵ Since the 'inner domain' would intersect with the arts, early nationalism's influence may be sought there and it perhaps began with the establishment of the Bengal School of Art, which had its genesis in the Swadeshi movement.⁶ This movement called upon Indians to reject the foreign influence and embrace the indigenous. Led by Abanindranath Tagore, the artists and critics associated with the Bengal School of Art and art criticism rejected lessons of Renaissance naturalism and instead advocated an authentic Indian style that concerned itself with emotional truth and piety. The Indian artist thus became, as Guha Thakurta sees it, indistinguishable from a yogi⁷ and artistic endeavour from a spiritual quest. Thus, Indians were successful in suturing religion and spirituality with the arts to distinguish themselves from the colonisers, and Partha Chatterjee's arguments about the inner spiritual domain seems particularly relevant here.

In some of his writings, Rabindranath Tagore went on to declare that India had never had a real sense of nationhood. 'This reign of law in our present government in India has established order in this vast land inhabited by peoples different in their races and customs. It has made possible for these peoples to come in closer touch with one another and cultivate a communion of aspirations.'[8] Brian McCully notes several such writings by other Indians too that attribute to the British governance of the Indian sub-continent the rise of a sense of unity among Indians and an idea of national life as owing to the establishment of British schools and colleges and, more importantly, English language education. However, the idea of nationalism as ideology was still to take root even when all this had happened. Lalmohan Ghosh, addressing a London audience in 1879, declared 'under the powerful influence of western education the various races inhabiting that vast peninsula are being gradually but certainly welded together into a common nationality; they are beginning to cooperate with each other in a manner that would have been absolutely impossible a few years ago'.[9]

As McCully notes, these early allusions to British influence creating a unifying idea for the future nation did not itself give rise to the idea of 'nationalism' (as we now understand it) although the acknowledgement of the benefits of English education was immediate. But in time, while the aim of introducing English education with the Education Minute Act of 1835 by Macaulay was to create a 'brown sahib', remaining in essence Bengali and helping with the administration of the land, what it ultimately led to was turning the Indian mind 'to politics and reforming the state'.[10] Panikkar, writing in 1920, notes the denationalising effects of early British education in creating religious reformism instead, finding expression in religious movements such as the Brahmo Samaj and the new Vedantism of Sri Ramakrishna and Vivekananda. However, he went on to concede that it was English education which acquainted 'Young India" with England's political growth and Whig political ideals.[11] In all, it can be said that intervention by the British in education and publishing, while it was not intended to produce nationalism but only an administrative class, had precisely that secondary effect. British initiatives made Indians acutely aware of their own culture (with a degree of homogeneity) that deserved to take its place proudly beside that of Britain, and that stirring in the 'spiritual domain' led to political nationalism.

These political ideals, unwittingly engendered by British intervention, thus led to the Indian national movement, which ultimately translated into the ascendancy of the Indian National Congress. J. Ghosh, writing in 1926, talks of the idea of nationality germinating in the Bengalis first (of which perhaps Bhupati in Ray's *Charulata* is an illustration), and modern Indian nationalism through the literature produced by the British and its subsequent consumption by the 'natives', who then proceeded to create their own indigenous culture. For our purpose, this led to the Bengal Renaissance, out of which reformism, primarily the need for educating women, and later nationalism was also to spring forth. The English language adopted as the lingua franca of India was, according to Dadabhai Naorji and several other nationalists, a potent tool for generating Indian nationalism.

The direct addressing of these political questions from a historical perspective is undertaken by Ray in both *Charulata* and *Ghare Baire*, and the filmmaker is true to representing the movement of history without himself becoming nationalistic, a much easier option. Satyajit Ray explores the influence of the print medium being introduced in Bengal, the use of the press as an instrument of nationalism and what it would produce (instantiated by Bhupati's newspaper 'The Sentinel' in *Charulata*) and, later, the influence of such newspapers in generating public opinion, a sense of public responsibility, a spirit of industrialism and finally Swadeshi – and a growth of the cooperative ideal in the Indian mind (explored in *Ghare Baire*). Although the two films were made far apart in time – *Charulata* in 1964 and *Ghare Baire* in 1984 – one still finds a connecting link in them, in the historical events as they transpired in the heart of British India.

The Bengal Renaissance and *Charulata* (1964)

To examine *Charulata* would mean not only looking at a slice of history that was later called the Bengal Renaissance, but also understanding the first stirrings of the sense of the future. Through *Charulata*, Ray tells the story of a society in transition, and the film focuses on the historic moment when two forces – one white, imperial and Christian and the other feudal, orthodox and Hindu, collided to give rise to a cultural phenomenon from which nationhood began to take shape. In 1835, as already indicated, Macaulay with his Minute on Education advocated the study of English for Indians, whereby a new breed of men would be produced who would be English in thoughts and habits while remaining Indian at heart. Western education was therefore introduced into India and Raja Ram Mohan Roy, who was one of the first reformers, gladly embraced it as he believed that it would rid his society of orthodoxy and insularity. Eventually a class did emerge – the bhadralok – the indigenous bourgeois elite, which having been exposed to European literature, science and philosophy ended up embracing and advocating Western liberalism, in effect becoming Englishmen while remaining oblivious of how to resolve the resultant crises when they arose in their own society. This chapter is a study of two such crisis moments created by the Bengal Renaissance.

The bourgeois class created by Macaulay's ideas in education, feeling politically aroused, brought out newspapers that discussed news from the cities, thereby trying to awaken their fellow Indians. Since Bengal was exposed to colonial influence for longer than the rest of India, Bengali modernity has come to be accepted as the prototype of Indian modernity. The 'Bengal Renaissance' began with the advent of Raja Ram Mohan Roy and his efforts to improve the lives of women alongside his efforts to remodel Hinduism on monotheistic lines as various scholars have noted. His mantle was then donned in the mid-nineteenth century by the educator and philanthropist Ishwarchandra Vidyasagar, followed by the novelist Bankimchandra Chatterjee and the reformist Keshabchandra Sen, culminating in the work of Rabindranath Tagore, whose winning of the 1913 Nobel prize in Literature called into focus the achievements of the Bengal Renaissance.

While the phenomenon became celebrated in latter-day India, with the decline of Bengal's fortunes – in war, famine and communal riots that ultimately led to partition – it was criticised by a young group of Marxist scholars in the 1970s, known as the Subaltern historians. They put forward the view that the modernity brought in by the colonisers was limited and even distorted in colonial Bengal. Ray's film *Charulata*, made in 1964, anticipates the findings by critiquing and putting to scrutiny the Bengal Renaissance, and Ray departs from its source, which is Tagore's novella *Nastanirh* (*The Broken Nest*, 1901).

In both Tagore's novella and Ray's film, Bhupati, Charulata's husband, belongs to the elite, bourgeois class just described. His newspaper *The Sentinel*, with its motto 'Truth alone Triumphs', to which he is committed, is 'his wife's rival for his affections'. Bhupati expresses his views in English and seems to be endlessly trapped in the world of the English language, writing his editorials and polishing them up by altering this phrase or that. The running of the household and being busy with its day-to-day activities he leaves to his wife Charu, and he has no time to spare for her or the household. While Charulata is the quintessential nineteenth-century housewife, trapped in the inner female quarters and made to do her husband's bidding, she is presented as someone bored with her limited role in life and who longs for excitement and freedom.[12]

However, unlike her husband, Charulata finds solace in the Bengali language and spends her time reading Bankimchandra's novels. From what was said earlier, the East-West conflict finds reflection in Bhupati's very household. While Bhupati converses with Charu in his mother tongue

Figure 2.1 Charulata eventually egged on by her brother-in-law and literary ambitions.

Bengali, his inner world is occupied by thoughts of British politics and political philosophies. Even the England he describes to his cousin Amal, to tempt him into a marriage proposal, is peopled by Burke, Macaulay, Gladstone and images of the British Parliament. To him, 'literature' does not convey important truths but politics he finds more palpable and alive, as he confesses to Amal. English literature itself is never mentioned and 'literature' is the Bengali literature that Charu is steeped in.

Bhupati takes no enjoyment in poetry, novels and the like that affect other people, as he tells Amal, and one senses the strange limbo that cosmopolitanism brought to the educated Indian. A sense of cultural confusion, which the Bengal Renaissance brought about, is implied by Nishikanta's offering of a puja at the Kali temple for a liberal victory under Gladstone.[13] Yet, this is of extreme importance as a liberal victory would mean better governance and perhaps less tyranny. Although a sense of nationalism is yet to be aroused in the class, one can still sense an awareness of politics in them. Ironically, however, Bhupati is unaware of the crisis brewing in his own household on account of his wife and the same Amal he has taken under his wing. Even as he celebrates the liberal victory in his Victorian drawing room, his wife is about to yield to Amal. Charu is drawn to Amal because both cherish the Bengali literature that Bhupati is distant from, and the triangle thus becomes infused with political significance. Bengali literature becomes a political force that pulls his own household asunder.

Amal is like a younger brother to Bhupati and it has been noted that Ray, while researching material for his film, found references to Tagore's own relationship with his sister-in-law.[14] The proximity allowed in the 'bhabi-devar' interactions makes eroticism possible and aspects of this have been also seen in popular Hindi films like *Hum Aapke Hain Koun ...!* (1994). Ray himself hinted at it in his later film *Shakha Proshakha* (1990).[15] Ray's film does not contain any explicit indication of a sexual relationship between Charu and Amal, but the outcome of estrangement with the husband is real.

Bhupati's newspaper, as his brother-in-law points out derisively, is purely political and bereft of gossip or entertainment, and hence finds few readers. It is also, as we come to know, established in imitation of Surendranath Banerjea's actual paper *The Bengalee*, which too was political. Through this particular set of characterisations, the plotting and dialogues, Satyajit Ray offers us a glimpse of the initiation of the nineteenth-century Bengal Renaissance and its conflicting politics as played out within the confines of Bhupati's home.

What is significant is that Tagore himself *did not include* this take on the Bengal Renaissance in his novella. Instead, his entire focus is on Bhupati, Charu and Amal's relationship and the emotional mess that it creates. When Ray researched *Charulata*, he found a draft copy of the manuscript with Tagore's notes in the margin that spoke of autobiographical connections. This focus by Tagore on the personal declines to contextualise the story within a larger whole and Ray's approach is a more historically nuanced one, where the inner and outer quarters of Bhupati's household come to symbolise not only the personal but also the cultural threads later to take on larger significances – implied by Partha Chatterjee when he speaks of the inner realm being nationalistic.

All three key characters in the film exhibit a sense of confusion as far as their cultural or political identities are concerned. While Bhupati is lost in bourgeois and political ideas, Charu, finding herself neglected and drawn to Amal because of their shared love for the Bengali language and Bankim's writing, is confused because her confinement to the inner quarters makes her unable to sense the changes in the outside world except through literature. Her husband, although a keen participant in this outside political world, is unable to bring its ideals into his own household. Amal's confusion lies in trying to be a cultural being that he is not; his bid is to establish himself as a writer but his efforts turn out to be more superficial than

Charu's. While he and Charu discuss Bankim's works, Charu's analysis of Bankim rings as more deeply thought out and truer. The confusion may be taken to mirror contradictions in the Bengal Renaissance, which was nationalistic in a nascent way without being fully aware of it. Its yearnings were thus unfocussed and without direction.

As other instances of the cultural confusion that Ray is portraying in *Charulata*, when Bhupati tries to tempt Amal into marriage, he tells Amal that his would-be father-in-law will be sending him to England for further studies. The image of England conjured up by Bhupati is that of political leaders and thinkers, while Amal's imagination involves Byron's poetry and the imagery of the Mediterranean – the sound of which he imagines as like the sitar, a stringed musical instrument. But it does not prevent Amal from playing 'God Save the Queen' on the piano. While Bhupati wears a dressing gown or is mostly seen in Western attire, Amal wears the kurta and dhoti as a quintessential Bengali would. Bhupati, enamoured of the English language, has a wife who loves literature although she is more at home with Bengali writers.[16] The men are ostensibly carrying forward nationalist ideals, but it is still Charu who is more in tune with the zeitgeist of the times.

Ray thus sets up this conflict between an alien modernity absorbed by an elite class without a deep understanding of its implications, and an indigenous form of it, a hybrid of the 'spiritual' owing to local tradition and a Western modernity. When Charu begins to write, it is in the same language in which she converses and reads – Bengali. The printing press was first introduced by William Caxton into Britain in 1476; when the British colonised India, many Indians took to this invention readily, appropriating it to publish newsletters and literary journals. It thus became an important medium for dissemination of information and knowledge and led to what Benedict Anderson refers to as 'print capitalism'. It was also a source that gave rise to notions of nationalism: social, economic and cultural practices were recognised as common with the rise of the printing press and the mass reproduction of printed material in the local language. Nationalism brought about by print capitalism includes the development of the vernacular and that is given emphasis in Charulata's literary efforts.

Nationalism scholar Steven Kemper echoes Benedict Anderson when he elaborates on the role of the printing press as 'making possible for enormous numbers of people to know of one indirectly, for the printing press became the middleman to the imagination of the community'. He further continues that for Anderson, the 'very existence and regularity of newspapers caused readers, and thus citizens-in-the-making, to imagine themselves residing in a common time and place, united by a print language with a league of anonymous equals'.[17] The revolutionary vernacularisation and the thrust of print capitalism were central to the creation of imagined communities, as the mass mechanical reproduction of printed works united people who would otherwise have found it difficult to imagine themselves as part of the same community, mainly because of extreme linguistic differences in the dialects they spoke.

An interesting strand in the film is Ray's critique of the Bengal Renaissance through Bhupati's character. Ray seems to hint that the Renaissance was essentially a male bourgeois fantasy which was backed by wealth, lofty ideals, self-indulgence and Anglophilia. Bhupati sprouts liberal ethics while he neglects his literary-minded wife at home; her idea that his newspaper could have an English political component as well as a Bengali cultural one even shocks him. Bhupati's Anglophilia is indicative of a part of the imperial project of colonialism. But it would, ironically, also be this elite class that would first raise the battle cry for nationalism and dream of a possible vision, that of a free India.

Nascent Nationalism, Swadeshi and *Ghare Baire* (1984)

Like *Charulata*, *Satyajit* Ray's 1984 film *Ghare Baire* too is an adaptation of a Tagore novel. Its focus is, however, on the various kinds of nationalism in conflict in the heart of India at a slightly later period. The Swadeshi movement evolved as a result of Curzon's decision to divide the Bengal presidency into East and West Bengal in 1905. Indians, especially the people of Bengal, protested by calling for a boycott of imported goods and the adoption of indigenous alternatives. Tagore wrote his novella based on what he saw taking place around him both in 1905 and later. The idea of Swadeshi meant different things to different people and this finds a reflection in his novel.

Ghare Baire (*The Home and the World*), published in 1916, is the story of Bimala and Nikhilesh, who decides to bring his wife out of inner seclusion, which was the practice of the day. He wishes to make Bimala a modern woman in every way and teaches her to speak English, sing and play the piano. Bimala meets Sandip, Nikhil's best friend, and falls in love with him. Sandip, a fiery Swadeshi leader with a particular brand of militant Swadeshi, stirs up trouble and a riot in the erstwhile peaceful Sukhshayar, eventually leading to the death of the zamindar, his own friend and Bimala's husband, Nikhil.[18]

The Swadeshi movement was not simply restricted to being an economic one. Many critics deemed it 'self-reliance' in diet, habits, in life, in arts, in literature, in science, in religion and in philosophy – aspects central to existence. It is evident that from the beginning the movement was ambitious in scope and attempted to cover all aspects of human life. Rabindranath Tagore, even then one of the leading literary and cultural figures of Bengal, was initially attracted to the movement, wrote some inspiring songs and also discussed the idea of *atmashakti* or building up the nation's strength. However, he withdrew from it in 1907 when the movement became too violent.

To Surendranath Banerjea, a 'moderate', the Swadeshi movement meant a revolution of sorts. However, later historians have not seen it as such and found it to be a Hindu crusade which alienated vast populations of Muslims in Bengal who remained aloof from it. Also, while the crusaders were able to establish indigenous businesses and industries, few of their products could supplant imported merchandise on a long-term basis. Culturally too, it did not have a lasting effect although it did give birth to the Bengal School of Art. While all Bengali Hindus opposed the partition of Bengal, not all of them wanted to sever their links with European art and letters. Upendrakishore Ray, Satyajit Ray's grandfather, was one of them. However, in the art arena, among practitioners led by Abanindranath Tagore, Rabindranath Tagore's nephew, there was a clamouring for infusing art with a 'spiritual', non-naturalistic style that was essentially Indian, and put aside Western naturalism.

Even though the 'Bengal School' and its artistic output complemented the Swadeshi spirit, they were also welcomed by the Raj as examples of a safe and legitimate Swadeshi – which could entice Bengali youth away from nationalism of a more political nature. Latter-day art historians and critics have pointed out that there was no such artistic style that was essentially Indian, only a mosaic of various regional styles. The foremost among such scholars were Gurusaday Dutt and Akshaya Kumar Maitreya. One of the major critics of the Bengal school was Upendrakishore Ray himself. Tagore also insisted that there was no need to stress this nationality aspect in art in his university.

The Many Spaces of Swadeshi

From 1908 onwards, the Swadeshi movement turned violent, and it is this moment in history in which Tagore's novel is located. Nikhilesh is the zamindar of Sukhshayar, in which there are both Hindu and Muslim subjects. Nikhil is a man with a modern outlook and kindly disposition, who thinks about his subjects a great deal. It is such thoughts that prevent him from practising Sandip's particular brand of Swadeshi, which makes him seem a weakling to his wife and prevents her from seeing him truly for what he is. He finds women's imprisonment within the household an

Figure 2.2 Sandip and Nikhil's fight over their individual ideologies stretches to that of possessing the woman's body.

offensive notion, and proceeds to release his wife from such household captivity in the *andar mahal*. He is an enlightened young man who wants his wife to become his equal and love him only of her own free will and not because he is her husband. He goes about getting for her an English governess, Ms Gilby, who will give her a thoroughly liberal English education, thus turning her into a liberal.

However, the timing opted for by Nikhil for his wife's liberation is all wrong. The winds of Swadeshi which have begun blowing inspire a young boy to pelt Ms Gilby with stones as an expression of hatred against all things foreign. This forces her to leave the Choudhury household and Bimala's education is prematurely terminated. Immediately after this, Sandip, Nikhil's best friend of many years whom Nikhil has supported with money to fund his activities, visits their house and sweeps Bimala off her feet with his fiery Swadeshi speech. Unlike Charulata in the earlier film, Bimala is well versed in politics and takes a keen interest in it, although her interests are quite diverse. She designs her own blouses, sings English tunes and to Sandip's surprise, even plays the piano. It is thirty-five years since Charulata's story and things have changed.[19] But it is Nikhil who actually decides to end her confinement by introducing her to Sandip – although to a personal end. He wants Bimala to love him even after she has been exposed to the world outside.

At the heart of *Ghare Baire* is the conflict between two similar but varying forms of nationalism. While Sandip's is the more radical and militant Swadeshi, Nikhil's is more pro-poor, socially conscious and gentler at the grassroot level. Sandip goes around Nikhil's estate burning foreign goods seized forcibly from Nikhil's poor Muslim subjects, scuttling their boats and forcing them to sell indigenous goods, but Nikhil, long before the call for Swadeshi, had tried to manufacture indigenous goods on his estate, resulting in huge losses for him. As his sister-in-law concedes, the indigenous goods, apart from being more expensive, were inferior products compared to British-made merchandise.

When threats do not work, Sandip takes to subterfuge to harass his Muslim subjects, aided by Nikhil's manager, who considers Nikhil a weakling. Time and again Nikhil warns Sandip of the divide that this policy will create, not only between his subjects but within the larger Hindu and Muslim population all over the country, and declares it unwise. Religious leaders now cross over from Dhaka to rouse the local Muslims against injustices done to them by caste Hindus and urging them to fight back; and the British ploy of 'divide and rule' emerges triumphant. Being a conscientious zamindar, Nikhil urges Sandip to leave his poor Muslim subjects alone. While the Hindu leaders call him 'anti-national', Nikhil remains unperturbed and civilly asks Sandip to leave Sukhshayar.

Several critics have argued that the character of Nikhil is modelled on Tagore himself, who enthusiastically led processions against the British and who was an active participant in the Swadeshi movement. When the partition of Bengal came through, Tagore wrote rousing songs to awaken the citizenry of the country, which proved influential and popular. However, as the movement came to inculcate violence, Tagore left it of his own volition and began protesting through his literature. One can perhaps see *Ghare Baire* as a form of protest literature. It tries to bring to light not only the consequences of the extremism adopted by the Hindus, but also of the unviability of the philosophy driving the movement forward. What Tagore's novel comes to highlight is the less thought-out sides to the Swadeshi movement, in which the likely future fissures are not anticipated.

Much like the Bengal Renaissance, which was a bourgeois fantasy, the Swadeshi movement also failed to take everyone along. Women were not included, and it is Nikhil's failing as much as Bimala's when she chooses Sandip over him, and Nikhil feels betrayed. If one scrutinises the film carefully, one will see that it is Nikhil's insistence on treating Bimala as a subject of his experimentation that destroys their marriage. He puts himself across as a superior human being through his achievements and impeccable conduct. Even when Bimala returns to him disillusioned with Sandip, he does not chastise her but feels vindicated in his assessment of Sandip. He insists on treating Bimala more as an apprentice rather than his political equal, and is surprised beyond measure when he finds her knowledgeable about the milieu and someone who keeps abreast of the political happenings in the country.

The novel is also an excellent explication of Tagore and Bankim's ideas of nationalism, which seemed to contest each other.[20] Both figures were important to the way the intellectuals thought about certain issues of the day. As is clear from a reading of the novel, which is polemical, Tagore was grappling with ideas of nationalism that were in conflict with those of the remaining nationalist leaders, and much ahead of its times. The novel, in many ways, is an introspective and dark one and Ray's film mirrors it with a few exceptions, such as when Ray imbues it with his own understanding of history. Tagore's novel is divided into three parts and styled on diary entries by the three protagonists. Ray's film, however, is more interactive and offers a greater agency to the woman, Bimala. Ray is faithful to the basic details of the text, except for the ending, which is a definitive one. Several characters, such as Nikhil's grandmother and Panchu, the lower caste man whom Nikhil helps, are done away with, as are some other characters. Ray's screenplay makes the story a crisper and sharper piece of narration that explores a certain historic moment in the nationalist struggle as it unfolded.

The overlapping narrative style of Tagore's novel is rejected by Ray in favour of a more linear chronological narrative. Interestingly, the political and the personal stories of love and betrayal are interwoven in the film, unlike in the novel. The 'home' and the 'world' so integral to the novel is retained to show the collapse of the personal one leading to the collapse of the social other. The central philosophical concerns of the text remain intact in Ray's treatment of Tagore's novel. Alongside the rhetoric on nationalism which divides the two friends, Ray makes much of the coming out of Bimala from her seclusion in the *andar mahal*. In a long shot lasting for several minutes, the two are seen walking along the passageway that divides the home from the world – according to Ray it is not only a transformative event in Bimala's life, but also a definitive one since Bimala as an individual is subsequently defined by it.

The outside world rushes upon Bimala in the only room outside the inner sanctum sanctorum – a large drawing room fashioned like an English parlour, decorated with English artifacts. This is where she comes into contact with Miss Gilby, Sandip and Amulya. It thus becomes a liminal space between the home and the world. As her relationship with Sandip grows, she longs to become a part of this outside world, whereas Nikhil gradually retreats inside/inward. When Sandip sees Bimala for the first time, the interaction is a curious mixture of the political and the erotic. Nikhil had already forewarned Bimala about this side of Sandip's character, and it hardly comes as a surprise to him when Sandip tries to win Bimala over to his side for his political cause. At the same time, unlike in *Charulata*, the film does not depart much from Tagore's story. Tagore was demarcating his own position polemically and, while Ray maintains a distance from Tagore and looks at the conflict in perspective, one cannot say that his film is a substantial reworking.

Ray does not, for instance, make much of the various other kinds of nationalism apart from Bankim's kind. Chandak Sengoopta notes the fact that the Sadharon Brahmo Samaj members were the precursors of nationalism in India.[21] Surendranath Banerjea lectured extensively on Mazzini and Italian nationalism, and inspired youth in Calcutta were forming secret societies imitating the Carbonari. English-educated Indians often tended to equate 'Indian' with 'Hindu' or mythically with 'Aryan', portraying centuries of Muslim rule as despotic, which was infinitely worse than British Raj; but we are not merely speculating actualities here and the treatment of Muslims had another aim.

Historian Anuradha Roy points out this Hindu emphasis was another way of imagining the culturally diverse nation as a unitary, powerful entity.[22] The 'Muslim invader' was used to symbolise all foreign rulers including the British, but in a form that would not attract their attention. James Todd's hugely popular *Annals and Antiquities of Rajasthan*[23] was used to encourage contemporary Hindus to rediscover the martial prowess and patriotism of the erstwhile Rajput princes as a universal model. *Anandmath* was one such novelistic effort to rouse the Bengalis of his day into action. As is evident from the above, this prompting through 'metaphor' only led to divisions along religious lines that would finally culminate in the horrific partition of the country into India and Pakistan – and bring about untold misery and trauma, which remains a festering wound even to this day. Tagore's novel on the other hand, as Ashish Nandy notes, 'offers a critique of nationalism but also a perspective on the form that anti-imperialism should take in a multi-ethnic, multi-religious society where a colonial political economy encourages the growth of a complex set of dependencies'.[24] In such a society, Nandy argues, the politically and economically weak may be dependent on the colonial system rather than the privileged ones of that society, and it is precisely this that Tagore wanted his readers to be made aware of. The treatment of the minorities is as crucial today as it was then, and Ray's treatment of the subject becomes especially important as it points out lapses in the way Indians thought about politics, living from moment to moment without paying heed to the future, without recognising that the present led there.

Conclusion: Failed Men and Strong Women

This book is about the men in Ray's films while, in the two films examined in this chapter, it is the women who shine brighter than the men. As already noted in the Introduction, there was a movement towards women's empowerment in the era we have just dealt with, and much of the Bengali literature of the period was preoccupied with the woman's question. Ray was probing historical issues through his two films, but the films themselves are adaptations of didactic writing – although Ray tones down the didacticism, which would be out of place today. Still, one should consider the possibility that the films are not realistic representations of women as they actually were in the nineteenth century, but an enactment located in the present of how they might ideally have been – showing courage and fortitude when the men in their respective lives singularly fail them. The term 'Bengal Renaissance' has a triumphant note to it but, judging by what Ray shows in his films, it was an era beset by much confusion, since it heralded the beginning of the nationalist movement; however, not only had there been no nation corresponding to 'India' before that, but even the colonisers did not see a single Indian nation as a possibility. The classes that Ray (and Tagore) deal with are only feeling the stirrings of nationalism and it is altogether scattered and confused. Ironically, in the nationalist Sandip's doings, it is not even the colonialists but the Muslims who are made to suffer the most. The irony is especially sharp when we see that while targets are ostensibly the colonial administration, the actual victims are neighbours disinclined to join the movement. Seen in this light, Ray's emphasis on the women is actually a way of pointing at a failure of the men. Since the movement was led by men, we could say that treating the men thus is Ray's method of approaching nationalist claims about the Bengal Renaissance with scepticism. Tagore, in both novels, is too preoccupied with the issues of the day to take a nuanced view of the changes underway but Ray, filming the novels a century or so later, is more interested in bringing a perspective to them. This is essentially the value he brings to the films: re-examining and picturing the Bengal Renaissance – as the embryonic and confused anti-colonial movement it might actually have been – by placing his emphasis on strong women suffering at the hands of weak men enlisted by causes, when the movement was led by male emblems of patriotism widely celebrated today.

But the failure of masculinity in nineteenth-century colonial India as portrayed by Ray in the two films merits further interpretation. Masculinity is either ineffectual or destructive (as in the case of Sandip in *Ghare Baire*) and this should be read in conjunction with the kind of nationalisms portrayed. In both films the nationalism is not strictly anti-British, in that it targets the Raj only indirectly and the worst sufferers in the later film are Muslim traders whose goods are destroyed due to Sandip's exertions. Indian goods could not compete with British-manufactured merchandise and the movement could only be gestural, in any case. Ray is, through the sexual triangles, implying political action ill-conceived or premature. The failed masculinity of the men leads to an untimely and ineffectual release; the women seem stronger because, having been excluded from politics by patriarchy and given only a limited social role outside their families, they try to be true to themselves as individuals within a restricted domain. In these films, as in later ones, the motif of the subjugated women emerging stronger than the men in their lives is used to critique India's history.

Notes

1. Benedict Anderson, *Imagined Communities: Reflections on the Origin and Spread of Nationalism* (London: Verso, 2006), 4.
2. Ibid., 6.
3. Bruce McCull, 'The Origins of Indian Nationalism According to Native Writers' in *The Journal of Modern History*, 7/3 (September 1935), 295–314. The essay takes up the particular case of the development of Indian nationalism and argues that it was a British product.
4. The Tagore family was industrious in running two newsletters, called *Bharati* and *Baalok*, which contained both literary as well as political issues in which even the women were encouraged to contribute.
5. According to Partha Chatterjee, articulation of anti-colonial nationalism rests on a division or separation between two distinct spheres, namely, the spiritual and the material. The material realm is one of economy, statecraft, science and technology, in which the superiority of the West, represented by the colonial power, is an established fact. In the material domain therefore, the historical task before the colonised was to imitate and reproduce for itself the benefits of the project of colonial enlightenment and modernity. The spiritual realm, on the other hand, represented true sovereignty of the colonised. It was a sphere of cultural distinctness from, and also superiority over, the colonisers of the colonised people, and hence needed to be preserved that way. If the material sphere represented the superiority of the colonial rulers, it was

the spiritual domain which was the main source of strength and autonomy of the colonised. Therefore, the spiritual domain was one that needed to be preserved from all colonial encroachments. This, according to Chatterjee, symbolised nationalism among the colonised people. Any kind of reforms or intervention in the said domain would be completely in the hands of the colonised masses. Therefore, the essence of the 'imagined' nation rested in the so-called spiritual or inner domain, in which the colonised masses were sovereign despite being ruled by an alien, foreign power in the material sphere. Partha Chatterjee, *The Nation and its Fragments: Colonial and Postcolonial Histories* (Princeton: Princeton University Press, 1993), 6–7.

6. The Swadeshi Movement was started as a protest against partition and got a formal proclamation on 7 August 1905 at a meeting held at the Calcutta Town Hall. It was a movement suggested by Krishan Kumar Mitra's journal *Sanjivani* in 1905. Swadeshi leaders appealed to Indians to boycott government services, courts, schools and colleges and foreign goods, while promoting Swadeshi goods and national education through the establishment of national schools and colleges. Hence, it was not only a political movement but an economic and cultural one as well. Several exclusive Indian industrial ventures, such as Bengal Chemical Swadeshi Stores (started by Acharya P. C. Ray), Lakshmi Cotton Mills, Mohini Mills and National Tannery were started.

7. Abanindranath Tagore, one of the founders of the Bengal School of Art, first came up with the image of India as Bharat Mata and painted her as such in 1905. She is painted as a saffron-clad woman, dressed as a sadhvi (woman ascetic), holding a book, some sheaves of paddy, a piece of white cloth and a garland in her four hands respectively. It drew from Hindu religious imagery, which equates multiple hands with immense power. Tapati Guha-Thakurta, *Art and Visual Culture in India 1857–2007* (Mumbai: Marg Publications, 2009). Also see Sumathi Ramaswamy, *Goddess and the Nation* (New Delhi: Zubaan, 2014) and Martin Jay and Sumathi Ramaswamy (eds), *Empires of Vision: Objects/Histories* (Durham, NC: Duke University Press, 2014).

8. See Rabindranath Tagore's book, *Nationalism* (New York: The Macmillan Company, 1917), 127, 133.

9. Lalmohun Ghosh, 'The Natives and the Government of India: an Address Delivered by Lalmohun Ghosh at the Willis Rooms on July 23rd, 1879,' (London, 1879), 7–8, 18. https://www.jstor.org/stable/10.2307/60226430 (last accessed 25 January 2020).

10. Macaulay's famous Minute on Education of 1935 eventually paved the way from religious/moral emphasis in English education to a secular/practical basis, one geared more towards worldly knowledge and the various occupations. The rhetoric of morality gave way to a scheme of education that aimed to create a middle-class serving as an agency of imperialist economy and administration. Education was differentiated on the supposition that division

of labor was the key to England's economic prosperity; to the masses it was to be limited to 'useful and practical' areas, but a small influential intellectual segment was also to be created out of the learned classes to eventually serve in the government. Gauri Viswanathan, *Masks of Conquest: Literary Study and British Rule in India* (New Delhi: Oxford University Press, 1998), 146–7.

11. K. M. Panikkar, *Indian Nationalism, its Origin, History, and Ideals* (London: Faith Press, 1920), 11–12.
12. A conscious effort was made by Ray to sketch out in great detail the woman Charulata's daily life, for instance in the celebrated opening segment with her viewing the street through opera glasses. These details are not to be found in Tagore's novella.
13. These are all additions made by Ray to Tagore's text in order to highlight his critique of the Bengal Renaissance.
14. Shohini Ghosh, '*Hum Aapke Hain Koun ...!* Pluralizing Pleasures of Viewership', *Social Scientist* 28/3/4 (March–April, 2000), 88.
15. Ibid., 83–90.
16. The men Amal and Bhupati come across as hybrids much in the sense of Macaulay's envisaging of native Indian men. Charu has no such qualms since she is immersed only in local culture.
17. Kemper, Steven. *The Presence of the Past: Chronicles, Politics, and Culture in Sinhala Life* (Ithaca: Cornell University Press, 1991), 4.
18. *Ghare Baire* is a polemical novel that looks at the two different kinds of Swadeshi in practice as Tagore saw it. Rabindranath Tagore, *The Home and the World*, trans. Sreejata Guha (New Delhi: Penguin, 2005).
19. Both *Charulata* and *Ghare Baire* are written by Tagore and were made by Ray into films in the space of twenty years, but *Charulata* is a more complex film while *Ghare Baire* is a simpler, more straightforward film. This difference can be attributed to the issues underlying *Charulata* being historically more complex, since it stands at the cusp of national feeling. The later film can simply be understood as a critique of Hindu nationalism, which has become pertinent in independent India. These aspects of the film will be touched upon later.
20. One could perhaps read the novel as Tagore's political dialogue with Bankim's ideas of nationalism, which were far more militant and of which Sandip's rhetoric may be seen as representative. Bankim keeps appearing as a recurrent trope in Tagore's novels.
21. Chandak Sengoopta, *The Rays before Satyajit* (New Delhi: Oxford University Press, 2016), 147–8.
22. Anuradha Roy, *Nationalism as Poetic Discourse in Nineteenth-Century Bengal* (Calcutta: Papyrus, 2003), 48–49.
23. James Todd, *Annals and Antiquities of Rajasthan* (London: Humphrey Milford/Oxford University Press, 1920).
24. Ashish Nandy, *The Illegitimacy of Nationalism* (New Delhi: Oxford University Press, 1994), 19.

CHAPTER 3

Breaking with the Past: The Apu Trilogy

Satyajit Ray shot to fame with his debut film *Pather Panchali*, the first part of The Apu Trilogy. *Pather Panchali* traces the birth and growth of Apu until he is six years old. *Aparajito* and *Apur Sansar* deal with his adolescent years and Apu attaining manhood respectively. One can read The Apu Trilogy as a bildungsroman[1] since that genre concerns itself with the individual discovering himself.

The birth of the bildungsroman as a genre is dated to the publication of *Wilhelm Meister's Apprenticeship* by Goethe in 1785–1796 or sometimes to Christoph Martin Wieland's *Geschichte des Agathon* of 1769. Although it originated in Germany it later spread to the rest of the world. As a genre it focusses on the psychological and moral growth of the protagonist from childhood to adulthood, in which character transformation or development is important. One however observes that bildungsroman novels usually focus on a male protagonist, as is the case with Ray's trilogy. One can attribute this male-centeredness of the bildungsroman to it being a genre dealing with individual self-discovery while woman protagonists learn to conform to gender givens, rather than discover themselves as individuals. *Anna Karenina* and *Pride and Prejudice* – which are about strong women – are, as instances, about women adjusting to patriarchal societies, either successfully or unsuccessfully, as the case may be. While in everyday life women have entered the public sphere and their voices can be heard in politics and the media, in gender conceptualisation they are still confined to the realm of the personal and the private, as Ljiljana Ina Gjurgain notes.[2]

In Apu's context, the fact that he is male becomes particularly relevant as his growth alongside the emergent nation partly informs the allegorical essence of the Trilogy. Apu's growth from childhood to manhood encapsulates in a way the conflicts, the paradoxes and histories of a nation in the making, although Ray is careful to allow it to be *our reading* through scrupulously realist storytelling. In the Trilogy – which is based on autobiographical novels by Bibhutibhushan Bandopadhyay – Apu grows up to become a writer, and it would be pertinent at this point to examine how the writer as creative artist was represented in popular cinema at around the same time. Evidently the creative artist had significance in the popular culture of the time to be thus represented.

Popular Cinema's Depictions of the Writer

The creative artist as protagonist is not a common one for Hindi cinema and presupposes, even in popular cinema, a filmmaker who is serious about himself or herself as an artist. *Pyaasa* made in 1957 and directed by Guru Dutt, is among the first of such films and the creative artist assumes the figure of a poet. A struggling poet, Vijay, tries to get his work published but is unsuccessful. But he gets unexpected support from a prostitute who falls in love with his work. Eventually his poems are brought out by a publisher – married to his former beloved – who profiteers selling Vijay's works. Eventually the poet rejects the city and goes away with the woman who loves him. Another film with a comparable theme was made by another doyen, V. Shantaram, in 1959, and portrays the writer-poet through *Navrang* (1959). The film is about a poet who is obsessed with his wife, who is also his muse. The film brings love for his wife and his inspiration from his muse into conflict.

Both films, it would seem, are about creative writers at odds with the world as it is. Although the socio-political world is not made much of in either film, it has nonetheless a presence which is eclipsed when the poets find or rediscover love. Neither film is 'social criticism' in the accepted sense. *Navrang* is set nominally in colonial India, and *Pyaasa*, which is contemporary, bemoans the self-serving attitudes of the bourgeoisie and may be similar to Raj Kapoor's *Shree 420* (1955). But there is a sense in both films of a retreat into a private space because of disillusionment with post-1947 society, where egalitarianism has not gained ground and privilege rules. Love triumphing over social issues in the consciousness of the protagonists arguably implies a retreat. Still, both films, through the figure of the poet, are affirmations of India finding its voice after 1947.

The two films along with The Apu Trilogy were made within a few years of each other, which suggests parallel concerns, although their respective treatment of the figure of the writer does not bear much comparison. In one sense *Pyaasa* is closer to the Apu Trilogy, especially in its reflection of the individual's growth into self-awareness, but *Navrang* is closer to *Apur Sansar* in privileging marital love over writerly ambitions. But before we go on to look at the significance of these later motifs, we should examine the first film of The Apu Trilogy, which is *Pather Panchali*.

Pather Panchali (1954)

Bibhutibhushan Bandyopadhyay's novel *Pather Panchali*, an adaptation of which Ray began his career in cinema with, is a novel containing autobiographical elements. It is a novel that reflects on a pre-independent Bengali society based in a fictional village, Nischindipur, and its inhabitants but whose central focus is a brahmin family called the Roys. But more importantly, it traces the growth of the young boy Apu, whose inner and outer journeys form the crux of the novel.

Bibhutibhushan Bandopadhyay's *Pather Panchali* is a rambling, romantic novel that constantly moves between elation and grief. Both the literary text as well as the film provide evidence of Bibhutibhushan's love of nature, although Ray's film is grimmer and more contemporary when highlighting its destructive power. Durga dies because of an illness caught after a soaking in the rain, but that is in Ray's altered rendering of the story. At the start of *Pather Panchali* Apu is not present and we first see him through an image of his eye opening as a child. Ray's *Pather Panchali* covers Apu's life only until he is six years old, and Apu is hence more an organising consciousness[3] than an individual.

Born to Harihar and Sarabajaya six years after Durga, their eldest child, Sarbojaya believes that Apu will alleviate their poverty. He is a shy little boy with an unquenchable curiosity. If The Apu Trilogy refers to the independent nation, specifically subjecthood within it, it is set earlier in the century. As indicated in the Introduction, it is about looking at the modern with new eyes, allegorising India awakening to a new reality. The film can, at once, be read as being about the hopes of independence and the arrival of modernity. Apu's curiosity is evidently directed towards the 'new'.

As a postcolonial artist too, arguably, Ray felt the need to examine the contexts that shaped his identity as an artist in an emerging nation, and one may even read the film through this lens. But what is important from the viewpoint here is the fact that the only conspicuous man in *Pather Panchali* is not Apu, but his father Harihar Roy, who has left his household responsibilities to his wife, and it is Sarbojaya who manages when there is not enough to feed the family. At one point we see her surreptitiously picking up a coconut fallen by the path and we sense the daily desperation dogging her. So there is a strange dichotomy operating here – Apu representing the young independent nation opening its eyes to a modern world, while his father, as a priest, is the product of tradition

Figure 3.1 The ancient and the modern, the past and the present – the father and the son in *Pather Panchali*.

and ineffectual. As already argued in this book, the weakness or 'femininity' of the male under colonialism is a recurring theme in Indian cinema, including Ray's films. Judged in that context Apu's task – what he needs to demonstrate through his development – is to be different from his father.

Apu, born to a priest father sometime in the early decades of the twentieth century, is like a link between the past (tradition) and an anticipated future. In the course of the Trilogy, he abandons his father's vocation of priest to pursue education and fulfil a desire to hold a job in the city. He also abandons his village to migrate there. Despite the scarcity of resources, Harihar had initially refused to be uprooted from his ancestral family home. At the end of the film, after Durga's death, when he does decide to move to Varanasi, a neighbour can be heard saying to Sarbojaya: 'It is not a good thing to get attached to any one place. It makes one's life become narrow, and the mind constricted.' But there is more to this move by the family than moving out, because it hints at a larger territory available to Apu than tradition bequeathed him, as he moves from Nischindipur to Varanasi, back to Mansapota in Bengal and thence to Calcutta. Later still, Apu will move around a great deal of India, finally leaving for Tahiti in Bibhutibhusan's novel. Ray evidently did not think

Tahiti a plausible destination for Apu, but Bibhutibhushan may have heard of Paul Gauguin as an artist who moved there, and made Apu do likewise as a writer. Bibhutibhushan did not anticipate an independent India with citizens loyal to a territory when he wrote the novel, and Tahiti is the unfettered 'anywhere' – which might be a difficult imagining for an artist moored to a nation.

But the motif of train journeys from place to place undertaken by the protagonist is also a common motif in post-1947 Indian cinema, in films like Bimal Roy's *Devdas* (1955) and Sohrab Modi's *Jailor* (1958), which has been interpreted as a geographical assertion of national unity.[4] The very fact of an independent nation with borders is enough for the citizen to envisage covering the space sometime in his or her life, and that is how I interpret Apu's movement. In the earlier chapters I dealt with Ray's films set before Independence, and in all of them, being confined to a place is a characteristic of the protagonist's existence.[5] Of course, Apu does not wander around India in the earlier parts of the Trilogy, but Ray is being careful here not to treat places as emblems, sticking to the locations that Apu and his family might actually have moved to. This aspect of the train as a way of linking spaces is quite different from it being an emblem of modernity.

The story of Apu is not told within a melodramatic consciousness that defines itself passively in relation to a changing world. It combines two narratives – that of an emerging modern sensibility, and that of a country emerging from its feudal and colonial past (represented by Harihar), into the dawn of Independence (Apu as a writer with a voice). 'We experience through the figure of Apu,' Dasgupta writes, 'the inevitable movement of one era into another.'[6] His growth from childhood to manhood then encapsulates, in a way, the trials and tribulations of a nation not yet made but in the making. It is this aspect that helps in our reading of the Trilogy as a bildungsroman of the nation.

Aparajito (1956)

If *Pather Panchali* represented Apu as a child, in *Aparajito* the dominant motif is that of Apu's education. Apu is displaced four times in the Trilogy and the most far reaching one (in consequence) is his move to the city, which brings him into a new world but also estranges him from his mother. The city space, rapidly transformed by modernity and Western education, has a decisive effect on his growth. In his search for independence, the move is not only away from his father's profession but also involves leaving behind his mother – who dies alone. The alienating solitude of the city, exemplified by sequences such as those of the riverside, the Victoria Memorial lawns et cetera, is in contrast with a lost life he lived in the lap of nature, in the proximity of family and community. Still, the compulsion to move away is overpowering to Apu, even if it involves forsaking his mother.

The second part of the Trilogy opens in the 1920s in Varanasi, where the family has relocated after the death of Durga. The family seems to be better off on account of Harihar having found some work as a priest, and Apu is free to wander about the ghats, the lanes and temples of the ancient city, driven on by his restlessness. Spatially and temporally *Aparajito* is divided into two sections – the first of which is located in Varanasi and the second in Mansapota. This film in essence traces Apu's journey from boyhood until the death of his mother, when he is seventeen and at the conclusion of the film's narrative. It also lays emphasis on education, associating it with progress and emancipation. Indeed, in *Apur Sansar*, Apu reiterates this when he exclaims to his friend Pulu that he has been able to get rid of his superstitions and been able to move forward only because of his (modern) education. It is no surprise that Ray upheld modern education as a liberating factor because of his Brahmo lineage and cultural inheritance. The Brahmos saw liberal education as a means of reforming orthodox Hindu society and Western learning was sought.

Apu first encounters learning at the local *pathshala* in Nischindipur, and he is seen receiving lessons from his father. There is a strong sense here of knowledge handed down from one generation to another, implying an awareness of Apu's privileged position as brahmin that entitles him to education.[7] Although other social segments are not invoked, we may understand this as Ray's acknowledgement of social stratification, that the Roy family's poverty is not the worst that India would need to engage with. Poverty is not even made the issue in *Aparajito* as it was in *Pather Panchali*, and signs of caste privilege are now visible. Gender privilege was seen in *Pather Panchali* – with men doing the writing – but not caste privilege, conspicuously. Indir threading a needle while Sarbojaya combs Durga's hair, even as Apu writes on a slate, is gender privilege.

Apu in Varanasi is gradually interacting with the world. From his friend Shambhu Apu learns English, and English evidently means more than just being the coloniser's language, since most modern knowledge is available only in English. But even though his self-worth in terms of learning is due to the coloniser's language, Apu will, first and foremost, be a good Bengali before anything else because he writes in his own tongue. As in *Charulata*, the dual attitude towards language remains embedded in *Aparajito*, another language for intellectual development and his own tongue for self-expression.

Figure 3.2 Breaking with the family past of being a priest.

After Harihar passes away, mother and son are forced to relocate to Mansapota, a village in Bengal, where Apu has to now shoulder the responsibility of providing for his family. He must revert to his father's profession even while harbouring a desire to go to school. Several worlds collide in this narrative as happened in *Pather Panchali* – the India of religion and rituals co-exists with the district school, which teaches the sciences along with English to show the way forward to willing learners.

Apu is a good student even while juggling his priestly duties and attending school in the afternoons. After a particularly impressive show before the school inspector, the headmaster begins taking a greater interest in Apu's education. He advises Apu an admixture of liberal progressive education in the form of Livingstone's travels, a book on the North Pole and another on men of science such as Archimedes, Galileo, Newton and Faraday. It is duly noted[8] that this emphasis on English, science and geography is an affirmation of Nehruvian values by Ray, duly imparted to his own protagonist. As the school headmaster is heard to remark: 'We may live in a remote corner of Bengal but that does not mean that our outlook should be narrow.'

Years pass and Apu moves to Calcutta to pursue a college degree. Sarbojaya and he quarrel since she is loath to see him go. Apu now faces the biggest challenge of all – to reconcile traditional obligations such as looking after her while pursuing his personal ambitions. The second half of *Aparajito* reflects this turmoil as Apu battles filial responsibility while the urban milieu is essential to his well-being. The globe gifted by his headmaster now acts as a marker of new worlds opening up. A long section of the film focusses on Apu's education in Calcutta alternating between lessons in English literature and mathematics, followed by shots of test tubes, burners and magnets as Apu continues his experiments. His encounters with 'knowledge' have become a part of his daily life.

When he returns to the village to the mother, it is almost reluctantly. She sews while he lies reading, seemingly self-absorbed. He now finds it difficult to reconcile the two very separate lives he leads and prefers his city self. There is a sense of alienation that Apu feels with regard to his village home. His estrangement from his mother culminates in her death before he can make time to meet her one last time, and this is tragic. But their lives were incompatible and it would have been worse for him to have been by her side, doing what she might have wanted him to do and becoming a priest like Harihar.

The film closes with Apu walking towards the railway station to catch his train to Calcutta to pursue his life in the city. He does not look back; he shows deliberation in pushing forward on his path, 'rejecting hindrances that serve no useful purpose'.[9] By doing so he cuts off ties with his mother's family and his life in the village and decides to perform his mother's last rites in Kalighat in Calcutta, and we realize that Apu has come to represent the aspirations of a whole generation – especially of Brahmins[10] – that migrated from the village to the city in anticipation of modernity.

It has been said that Satyajit Ray did not return to the lyricism of the Trilogy later in his career, but this movement away from lyricism also reflects the journey to the city in his films. It is easy to be lyrical about nature but much more difficult to be equally so about the chaos of Calcutta. We may also see *Aparajito* as the film in which, by deciding upon a 'modern' course of life for himself, Apu moves away from Harihar's legacy, embedded as that was in the consciousness of the colonised.[11]

Apur Sansar (1959)

Just as Sarbojaya's presence dominates the world of *Pather Panchali*, it is Apu who is at the center of *Apur Sansar*, as should be evident from the film's title. *Apur Sansar* opens with Apu having to give up his studies since he cannot afford college. Instead, he begins to look around for employment to sustain himself. But living in an attic room on the top of a tenement building – in which there are other tenants and where water frequently runs out – he still does not seem unhappy. Poverty, which was an issue in *Pather Panchali*, is no longer one, although there are no material reasons to think so. It just seems that Apu, being independent in spirit, does not allow it to dampen his outlook. The film is set in the precolonial era, but the consciousness of Independence permeates the film through Apu's attitude towards life. He plays the flute, bathes and washes in the rain, sells his books to pay the rent and eats what he can afford, but is nonetheless happy.

Apu enjoys being alone, is reluctant to give up his independence and, more importantly, dreams of becoming a writer; and the novel he writes has autobiographical elements in it – as did Bibhutibhushan's own novel on which the film is based. Apu's protagonist in his novel resembles him a great deal, as he tells Pulu, 'Through education, through struggle ... . he wants to live!' Apu continues talking about his novel, and over the soundtrack can be heard the familiar musical motif from *Pather Panchali*, recalling the young boy who once frolicked in the company of his sister.

One day Pulu coaxes him to join him on a trip to his village in Khulna to attend the marriage of a cousin named Aparna. At the marriage, it is revealed that the bridegroom has a serious mental disorder. The bride's mother cancels the marriage, despite the father's protests. But the father and the other villagers believe, according to tradition, that the bride must be wed during the appointed auspicious hour or she will remain unmarried all her life. Apu, after initially refusing, when requested by a few villagers, ultimately decides to take Pulu's advice – and comes to the rescue of the bride by agreeing to marry her. He returns with Aparna to his apartment in Calcutta after the wedding. Once married, Apu sees the need for candor. He tells Aparna that he has no family, also of his lack of prospects. However, he gives her the choice to remain behind with her parents in relative opulence while he returns to Calcutta, but Aparna accepts her husband and thus begins a beautiful relationship.

It is also at this moment in his life that the writerly Apu is brought down to earth. While earlier, he was not particular about how he lived, marriage awakens him to a different kind of existence. Earlier he had dismissed the notions of working as a clerk because he was a 'free man' with no dependents, but he now works as a clerk and also gives tuitions. Apu's in-laws are well-off but he wants to be able to support his wife as men are required to. It would also seem that he has to move away from becoming Harihar, and self-reliance is therefore essential. But Apu is saved all possible humiliation by having an uncomplaining wife; Sarbojaya in both *Pather Panchali* and *Aparajito* does complain but Aparna makes do with what she has and performs all the household duties cheerfully – even as Apu is aware that back in her paternal home domestic servants would have attended to every menial task.

The two transcend the apparent handicaps confronting them and still find joy in their life together, and Apu's writing begins to take a back seat, without much regret on his part. But soon enough Aparna conceives and will go home to Khulna in the last two months of her pregnancy, as Bengali customs dictate. On the way home a saddened Apu feels the weight of her impending absence and defines her importance in his life to her. Comparing her import to the one great love in his life – his writing – Apu says, 'My writing is important to me, but you're more important to me. I'll dedicate the novel to you.'

This obsession with marital state, so much as to confine the writing ambitions of someone who has yearned to be a writer to the sidelines, needs examination, and it is interesting that the motif finds reflection in Shantaram's *Navrang*, as noted earlier. What could this mean, since Apu abandons his completed novel that already been praised by his friend Pulu, as though it were of no worth? Shantaram's film, at least, can be explained in terms of the habitual inwardness inculcated, according to which all solutions to problems are directed inward. Love is often the only subject matter in some popular films and social issues – of any kind – do

Figure 3.3 Marriage as friendship and mutual respect.

not intervene in destinies. But Ray has chosen a different path and modernity is what Apu has consciously immersed himself in.

But one must also draw attention to the fact that while it is the poet who represents creativity in the popular films, Apu is trying to become a novelist. This view may be contested, but poetry as represented in popular cinema is otherworldly or steeped in metaphor – and implying universal values – while the novel is a modern form engaging strongly with the real world of today, even when it is set in the past. Divakar in *Navrang* is essentially a receptacle and emblem for romantic emotions, but Apu is individualised and his psychological trajectory is part of the Trilogy's design. Apu chooses as his vehicle the novel, which, as Ian Watts notes in his seminal book,[12] emerged in the eighteenth century due to the rise of the middle-class. Ray, in depicting Apu's literary choices, links it directly with the young Nehruvian nation, with a direction imparted to it by middle-class consciousness, since it was the educated middle-class that was the cultural fulcrum of Nehruvian modernity. However, given this aspect, it is still difficult to understand Apu's passionate immersion in marital life at the expense of his literary ambitions, and for that we need to look at the whole Trilogy. Apu is not only an emblem of national awakening after 1947, but also an individual made by his past and we have also to understand him as such – which is not to say that the two are not related. Apu faces tragedy once again when Aparna dies in childbirth, but we will examine that later.

Conclusion: Shouldering 'Manly' Responsibilities

In *Pather Panchali* Harihar Roy, in failing to provide for his family, his wife having to become provider for the family, can be understood as the 'failed masculinity' of a people under colonisation. The crisis of masculinity variously noticed and described in Indian cinema provides enough evidence. Harihar refuses to move with the times and would rather continue as tradition dictates and also follow caste hierarchy. We recollect a sequence in *Pather Panchali* when Harihar desists from giving *diksha* to a person with means entirely because he belongs to a lower caste. In one stroke Harihar's personal ineffectuality – his refusing an opportunity to help himself when he needs money – is conjoined by Ray with the worst aspects of tradition, caste being its basis.

When Harihar is travelling and looking around for work, he forgets his family altogether, evidenced by the scarce mail they receive from him. It is also during his absence that Sarbojaya is forced to move into the role of the provider and takes to selling household utensils to keep hunger at bay. As we are told in the film, Harihar had previously left Sarbojaya in her paternal home for eight years after their marriage while he resided in Varanasi, and he has been habitually like this, someone whose masculine presence in the family is not comforting.[13] The only activities we see Harihar engaging in are those of writing (he too has literary dreams and Apu inherited them), teaching Apu, eating the food cooked by Sarbojaya, doing ritual obeisance to the gods and later, in *Aparajito*, reading from the scriptures to the widows in Varanasi. But from the very beginning Sarbojaya is associated with doing the work in the household. Not only does she perform her womanly duties, but she also performs masculine ones: providing for the family when Harihar is away, pushing him to help fix the house, and providing money for Apu's education.

We could propose that since *not becoming Harihar* is a key desire in Apu's construction of himself, he devotes himself to marriage with a vengeance, since that was where Harihar failed abysmally. When Aparna dies in childbirth, Apu is unable to bear the loss and throws away the completed manuscript of his novel. His son Kajal (whom Apu instinctively blames for Aparna's death) is being brought up by Aparna's parents and is growing wild, a factor brought to Apu's notice by Pulu. Apu has been wandering about the country drifting from job to job, his unkempt beard becoming indicative of his inability to keep himself stable, but Pulu's entreaty to take up his responsibilities as a father touches him; he consents.

It is customary for critics to see Apu's loss of his wife sentimentally, but what is its true meaning in the context of the Trilogy as a whole? My own sense is that after having invested emotionally in his relationship with Aparna, her death shatters him so much that he begins to slip back into a Harihar-like condition. If the object of his responsibility is removed, what should he live for? His abandonment of his completed novel seems important, but that is autobiographical and deals with his own past, which he is only reflecting upon through it. Even unpublished, therefore, its purpose has been fulfilled – as an effort at self-understanding – and there is perhaps no need to go back to it. While Harihar dreamed of being a professional writer, Apu wants only to express himself – and perhaps exorcise the past. Although his novel was appreciated by Pulu, there is no indication that Apu wants to make something out of it. The positive ending in the film is therefore not Apu recovering the novel but *manfully* accepting the responsibilities that his own father had eluded.[14]

The Apu Trilogy is among the most important of Satyajit Ray's works because it appears to be a statement on the independent nation, especially its agenda to break with an outmoded past and embrace modernity. We earlier regarded Apu's eye as the key element in *Pather Panchali*, but Apu's experience of his father has unconsciously imprinted itself upon him, and his endeavour as a family man is to move away from that. We do not see him paying much attention to Harihar in *Pather Panchali*, but the later films imply that impact. His efforts to be modern therefore also involve moving away from traditional modes of conduct, which is what Harihar represented to him.

Based on whatever has been said, The Apu Trilogy has more complex implications than simply being an allegory of the independent nation awakening to modernity. Apu also emerges from it as a psychologically distinct and complex individual, dealing with personal issues even as his presence and doings serve the ends of allegory. There are no public events named in the films to historicise the happenings, but there is an indication in the two later films that the period is India before 1947. The motif of a writer in fiction usually implies a milieu that has found its voice, and both the Hindi films named earlier were made in the 1950s, although *Navrang* was set in colonial India. The same is true of *Apur Sansar*, which merely anticipates a milieu that *will* find its voice with independence. But I would still argue that more important to the Trilogy than Apu becoming a writer is his accepting the responsibilities ahead of him, which would include mentoring a generation to make it fit for independence. Apu is not a 'national subject' since the nation is yet to be, but it is his responsibility to make his son Kajal one – when the nation does happen. This acceptance of his role perhaps makes Apu the most 'masculine' of all Satyajit Ray's male protagonists.[15]

Notes

1. Erich Neher, 'Satyajit Ray's Apu Trilogy Restored', *The Hudson Review* 68/2 (Summer 2015), 281.
2. Ljiljana Ina Gjurgian, 'The (Im)possibilty of Women's Bildungsroman', *SRAZ-LVI*, 107–21 (2011).
3. Suranjan Ganguly, *Satyajit Ray: In Search of the Modern* (New Delhi: Penguin, 20).
4. M. K. Raghavendra, *Seduced by the Familiar: Narration and Meaning in Indian Popular Cinema* (Oxford: Oxford University Press, 2008), 147. Raghavendra notes that the pre-Independence version of *Jailor* (1938) does not include the railway journey.
5. In three of the four films dealt with – *Shatranj ke Khiladi*, *Jalsaghar* and *Ghare Baire* – the insularity of the protagonists is made an issue. In the last of the films Sandeep comes from outside, but he is also a nationalist with larger loyalties than to his immediate space. In *Charulata*, the subject is incipient nationalism, which naturally enlarges the space of the action.

6. Chidananda Dasgupta, *The Cinema of Satyajit Ray* (New Delhi: National Book Trust, 2001), 35.
7. Suranjan Ganguly, *Satyajit Ray: In Search of the Modern* (New Delhi: Penguin, 2000), 24.
8. Ibid., 30.
9. Dasgupta (2001), 47.
10. The urbanisation of Brahmins in search of professional employment from the nineteenth century onwards has been widely noted. For instance, see the following about Tamil Brahmins: C. J. Fuller, Haripriya Narasimhan, 'From Landlords to Software Engineers: Migration and Urbanization among Tamil Brahmins', *Comparative Studies in Society and History*, 50/1 (January 2008), 170–96.
11. I am describing this as the 'consciousness of the colonised' based on Harihar's ineffectuality, which finds correlation with the portrayal of males in the colonial era in popular films like P. C. Barua's *Devdas*, already discussed in the earlier chapters and also with regard to *Shatranj Ke Khiladi*.
12. Ian Watts, in his seminal study of the novel *The Rise of the Novel*, discusses this at length. Ian Watts, *The Rise of the Novel: Studies in Defoe, Richardson and Fielding* (Berkeley: University of California Press, 1957).
13. The ineffectual and wayward man who abandons his family is a motif noticed in *Aurat* (1940), of which *Mother India* (1956) was a later remake. That film is associated with the crisis of masculinity in Hindi cinema in the pre-1947 period. Raghavendra (2008), 87–8.
14. It has been noted that 'The world of Apu' is an imperfect translation of *Apur Sansar*, since the term 'sansar' also includes 'family life' as one of its meanings. This gives a different meaning to the title altogether. Peter L. Bertocci, 'Bengali Cultural Themes in Satyajit Ray's "The World of Apu"', *Journal of South Asian Literature* 19/1, Miscellany (Winter, Spring 1984), 21.
15. We noted that Wajid Ali Shah being 'artistic' instead of being a leader made him less masculine, and performing one's given social role effectively is a key way of judging 'masculinity' in Ray's films.

CHAPTER 4

'For all we have and are':
The Post-Independence Bourgeoisie in *Kanchenjungha* and *Kapurush*

Ray's cinema, as noted before, offers a consistent and perceptive critique of the nation and the citizenry it created. His 'locatedness' – in inhabiting the imaginative as well as geographical terrain of the nation – is clearsighted. To either take a position as a critic of the nation – as many leftwing filmmakers did – or embrace it patriotically as many popular films did after 1947 was not an option to him; what was possible and necessary however was to lay claim to it even as it was being spoken for by sectarian economic and cultural interests, not to forget political ones at the time of Independence. Without taking these paths, Ray instead laid claim to Indian history, seeing it unfolding under the first prime minister of India, Pandit Nehru, and then his later successor Indira Gandhi. One recalls here what Edward Said proposed about the role of the intellectual: 'With regard to the consensus on group or national identity it is the intellectual's task to show how the group is not a natural or god-given entity but is a constructed, manufactured, even in some cases invented object with a history of struggle and conquest behind it, that it is sometimes important to represent.'[1]

Postcolonial 'masculinities' have been studied by Mrinalini Sinha, Rosalind O'Hanlon, Sikata Banerjee and Sanjay Srivasatava, but these studies have mostly been studied in conjunction with violence, religiosity et cetera,[2] the most blatant manifestations. In dealing with the Indian male, Ray was not concerned with 'Indian masculinity' per se as much as the Indian subject actively interacting with the nation, being created by it and directing its future. In patriarchal societies national subjecthood is usually exemplified by the male citizen. If the male subject's masculinity is problematic, it could be interpreted as a critique of emergent India – which is how I propose to read Ray's films set after 1947.

From the Colonial to the Postcolonial

India and Pakistan became two sovereign states on 14–15 August 1947, which marked the formal transfer of power from the British imperial government to the newly formed governments of India and Pakistan. This moment in Indian history is specially marked by Nehru's historic speech 'Tryst with destiny'. While there were celebrations on the streets, there were also riots. It would be quite some time before things settled down and the two countries found their own rhythms of political life and dealt with the making of a new society. These developments have often been read in terms of the process of decolonisation in Asia and Africa in the 1950s and 60s.

The expression 'postcolonial' refers to a historical process that is inherently incomplete – that is fragmentary[3] if by decolonisation one refers to inspiring anticolonial visions of complete freedom from all possible cultural and institutional acts of domination by the coloniser. But 'decolonisation' is only a theoretical notion – especially in India's context – and in the actual historical context the coloniser and the colonised are often in a hybridising encounter. Both mimicry and hybridity are concepts we owe to Homi Bhabha and closely associated with postcolonialism. The terms were used by Bhabha to describe certain conditions in a postcolonial society.[4] Hybridity on a basic level refers to any mixing of Eastern and Western culture. Within colonial and postcolonial literature, it most commonly refers to colonial subjects from Asia or Africa who have found a balance between Eastern and Western cultural attributes. However, Bhabha, in his essay 'Signs Taken for Wonders',[5] argues that it can also be a subversive tool whereby colonised people might challenge various forms of cultural domination.

But becoming postcolonial, as Chakrabarty proposes,[6] is a process and a gradual one that occurs over a significant period. Without using the Fanonian viewpoint that theorises about the process of decolonisation from a radical perspective, society in India today must be studied taking into account a very different scenario, since significant changes occurred even when India was under British rule. The slow changing process has never, in fact, implied a rejection of political and social attitudes in the subcontinent under the British raj, which is what Fanonian 'decolonisation' would posit. One may instead apply Bhabha's term to understand Ray's films under study in this chapter.

While Ray's characters who will be dealt with in this chapter – Indranath Choudhury (*Kanchanjunga*) and Bimal Gupta (*Kapurush*) – are 'hybrids' in the broad sense of subscribing to both Eastern and Western values and being 'brown sahibs', Satyajit Ray's case – although he had imbibed Western values – as a postcolonial artist was more complicated. While Ray can be justly seen as an anglophile – the cultural influences on him, his comfort with the coloniser's language – in his choice of subjects, he has always been an Indian who observes sympathetically but critically. So, for every Indranath Choudhury there is a more 'resisting' Ashok and for every Bimal Gupta an Amitabha, although in the latter case Amitabha is not a character Ray sympathises with. This chapter is then an analysis of such complexities as arising from a postcolonial situation as portrayed by Ray.

While in the colonial period, as Partha Chatterjee argues, the reformers looked to the colonisers to help in the reformation of an orthodox conservative Hindu society, by the time we come to *Kanchenjunga* (set around 1960), the milieu being a post-Independence India, Bengali society has changed significantly but is still in need of 'reformation'. In the colonial period, Macaulay's 1835 'Minute on Education' had successfully been able to create a breed of Indians who were Indian by birth but part Englishmen in thought, speech and action. While the need for change was not disputed, there was strong resistance to allowing the colonial state to intervene in matters affecting 'national culture'. This period of resistance was the period of nationalism, but what is interesting is that even years later after Independence, this resistance can still be noted in the various characters peopling *Kanchenjunga* – in Anima, Ashok and Monisha. To the anglophile Indranath they offer 'resistance' by using their other tongue – Bengali – and talking about Tagore, an iconic figure of Bengali literature and culture but also a nationalist figure comparable to Mahatma Gandhi. What this suggests is that Ray is noting a 'colonial' conflict a decade after Independence with the anglophones still exercising authority and being 'resisted' as in the colonial era. We may recall here the conflict between the English language and Bengali in *Charulata*.

The Postcolonial Elite in Popular Cinema

Before we go on to study *Kanchanjunga* it will be helpful to examine the effect of Independence on popular cinema, where too the anglophone postcolonial elite must have been represented in the 1950s at least. In Hindi cinema this class features, but more as caricatures and there is no concern on the part of the director to understand or make sense of it in historical terms. Ray, being anglophile himself, was more drawn to portraying this class, but not as in Hindi cinema which addressed a pan-national public, including a majority that had smaller dealings with the British in everyday life.

In *Kaagaz ke Phool* (1959), a film made by Guru Dutt and representative of Hindi cinema of the 1950s, a portrayal particularly pertinent to this chapter is the representation of this anglophile class. Suresh Sinha, the protagonist, is a film director who is estranged from his wife, the daughter of a wealthy man – a 'Ray Bahadur', an honorary rank bestowed under colonialism. Although it is not clear what his background is, it comes out that he is keeping his daughter away from her husband, as well as putting his granddaughter through an expensive public school. Sir B. P. Varma is a figure of ridicule, with his accented English and his affected mannerisms, and his son Rakesh (Johnny Walker) goes by the name of Rocky. His mannerisms are as affected as his father's, although as the narrative progresses, he is revealed to be essentially a good soul. The Ray Bahadur follows British customs and emulates their publicised ways, like insisting on appointments before meeting people, keeping dogs with English names and sporting a fireplace in his manor house like his erstwhile colonial masters. In this film there is a clear-cut difference between self-made men of the independent nation (Suresh Sinha) and the former officers of the British empire, or a generation with accrued money based on working for the British in whichever capacity (like Sir B. P. Varma).

In Raj Kapoor's *Awaara* (1951), Judge Raghunath (Prithviraj Kapoor), who is Raj's father, is not anglicised in the same way as Sir B. P. Varma, but can be read as a figure of postcolonial authority and is much more overbearing. He lives in a huge house, wears a dressing gown, eats English-style meals and travels in a foreign-made car. Raj's friend, Rita's father, is also a pipe-smoking, anglicised gentleman, although like Raj, he always speaks in Hindi. But given the constituency of Hindi cinema, using English for key conversation in 1951 might have been problematic for the general audience. Strangely, even though Judge Raghunath is well educated, he harbours bizarre notions about 'breeding' and believes that criminals are produced by criminals while gentlemen engender gentlemen. This causes a crisis in the film in the Judge's own family, but it can be argued that the sense of moral qualities being inherited was largely a product of colonialism's misunderstanding of caste, since the British also identified 'criminal tribes' who were said to owe their moral qualities to their jatis. The 'Thugees' were even considered to be murderous by birth. Whether this had any basis in the caste system can be questioned, but it would seem that the British were so confused by India's social complexities that 'criminal tribes' may have seemed logical. Judge Raghunath, then, is perhaps postcolonial authority inheriting irrational colonial attitudes.

The Hindi films of the 1950s, it has been proposed, can often be read as allegories of 'postcoloniality' and M. K. Raghavendra reads the mother (living in poverty when cast out by her husband) in *Awaara* as the land which is unable to provide bread for her son.[7] Significant here is the fact that Judge Raghunath married a widow. Interpreting this alongside the mother as allegorising the land, one could propose that postcolonial authority, which was anglicised, became 'second master' to the land, and quite a heartless one at that, judging by Raghunath's conduct. This sounds uncharacteristically radical for a popular film, but it was scripted by K. A. Abbas, a Communist who had directed *Dharti Ke Lal* (1946) for the Indian People's Theatre Association (IPTA).[8] The observation here is that postcolonial issues engaged all Indian cinema in one form or another immediately after 1947, but Ray's cinema, being realistic, looked at social history in a much more observant way and we can see his portrayals as 'representational' – as popular cinema was not.

When we come to Bengali cinema, Ray's celebrated contemporaries – Ritwik Ghatak and Mrinal Sen – did not study this class. Ghatak dealt usually with rural lives (often migrants) distant from such figures of authority, while Mrinal Sen made his political films much later (*Interview*, 1971), when the anglicised Indian had virtually become a figure of fun. Ghatak, who for all his life was obsessed with the trauma of partition, chose partition as his subject in most of his films and dealt with the classes most affected by it (*Meghe Dhaka Tara*, 1960). One does not detect inscriptions of the 'nation' in his films and Bengal seems the subject. The issue of the postcolonial bourgeoisie is, however, a national one, since the class was pan-national and Satyajit Ray chose to deal with it.

Indranath Choudhary in *Kanchenjungha* (1962)

Indranath Choudhary, the central male character of *Kanchenjungha*, belongs to the upper-classes and is described as a director on the boards of five companies. He is an influential man, also the holder of the title given to him by the British and one which was also given to Suresh Sinha's father-in-law in *Kaagaz Ke Phool* – 'Ray Bahadur'. When the film begins, Indranath is on a holiday with his family in the picturesque hill station of Darjeeling. However, it is the last day of their holiday and a day when he is hoping that Banerjee, an eligible bachelor with a degree from Glasgow, will propose to his youngest daughter Monisha. The patriarch also hopes to catch a glimpse of the *Kanchenjungha* on this trip, but he also wants everything to come together like clockwork. Whether Monisha will agree to marry the UK-educated engineer who is courting her with her father's evident approval is the question at the centre of the film. Manisha's feelings about this coercion, along with the sympathetic responses of her mother and brother-in-law, form the substance of the film.

The story includes several conflicts, between the older and the younger generations, between vestiges of British India and the young independent nation, between male assertion and the beginnings of female resistance, between postcolonial authority personified by a patriarch and a young man trying to find his own independent path. Ray avoids high drama yet awakens us to the dimensions of change taking place in a postcolonial society, holding up the pompousness of a class to subtle mockery. The subaltern studies historians[9] argued that the movement of national literature which had produced visons of independent India had been flawed in that it copied the colonial regime, both in the form of the state it envisaged and in the notion of citizenship it espoused – both of which ignored the reality and complexity of Indian history and experience.

In class terms the native bourgeoisie had conceived the national liberation struggle in terms of their own production of citizen-subjects worthy of participation in a modern nation. But these new citizen-subjects – modelled on British politics – ruled the subaltern classes with as little attention to their particular experience as the former masters of the days of the Raj had done. And so, Indranath acts highhandedly when he meets his son's former tutor and is rude to his nephew. Indranath's unnamed son, who does not have to earn his keep, goes around flirting with young women on his holiday, this perhaps indicative of the ultimate results of colonial discipline and instruction on the young nation. Much like the colonies in Africa that gained freedom in 1950 and afterwards, society in India too was ruled by a class that had attained education and a livelihood at the hands of the erstwhile colonial masters. More importantly, they were a class that felt at home with the English language and with British customs and manners; they also lived in huge bungalows with signs on them that said 'Beware of Dogs' – as Ashok snidely remarks to Monisha.

There is a popular nativist critical approach to Satyajit Ray's cinema that tends to make him Bengali-centric. The implicit theory of this approach is that the normative postcolonial cultural worker is one who is close to his regional culture and has an organic relation to his language, his people, and his homeland. The telos of this critical approach is to suggest that only the Bengali movie viewer truly understands the inflexions and nuances of a Ray film. There is no doubt that Ray lived and breathed his regional culture in a way that enriched his art, but Ray's political vision was freed of regionalist associations when he travelled out of Bengal and made films about other spaces, signalling larger concerns.[10] As already noted, Ritwik Ghatak had a Bengal as his focus much more than Ray.

From the middle of the nineteenth century onwards, both the English in Bengal and the Bengalis used to flock to the hill stations to escape the worst heat of Calcutta. A thoroughly anglicised atmosphere was created there, which influenced both Satyajit Ray and his father Sukumar Ray, who had stayed there with relatives – some of whom must have been brown sahibs – at least outwardly. This came to bear a lot of influence on their work. In fact, Sukumar Ray had also gone to Manchester for higher studies during his time.[11] Therefore, it comes as no surprise that this particular class was something Ray was familiar with firsthand and perhaps was also in sympathy with to a certain degree; or to put it more succinctly, a class which he sympathised with, but with some irony.

In early 1962, Ray, in a letter to Lester Peries,[12] described his ensemble of *Kanchenjungha* as 'a domineering, British-title-holding father, brother-in-law, brink-of-divorce elder daughter and husband, playboy son, sensitive younger daughter, eligible prosaic bachelor suitor, and young unemployed intellectual stranger'. Indranath Roy Chaudhary, played by the formidable Chhavi Biswas, is a bully – he belongs to the class that served the British Raj but gradually ceased to exist with the passing of that generation. As Andrew Robinson puts it,[13] it is very evident that Ray's sympathy does not lie with him – not because he made himself rich and influential by serving the British but because he is a philistine. He suppresses his wife's talents and thinks of his younger daughter as a marketable commodity, even though she has proved herself intellectually superior. In the film, his brother-in-law and the younger man Ashok, and to a certain extent his son-in-law Shankar, act as foils to his character. This is set up quite early in the film when his brother-in-law notices a rare bird when Indranath interrupts to ask him whether it can be eaten. When his brother-in-law answers in the negative, he expresses disgust at his lack of practical sense and walks off.

Language and Resistance

Earlier I noted the 'resistance' offered to the anglophile Indranath by members of his family when they discuss Tagore and insistently speak Bengali. The language of communication in *Kanchenjungha* is Bengali interspersed heavily with English words and phrases. While this may be disconcerting to a person ashamed of India's colonial past as Robinson proposes,[14] for Indranath it is a happy state of linguistic being, and one which makes him feel at home. He is proud of having lived in an era in which the British ruled, but also perhaps grateful because he reaped the

Figure 4.1 The beauty of the Himalayas with its rich flora and fauna is lost on the Ray Bahadur.

benefits of an elite colonial education and which helped him achieve great success and prestige in life.

When Labanya, his wife, expresses her hesitation to get Monisha married off so early while she is still pursuing her BA, Indranath makes a pun on it, as it being less important than her *biye* – the Bengali word for marriage. This is a faithful reflection of one type of Bengalis who used to holiday in Darjeeling. They were the hybrid characters – products of 200 years of colonial interactions. Ray planned to make him even more conspicuous by the clothes that he wears, which Ray felt to be true of the upper-class.[15] So, Indranath struts around Darjeeling dominating the others and trying to orchestrate a 'happy ending' for Monisha, or so he thinks. It is not only his daughter whom he thinks of as a commodity to be transferred. Even the eligible bachelor Banerjee is referred to as 'acquisition' to his brother-in-law. To Indranath life is all about family prestige, money and acquisitions.

He looks down on fellow Indians, except to grant favours, which allows him to patronise them. When he feels that Ashok is needy and could do well with a job, he warms up to him, only to harangue him with nostalgic tales of his cricket-playing days. Cricket being the sport of the British upper-classes, he naturally speaks very highly of the game. While Indranath persists in speaking about the British race, especially their superiority, his wife maintains silence. Ray is quick to point out that despite his anglicised lifestyle, his worldview is governed by local superstitions, suggesting that Indianness runs very deep.

Although Ray's own family was Brahmo as well as patriotic, there is no doubt that the family absorbed much from the British. In fact, when Tagore's nephew Abanindranath Tagore, a leading painter and founder of the Bengal School of Art, called for a boycott of the imitation of Western art, both Upendrakishore and Sukumar Ray stayed away and even advocated the opposite.[16] Even though Abanidranath's stance was a nationalistic one – which produced a painting of the 'Bharat Mata' – both father and son were convinced of the superiority of the Renaissance naturalistic style. No one denied the superiority of Western art except a certain section of the Bengal school movement. Rabindranath Tagore himself made it quite plain that in Viswabharati University there was no need to favour Indian perspectives in art at Kalabhavan. Ray himself worked in a British advertising agency, where he was thought of highly by his superiors and may have been influenced by them.

The Westernised and the Traditional

There are several ways that Indranath Choudhary is observed in Ray's film – several aspects of his character exposed in his interaction with various people. But there is arguably something more to him and that is the conflict between his anglicised Western side and his traditional superstitious side. As already suggested, Indranath Choudhary seems representative of a postcolonial class that wielded authority after 1947, and the question is what its relationship with tradition was. If he is a 'conservative' – and the term seems eminently applicable – there is some doubt expressed about what the term meant in the 1950s. Attention has been paid by political scientists to traditional societies, the ways in which political leaders have sought to draw upon traditional culture for symbols and slogans in order to provide a sense of continuity for contemporary regimes. But as far as India is concerned there was no party that chose to call itself 'conservative', with such an agenda as its basis:

> It is one of the paradoxes of Indian politics that India's *ancien regime*, surely one of the oldest and most deeply rooted in the world, produced no reaction ... Only a few

local parties today stand for a full return to the rule of Brahmins and Kshatriyas according to the precepts of *dharma* or traditional duty and they are ineffectual.[17]

The situation may be less valid today, but it is interesting that the above quote is from 1960, roughly around the time of *Kanchenjungha*. What it implies is that it would have been difficult after 1947 not to profess being modern in one's outlook and the most evident representative of that was British-style education and Anglophilia. At the same time India's ruling party under Nehru found it difficult to push reform bills because of conservative resistance. A Hindu Code Bill unifying Hindu practices was proposed, but that too met with opposition. Eventually, that was split up into several separate bills, The Hindu Marriage Act in 1955, the Hindu Succession Act in 1956, the Hindu Adoption and Maintenance Act in 1956 and the Dowry Prohibition Act in 1961.[18] What these contradictory aspects suggest reflects on Indranath as well, although Ray, being a creative artist rather than a political scientist, evidently did not make such connections explicitly. Indranath's insistence on an arranged marriage with an eligible bachelor for Manisha alongside his superstitious nature suggest a traditional Indian underneath the Westernised mien, perhaps someone who harboured deep caste feelings as well. The fact is that the British, for all their efforts to create an elite who thought like Europeans through education, did not change the Indian mindset, specifically of the upper-castes,[19] to which Indranath Chaudhary evidently belongs. Ray, as an anglophile, stands demarcated from him.

Bimal Gupta vs Amitabh Roy in *Kapurush* (1965)

Ray's *Kapurush*, made in 1965, resumes the same argument as in *Kanchenjungha* when the filmmaker represents two different kinds of Bengalis – one, a sophisticated anglophile tea plantation owner named Bimal Gupta and the other representing popular Bengali culture – the film scriptwriter, Amitabh. The setting is somewhere on the border of Bengal and Assam in a tea plantation. The evening is gloomy with very few people around depicting isolation and leaving the film a kind of chamber piece with three characters. In a car mechanic's shop, Bimal Gupta meets Amitabh, whose car has broken down and is in need of repair as he is making his way to Hashimara on work. However, unable to make further ground, he allows himself to be invited to Gupta's house for the night.

In the bungalow he meets Karuna, once his lover and someone he had let down when he did not marry her. While he is startled, the uncomfortable Karuna, now Bimal Gupta's wife, shows no signs of recognition.

She is formal and courteous and sets about attending to the guest. As Bimal Gupta reiterates through the film, he is starved for company. As a plantation owner, he needs to maintain hierarchy and cannot be mixing with others lower down. It is a part of a rigid system of British devising that keeps Indians away from each other – although one cannot absolve Indian hierarchy of being implicated in the arrangement. But the names that Gupta iterates are indicative of the fact that it is largely the British who reach a high rank. The strict code ensures that only a manager socialises with another manager and a proprietor with another. Perhaps this imparts a certain efficiency to the system, but it also condemns the bearers to alcohol and solitude. Life is indeed tough for this class, not only in terms of work but also in terms of living their lives. As Gupta informs Amitabh, not only do the various tea gardens have distinctive flavours in tea, but come rain, sun or inclement weather, Gupta and Company have to carry on. His regret is that in spite of being a promising student with a first in economics, and a debater with a reputation, he ended up in a life like this.

In *Kapurush* Ray makes a distinction between the two different kinds of Bengalis through several markers – one of which is clothing and the other, décor. Gupta's bungalow is spacious and large with clearly marked out spaces. The décor in the large living room is urbane, sophisticated with table lamps, curios, portraits, prints of paintings and, most conspicuously, a defunct fireplace and two tiger skins adorning the walls. Not only is there aspiration towards a 'British' lifestyle, but one can also discern a covert admiration for their system. Gupta speaks English, does not seem too familiar with the Bengali language, reads comics (possibly another British import), drinks good and expensive whisky, keeps a plethora of servants and has British-style courses for his meals. While his wife dresses in a saree, Gupta is in a mackintosh worn over a khaki shirt and shorts, while Amitabh his guest wears a plain shirt and pants like other Bengalis. For drinks and dinner Gupta changes into a dressing gown, while his guest changes into a simple kurta pajama like a quintessential Bengali.

Bimal Gupta is clearly at home with the English language – reminiscent of Bhupati in *Charulata*. Their respective wives, however, love Bengali literature, and in Karuna's case she is enveloped in Indian culture. It is Bismillah Khan's shehnai that greets Amitabh in the morning at breakfast, and it is Tagore's *Shapmochan*, the dance drama, that greets him when he first meets her in her husband's bungalow. Amitabh is rather a strange character who does not come across as 'rooted'. While he works for the Bengali film industry as a scriptwriter, he does not seem overtly confident about its merits.

In the earlier sequence before dinner, Bimal Gupta and Amitabh engage in a conversation that borders on a discussion about Bengali characteristics. Gupta denounces the present generation as lacking in moral fibre, which is reflected in everyday pursuits and popular cultural forms such as politics and cinema. However, when Gupta reads *Cartoons and Gags* it is reflective of not only a certain shallow standard of British managers in India, but still one that Gupta maintains and aspires to. While talking about Bengali cinema he bursts into derisive laughter that Amitabh probes, but still cannot follow up with a convincing defense. As far as the food in the Gupta household is concerned, it too is influenced by English ways, beginning with soup. Significantly, Judge Raghunath in *Awaara* follows the same regimen.

Kapurush is adapted from a story, but Ray's text is more nuanced and includes a detailed contextualising of the milieu in keeping with his chronicling of history, whereas Premendra Mitra's text is not. There the focus is much more on the unfolding drama between the two former lovers. The narration is a first-person narrative which makes the perspective narrow and subjective. Throughout the original short story, the narrator is intent on seeing Karuna break down and the setting is vague

Figure 4.2 The décor and the sartorial style of the key protagonists reveal a lot about the milieu.

and under-determined. The husband works in a colliery and Karuna confesses to knowing Amitabh, which takes away much of the edge and tension that we witness in Ray's film. The husband in the story by Mitra hardly appears for more than a scene or two.

The original story is a long-drawn-out reaction of the narrator's to meeting his former lover Karuna and his desire to see her suffer and break down because of her presumed unrequited love. However, no such breakdown happens and the man is left to nurse his wounds at the end. There is of course no doubt that the story has a feminist slant to it or, rather, it shows women in a particular light informed by gender concerns. Even though Ray's film adapted Mitra's story it shows the same slant; however, Ray's intention goes beyond that to include an analysis of a particular class as well. Ray's film tries to capture the very special kind of mood prevalent in a tea plantation – the languor, the sense of remoteness, the physical labour and the boredom, but most importantly an influence that is colonial.

This leaves us with the task of interpreting Amitabha or, rather, the relationship between him and Gupta, which evidently carries more weight than it does in Mitra's story. *Kapurush* was made in 1965 and we already see the colonial class becoming slightly ridiculous, which was not so in the 1950s. It was earlier noted that Ray, even while being critical of the postcolonial anglicised elite, could see from their viewpoint in *Kanchenjungha*, and the same is true of *Kapurush*, in which Bimal Gupta castigates Bengali cinema, Amitabha Roy is deeply involved, and the latter has no answer. We know that Ray was not sympathetic to Bengali popular cinema and could well have shared Bimal Roy's feelings about it, which makes his portrayal of Bimal Gupta more ambivalent.

Conclusion: The Trajectory of the Anglophile Indian

Both the films under exploration in this chapter investigate the postcolonial Indian male subject who displays certain characteristic traits. These traits are in consonance with the milieu to which they belong. Ray is perhaps the only Indian film director to have acutely studied the social conduct of this class. Hindi popular cinema also dealt with the class but as emblems of a fading past, though still vested with authority.

Both Indranath Choudhury and Bimal Gupta display a certain surety, a sense of purpose that others do not. They are, in a sense, rooted in a world created by the colonial past, but it confers on them some kind of authority that the others submit to – or are struggling to gain. Karuna's position vis-à-vis Bimal Gupta's in the narrative can be compared to one of Ray's earlier films, *Charulata*. Here too, the wife is someone who finds solace in Bengali literature and culture, as opposed to the husband, who finds it in English customs and the colonial world. Indeed, much like *Charulata* the atmosphere is an anglicised one in *Kapurush*. The Bengali spoken is littered with English phrases and expletives, with Bimal Gupta even fumbling to understand the Bengali word for economics.

Kanchenjungha and *Kapurush* have been considered together in this chapter, but a subtle distinction can be made – Indians with proficiency in the local languages and culture gradually gaining in importance. Ashok in *Kanchenjunga* is of the new generation that does not speak English and is more comfortable in Bengali. However, he is unemployed, having to earn a living by giving tuitions. In the later *Kapurush* Amitabh is partly in Ashok's place, in the sense that he is of the 'local culture' as opposed to the anglophile way. But now he is someone already with a foothold having worked in two films. He is not 'sophisticated' in Bimal Gupta's sense but by casting Soumitra in the role, an actor with a strong presence, Ray suggests the growing sense of indigenous culture gaining ground.

The anglophile class would once again make an appearance in Ray's 1971 film *Seemabaddha* in the form of Sir Baren Roy, an erstwhile ICS officer, but he now comes across as a figure of ridicule. By the 1970s, with India having experienced two decades of freedom, suffered the death of its first prime minister in 1964 – one who was himself anglophile – the anglophile world seemed to have undergone a huge change for Indians like Ray. Apart from being anachronistic this class seems to have no place in the India of the 1970s. Indeed, Sir Baren Roy has been portrayed in a comical way, which is a far cry from the portrayal of either Indranath Choudhury or Bimal Gupta. He is shown to doze off at meetings, leer at young women and has none of the authority or dignity that Indranath Choudhury and Bimal Gupta are allowed, despite their negative characteristics.

This leaves us with the notion of the masculinity of the male characters and, if Indranath and Bimal Gupta are more authoritatively masculine,[20] there is a deliberation in the way the other men – principally Ashok and Amitabha – are made subdued. Ashok, the most sympathetic male character in the two films, is admirable, but there is a frailty to him that one tends to extend to his sense of resolve. The contrast between Bimal Gupta and Amitabha is also significant here, since the former wears work clothes (until he changes them for a dressing gown in the evening), while Amitabha – as a songwriter in the film industry – exudes effeteness, made stronger by his past failure to meet Karuna's romantic expectations. Ray is dealing with the 1960s here and the British have long since departed, but the seeming inheritors of their mantle still exude masculine authority. Ray may not be in sympathy with these masculine characters, but the gravity they display is arresting. Still, nothing definite can be said about where Ray stands vis-à-vis these characters, except that the films are much more ambivalent about his position than might be imagined, and colonial masculinity is the notion that lends his vision such tantalising ambivalence.

Notes

1. Edward Said, *Representations of the Intellectual* (New York: Vintage Books, 1996), 11–12.
2. For instance, Sikata Banerjee, *Make Me a Man! Masculinity, Hinduism, and Nationalism in India* (Albany: SUNY Press, 2005).
3. Dipesh Chakraborty, Rochona Majumdar and Andrew Sartori, *From the Colonial to The Postcolonial: India and Pakistan in Transition* (New Delhi: Oxford University Press, 2007), 3.
4. The term hybridity has become one of the most recurrent concepts in postcolonial cultural criticism. Homi Bhabha is the leading contemporary critic who has tried to disclose the contradictions inherent in colonial discourse to highlight the coloniser's *ambivalence* in respect to his position toward the colonised Other. Mimicry in colonial and postcolonial literature is most commonly seen when members of a colonised society (say, Indians or Africans) imitate the language, dress, politics or cultural attitude of their colonisers (say, the British or the French). Under colonialism and in the context of immigration, mimicry is seen as an opportunistic pattern of behavior: one copies the person in power, because one hopes to have access to that same power oneself. Postcolonial hybridity can be quite slippery and broad. At a basic level, hybridity refers to any mixing of East and Western culture. Within colonial and postcolonial literature, it most commonly refers to colonial subjects from Asia or Africa who have found a balance between Eastern and Western cultural attributes. For a useful summary see Cherry Lou C. Sy, 'Mimicry and Its Discontents: Examining Bhabha's Multiculturalism as Mimicry and Hybridity', *Inquiries Journal*, 3/10 (2011) <http://www.inquiriesjournal.com/articles/583/mimicry-and-its-discontents-examining-bhabhas-multiculturalism-as-mimicry-and-hybridity> (last accessed 8 January 2022).
5. Homi K. Bhabha, 'Signs Taken for Wonders: Questions of Ambivalence and Authority under a Tree outside Delhi, May 1817', *Critical Inquiry*, 12/1, 'Race', Writing, and Difference (Autumn, 1985), 144–65.
6. Dipesh Chakraborty, 'Introduction', in Dipesh Chakravarty, Rochana Majumdar and Andrew Sartori, *From the Colonial to The Postcolonial: India and Pakistan in Transition* (New Delhi: Oxford University Press, 2007), 3.

7. M. K. Raghavendra, *Seduced by the Familiar: Narration and Meaning in Indian Popular Cinema* (New Delhi: Oxford University Press, 2008), 171.
8. A short while before Ray made *Pather Panchali*, two films which tried dealing with the same issues were Nemai Ghosh's *Chinnamul* (1950) and K. A. Abbas's *Dharti Ke Lal* (1946). Both deal with agrarian life in a lyrical way that anticipates *Pather Panchali*. Both were Communist-inspired, with little faith in the 'bourgeoise democracy' ushered into India in 1947, and both are deeply pessimistic; the fact that one film came after Independence does not make it different from the other.
9. Historians such as Ranajit Guha and Gautam Bhadra belong to the Subaltern Studies school. The term 'Subaltern Studies' is sometimes also applied more broadly to others who share many of their views, and they are often considered to be 'exemplary of postcolonial studies' and as one of the most influential movements in the field. Their anti-essentialist approach is one of looking at history from below, focussed more on what happens among the masses at the base levels of society than among the elite.
10. Here is critic Robin Wood pointing out the absence of distracting local specificities in Ray's films: 'What is remarkable is how seldom in Ray's films the spectator is pulled up by any specific obstacle arising from cultural differences.' Robin Wood, *The Apu Trilogy* (New York: Praeger, 1971), 7.
11. Sukumar Ray was sent for studying Printing Technology at the University of Manchester so that he could help in his father's business. Upendrakishore Ray Chaudhury, his father, ran a moderately successful printing press which was called 'U. Ray and Sons'.
12. Andrew Robinson, *The Inner Eye: The Biography of a Master Film-Maker* (New Delhi: Oxford University Press, 2004), 183.
13. Ibid., 189.
14. Ibid., 138.
15. Ibid., 139.
16. Ibid., 141.
17. Chandak Sengoopta, *The Rays before Satyajit* (New Delhi: Oxford University Press, 2016), 166.
18. Lloyd and Susanne Rudolph, 'The Political Role of India's Caste Association', *Pacific Affairs*, XXXIII/I, March 1960, 5–22.
19. Reba Som, 'Jawaharlal Nehru and the Hindu Code: A Victory of Symbol over Substance?', *Modern Asian Studies*, 28/1 (1994), 171.
20. A missionary apparently remarked: 'I am not certain that a man's being able to read Milton and Shakespeare, or understand Dr. Johnson, would make him less susceptible of the honour of being a Brahmin.' Gauri Viswanathan, *Masks of Conquest: Literary Study and British Rule in India* (New Delhi: Oxford University Press, 1998), 152.

CHAPTER 5

The Hollow Men: The Complacent 'Achiever' in *Nayak, Aranyer Din Ratri* and *Seemabaddha*

By the time we come to the 1960s and 1970s, the newly emergent class is an indigenous segment that may be seen as an offshoot of the class under observation in the last chapter – the anglicised postcolonial bourgeoisie. The era was, however, different from the previous one, with more disaffection. While the early 1960s, dominated by the Sino-Indian War and alarming food shortages – when the Green Revolution was initiated with massive investment in agriculture – was politically 'stable', the last years saw the rise of Maoism. This was a radical period around the world and culminated in 1968 in Paris, even being described as a 'World Revolution' by political thinkers.[1] Maoism in the late 1960s was associated with a village in North Bengal called Naxalbari, and for this reason has been called 'Naxalism' ever since. It was only in the early 1970s when Naxalism was finally suppressed through the concerted efforts of the then Bengal government – the United Front – but it keeps reappearing in one form or another. It is therefore impossible to deal with the Bengali cinema of the period without invoking Naxalism.

A strategy used in this book is to invoke the popular Hindi cinema of the period to which Ray's films in the chapter pertain, and that is not because the two kinds of cinema are similar. It is rather because the two are different responses to the same socio-political reality which needs to be understood first. Looking at that reality from the perspectives of the two cinemas may be helpful. It is interesting to note that the decades under examination here produced Hindi films that were held to be 'escapist'.[2] Foreign location and hill stations were the norm after the Sino-Indian War, read as an escape from the Nehruvian nationalism of the 1950s,[3] but the trend continued after 1965 when India had fared better in a war against Pakistan. The years immediately after the military disaster against China were dominated by food shortages, but the Green Revolution, with massive investment in agriculture, also mitigated conditions. Whereas farmers were indebted and poor in the earlier cinema (*Ganga Jumna*, 1961), the progressive farmer is the motif in *Upkaar* (1967), in which the war of 1965 is also invoked and agrarian want is less of an issue.

But the 'escapist' fare was represented largely by films like *Teesri Manzil* (1966), *Love in Tokyo* (1966), *An Evening in Paris* (1967) and *Jewel Thief* (1967). The motifs in these films are foreign locations, glitzy cabarets featuring Helen and technology like sliding doors, perhaps inspired by the 'modernity' in the James Bond films and largely simulating the 'foreign'. The rise of Rajesh Khanna through *Aradhana* (1969) happened thereafter and a romantic hero arguably manifests lower social concern – since so much of the film is taken up by personal appeal. Inferring the conditions in the years after 1965 on the basis of this escapism of popular cinema, we could propose that while there were some opportunities being created, they were for the few. Escapism presumes some hope in the populace, at least enough to dream of a better life. The Indian Institutes of Management, Ahmedabad and Calcutta had been established in 1961 and the career opportunities they created were also being noticed by the turn of the decade.[4] Ray's films dealt with in this chapter are about successful men, describable as the achievers of the period. The first of the achievers is from the film industry, while the others might be corporate executives today.

Arindam Chaudhuri in *Nayak* (1966)

As just indicated, the first of Ray's three films to deal with the 'achievers' of the period is *Nayak*, a film actor, perhaps from the same kind of cinema described as 'escapist'. Based on yet another original screenplay by Ray, *Nayak* follows the life of Arindam Chaudhuri, a matinee idol, played by the real-life superstar Uttam Kumar. Uttam was on Ray's mind while he wrote the script for *Nayak* and also because he had read somewhere that in order to portray a matinee idol, one must cast a star. However, to Ray, Uttam Kumar was interesting more as a phenomenon than as an individual. 'Success gave him a personality', Ray said of Uttam once.[5] This notion is seminal to this chapter, but Uttam Kumar's real-life characteristics perhaps did not bear much importance in Arindam's characterisation. Andrew Robinson notes[6] that while Ray was writing his screenplay, he was driven by a desire to investigate the psychology of such a star outside his own kind of cinema. The central thread of *Nayak* revolves around the exchange between the star and Aditi Sengupta, a serious young journalist. There are however a number of subplots that revolve around the main plot, helping to augment it, largely through recollections.

In *Nayak* a film star is travelling to Delhi to collect a prize from the Government of India, but with the ulterior motive of getting away from the news hungry media, abuzz around him because Chaudhuri has slipped up on a personal matter. Ms Sengupta, also on the train, is a charming woman whose glasses and severe expression do little to conceal her feminine charm. She is egged on by her travelling companions to get Arindam's interview for her magazine and that is how she makes his acquaintance. Arindam is very conscious about his star power and charisma from the very beginning, but Aditi is different. He has turned a producer away with a refusal and maintains a confident front, even though a scandal pertaining to his personal conduct and dealings is brewing in the media.

In the first third of the film Arindam comes across as someone accustomed to public adulation but who does not value it very highly. Although courteous to the people around him, he emerges as cocky and too sure of himself. However, he manages to hide his insecurity well under a veneer of personal style until Aditi asks probing questions that open up a new line of thinking for him. Aditi provokes this with, 'In the midst of having so much don't you feel there's something missing? Some emptiness somewhere?' Arindam is the quintessential complacent achiever. He has moved in stature from a 350 rupees a month job to 30,000 rupees a film thanks to hard work and boundless ambition. While his former mentor in the theatre (Shankar da) was against cinema in general and film-acting in particular, Arindam has been trying to prove him wrong. He has proved to be successful as he climbed the unsure and slippery steps of fame and filmdom, but he is abruptly shaken up by Aditi's question. The question may not seem probing to the reader, but must be regarded in the light of the gossip that film magazines feed their readers on, largely revolving around lifestyle issues. Very rarely do questions from journalists invite introspection.[7] Ray has Arindam sweating in a nightmare at this point, one that fuses material success with death.[8]

In a series of conversations with Aditi over the length of the train journey, Arindam reveals aspects of himself to her, about his mentor's dismissive attitude towards film actors, treating them as mere puppets in the hands of the technical people and especially directors. Taking to alcohol to suppress untoward anxieties, Arindam admits his betrayal of an old friend Biresh over union politics – committing himself politically might have hurt him and Arindam turned tail. Much of this is shown in flashback and it is hence not simply Arindam 'coming clean' to Aditi, but also recapitulating his own past to himself – including parts that might be too inconvenient to reveal to a stranger.

The other passengers on the train who interact with Arindam help highlight his character to some extent. The factors highlighted in these asides involve women prepared to hand out sexual favors in order to get

Figure 5.1 The actor who can be himself for a day.

ahead, even married women egged on to do so by their husbands, or at least to flirt with possible benefactors. Some of these events happen on the train (not always to Arindam) while others are in flashback as characteristics of routine film-industry conduct. Aditi holds Arindam in some scorn for his films and his career, which could echo Ray's own feelings towards popular Bengali cinema. In the decade when this film was made, other contemporary films were abhorred for their crassness and became a reason for state intervention around 1970 to promote a more socially responsive cinema.[9]

Arindam's self-loathing is revealed as the film's narrative progresses, becoming a key aspect in the story and Aditi offers some hope that he will be able to respect himself. She might have held up a much-needed mirror to him as a partner, since there is a certain chemistry between the two. But Aditi's conduct does not suggest desire for him, even though we in the audience unconsciously pair off the two. A key motif in the film is Arindam's alcoholism and it is his reflection in a broken mirror at a drunken moment that prompts him to contemplate suicide. When he is drunk enough, he would like to confess his misgivings to Aditi, but she has already guessed much, and guessed correctly, and would rather not hear it. There is little doubt here that Arindam is weak and Ray is using alcohol as a trope to imply moral weakness in men. That Arindam is not the only man judged is evident since there are others – one trying to get his wife to flirt with a potential client, another pronouncing uncharitably about the film industry and film actors like Arindam. Except for Aditi, the women themselves seem to be playing second fiddle to some man or other.

But an issue in *Nayak* is why this flat character of Aditi, about whom we are told little, should be placed here as moral arbiter. Nominally, Aditi is 'strong', but 'strength' in a person also means that he or she should have *human* weaknesses that he or she overcomes. Just as courage is not fearlessness but doing what needs to be done despite being afraid, being strong is doing things that one might wish to avoid doing, i.e. taking risks. One does not get the sense that Aditi is risking anything in *Nayak* and she seems placed there only to strike a cautionary note towards career success. That Ray picked the film industry as emblematic of the flimsiness of material success in the period is significant because of the kind of cinema the era was producing. It is even more significant that he picked the same actress (Sharmila Tagore) to play similar roles in all three films covered in this chapter – as a 'non-character' who does not participate in the action,[10] but is present only to hold up a cautionary hand to a man at the moral crossroads – a woman as a message bearer.

Ashim in *Aranyer Din Ratri* (1969)

Ray's 1969 film *Aranyer Din Ratri* revolves around four young men who take a short holiday in Palamau, a wild forested area in neighbouring Bihar. They have read an account of it in Sanjib Chatterjee's 1880 eponymous travelogue, and it appeals to their sense of adventure; in other words, they seek to 'escape the rat race' and they travel to it in Ashim's car. The group is a motley one: Ashim, who is the most successful of the four and a sort of leader of the group; Sanjay, a labour welfare officer in a firm; Hari, a cricketer who wishes to escape a disappointment in love; and the unemployed and gambling Sekhar, who keeps the group together with his antics – played by comedian Robi Ghosh.

Once in Palamau they attempt to live out a 'wild' life through conduct that might have shamed them in the city. They elbow their way into a forest bungalow on the strength of their urban sophistication, bribing the poor caretaker who does not have much of a choice with an ailing wife and several children. Even as he bribes the caretaker Ashim is heard saying, 'Thank God for corruption.'

The film was based on Sunil Ganguli's novel of the same name, which included autobiographical elements, but Ray altered it considerably. Instead of being unemployed and travelling ticketless by train, the men journey by car and three of them have jobs. There is, actually, a hierarchy within the group and one takes them to be former classmates who have progressed differently. When they decide to adapt to the 'wilderness' by ceasing to shave and ceremonially burn a newspaper, they are covertly trying to erase the sense of hierarchy between them.

While the people in the novel are cruder and confused, in Ray's film they are more refined and this 'refinement' goes along with them being well-placed in a society that is facing hardship. To relate the story of the film, the four friends meet a family also from Calcutta staying at their own forest bungalow: a father, a widowed daughter-in-law Joya, an unmarried daughter Aparna (Sharmila Tagore) and Joya's little son. With the women becoming an attraction in this wild place, the men make themselves presentable and relationships are soon established. Ashim woos Aparna while Joya tries to establish a relationship with Sanjay. Hari finds a drunken tribal girl Duli (played by Simi Garewal), and has a brief sexual liaison with her.

These four characters, especially Ashim and to a certain extent Sanjay, are representatives of the upwardly-mobile Bengalis of the period, lacking the ideals of Apu or Ashok the unemployed young graduate in *Kanchenjunga*, who were still seeking something apart from careers. They do not measure themselves by the values that the erstwhile Bengali bhadralok believed in. These characters, along with Arindam in *Nayak* and Shyamlendu in *Seemabaddha*, seem to be 'nowhere people' or a hybrid of some sort created after Independence. The bhadralok were culturally nationalistic, but not so this self-seeking bunch. Much like Arindam, who has everything materially but lacks for something to genuinely satisfy him, Ashim too is empty at heart. When he meets Aparna for the first time he seems very much in control of the situation. He demands to see her personal and private space, or rather her 'meditative retreat' as her father calls it, and even gets her to show it to him.

But Ashim, when driven to it, actually laments his life. He has had to compromise far too much; and the higher he aspires to reach, the lower his dignity plummets. His confident bearing at Aparna's residence the first time is undone when he is caught bathing half naked at the well in the bungalow. He and Aparna have exchanges in which he is seeking approval from her but is unsuccessful. The group's drunken 'tribal twist' in the night also contributes to Aparna gaining the 'upper hand'. The men, half unclad, are dancing in the middle of the unlit road doing what they imagine is tribal dancing when the women drive up. As the group blocks the road, Ashim shouts, 'Do you know who we are? We are very important people!' Inside are Joya and Aparna, who can barely control their laughter but do not bring it up the next day when the men visit them. The film oscillates

Figure 5.2 The game that brings them together but also divides.

between moments of dignity for the men when sober with the women, and their ridiculous conduct when by themselves.

The memory game is an interesting sequence in *Aranyer Din Ratri*. Each participant needs to name one famous person apart from all the preceding ones named, and the names keep piling up. The game has its own techniques and it is strategically preferable to stay away from obscure names that cannot be recollected. The choice of names that each player comes up with reveals something about him or her. Ashim, the literary-minded one, comes up with Shakespeare while Sanjoy comes up with Karl Marx and Mao Tse Tung, being directly involved in politics because of his labour associations. Aparna's choice of names is eclectic – from Cleopatra and cricketer Don Bradman to Bobby Kennedy. The less adventurous Joya comes up with the iconic Tagore, a name someone traditionally Bengali might choose. Shekar names 'Helen', although the issue of whether it is Helen of Troy or the Bombay actress who played vamps in Hindi films is not resolved. As Andrew Robinson describes it, this is a sequence that Ray was rightly proud of: 'It makes use of the fullest scale of possibilities for psychological probing through acting, dialogue and editing.'[11]

At the same time there is a degree of competition between the participants, that Aparna plays down by withdrawing. In each of these encounters between the men and the women, the men seem wanting while Aparna, without trying, appears superior. After so much in which the men discredit themselves, Ashim is eventually chastised by Aparna for being immature and inconsiderate; but he apologises and she seems to relent. Ashim may have the capacity to feel regret, but we are still dissatisfied. Perhaps it is in that a self-confident person in such a social situation should submit so unequivocally to the judgement of someone of the opposite sex, purely because that other person has allure. Would a real Ashim submit so willingly to an actual Aparna, with vulnerabilities of her own? This trope of the intelligent woman pointing out the man's foibles – and being heard – is moot but perhaps deliberate. In any social situation there would be contrary responses to someone else's 'truth-telling' voice about one's own errors; the more generous one would be to accept the truths, but a contrary one would be to see an attempt at domination. It is the absence of these contrary impulses that one misses – since Ashim puts up no resistance. He seems to see Aparna more as a truth-telling voice than as someone human with foibles of her own.

Shyamalendu in *Seemabaddha* (1971)

Ray described *Seemabaddha* as 'a definitive film about the boxwallahs' – a class which came to be called so because they worked in Western-oriented large companies and businesses. Their lifestyles mainly revolved around the office, cocktail parties, clubs and the racetrack and they were routinely seen as anglicised. Shyamalendu the protagonist is essentially a decent fellow who has qualms and is ready to heed the advice of the beautiful and idealistic Tutul, his sister-in-law (Sharmila Tagore), but the ambition of becoming a director gets the better of him. Ray draws up an intimate portrait of the world of the boxwallahs, depictions of their personal and professional lives and the intertwining of the two. Ray, who had many friends in advertising firms and who rose through the ranks, exhibited many of these characteristics; he himself would have perhaps become a 'boxwallah' if he had not left the corporate world in order to pursue filmmaking. Although one feels a sense of admiration for Tutul and her correctness, one cannot help but feel Ray's sympathy for Shyamalendu too – although Ray does not approve of what he does.

The film begins with an ironic introduction to Shymalendu, the kind of tone Ray had a penchant for and which marks the beginning of *Shatranj Ke Khiladi* also. Ray provides his protagonist's background – a good student of English literature, a conscientious college teacher until his job at Hindustan Peters and his steady rise took their toll on his attitudes.

Figure 5.3 Shyamlendu revealing his most private thoughts to Tutul.

Ray lists his achievements, among which is his acquisition of his wife Dolon. *Seemabaddha* is a story that belongs largely to Shyamalendu; not only does it portray his kind of life, but the film also successfully depicts an admired and emulated social segment. Much like the other two films under exploration in this chapter, Ray attempts the critique of a class of successful young people who have risen through compromises.

It is interesting that the observations made about Shyamalendu are from Tutul's perspective. Tutul is the quintessential outsider to the city – a native of Patna, she comes to visit her sister and brother-in-law and much of the action is recorded through her viewpoint. In fact, a study of Shyamalendu would be incomplete without Tutul's observations of him. We see Tutul and Shyamalendu engage in friendly banter the day she arrives in Calcutta. We are made wise to the fact that Tutul is not Dolon; she is well-educated, having completed her master's degree, and is on the verge of entering a profession. She is curious and observant but also reserves her judgement. Even though Tutul declares at the outset that she is 'studying' Shyamalendu, the city of Calcutta too comes under her purview as she visits the famous Eve's – a beauty parlour – the racecourse and Shyamalendu's club and looks at them all with eyes full of intelligent curiosity. She is not strictly like Aditi in *Nayak* in that she partakes of the things that boxwallahs do without protest. But she is not from this city but from Bihar, which is without the colonial trappings of Calcutta.

When at the races with her, not only do we see the location through her eyes as she takes in the atmosphere, but we see the people there as well. The upper-classes in Calcutta, Anglo-Indians and a few British who still run firms in Calcutta seem to descend on the race track on Saturdays. Tutul being sprightly and intelligent asks Shyamalendu questions not only about the raging Naxalism in urban Calcutta, but about his beliefs, his professional world et cetera, which helps us gain a perspective about Shyamalendu filtered through her sensibility, that of an intelligent outsider impervious to glamour.

Certain sequences in *Seemabaddha* also help highlight the milieu. When Shyamalendu takes his wife and Tutul to lunch at an upper-class club he remarks that even ten years earlier Indians would not have been allowed to enter, it being exclusively British territory. Shyamalendu seems actually proud to have become a member of a club that would once not have had him as a member! Another indication of Shyamalendu being cultural heir to the British is the character of Sir Baren Roy, a director in his company and a decrepit old clown who leers at young women at the club.

Much of the film is given to the delivery of information pertaining to the period. Naxalism is mentioned; Tutul's own fiancé is apparently a left-winger in Bihar although not much is said about him. The film was made in 1971 when Maoism was drawing the younger crowds and Ray was perhaps under pressure politically to take a stand. There is a discussion of Naxalism in the film at a cocktail party and, as may be anticipated, Shyamalendu's friends and colleagues are unsympathetic. Still, much of the conversation stays away from siding politically with ideologies and the film tries only to be informative. Naxalism was not all 'idealism' as some left-wing cinema/literature of the period has it.[12] There were too many casual political murders that could not be justified through any political logic. It should however be mentioned that the Naxalism of 1970 finds no response in the Hindi cinema of the period – since it was perhaps a 'Bengali' phenomenon by its own reckoning and not pan-national – but Ray, being Bengali, needed to engage.

Some of the well-heeled characters at Shyamalendu's party also express dissatisfaction with the country, but we are made to measure the remarks against their own class backgrounds, lives and personal profiles. Perhaps their deepest grouse is in the lack of opportunities in the milieu, since we may be certain that even within their own middle-class families, such material success would have been exceptional. Shyamalendu eventually gets out of a tricky situation by engineering a strike at his own company's factory, and this comes to the attention of Tutul, in whose esteem he plummets morally.

Tutul is the moral arbiter in the film the same way Aditi was in *Nayak* and she is played by the same actress, almost identically. But unlike in the earlier film, Tutul and Shyamalendu have had a past relationship, since Tutul is his sister-in-law, someone he was close to during his days as an idealist and student. When Tutul arrives, she sees him as the old Shyamalendu and only gradually is it established to her that he has transformed. Her acquiescence to partake of the 'good life' in Calcutta is therefore part of her efforts at seeing life from the viewpoint of someone who she once admired but is now different; she is not cold to him as Aditi was to Arindam in *Nayak* and she does not judge him until he actually stoops morally.[13] Being an outsider to Calcutta from a space that has not seen the same wealth, we can take Tutul's gaze to stand for that of someone studying the mechanics of success. Tutul's scrutiny of Shyamalendu stands for an outsider's survey of the city's glitterati and their attitudes and (hence) the trajectory of post-Independence India in terms of the sensitivity of its salaried upper-classes. The argument offered here is that someone travelling from the 'provinces' to the metropolis in space would experience something like travelling forward in time – since the two spaces also exist in separate temporal planes.

Women versus Men

All three films dealt with in this chapter are about successful men brought face-to-face morally with the scrutinising gaze of intelligent women. The bespectacled Aditi is put across from the beginning of *Nayak* as a 'person' in her own right, who along with two others runs a magazine for women called 'Adhunika' or 'The Modern Woman' as she informs her travelling companions. A pen clipped to her blouse, together with no trace of make-up and square glasses, lends Aditi a thoughtful appearance. Aditi has the air of someone who relies heavily on her capacity to articulate rather than her good looks. Her appeal is largely intellectual, though as Arindam is to find out later, that it is not without allure.

With the glasses on, she is Ms Aditi Sengupta, editor of Adhunika or 'The Modern Woman' but without her glasses she is Aditi, another pretty face. Even though Aditi tries to draw a line between their two worlds – that of Arindam and hers, a discerning reader of the film text will not fail to notice that the two are not unalike in being guarded and only gradually allowing others to see them for what they are. Aditi, a very confident and independent woman who can be blunt to a fault, reveals her considerate and sensitive nature when she refuses to cash in on the intimate inputs that Arindam gives her about himself, which she might have used to further her own ends by publishing and enhancing the appeal of her serious-minded women's magazine.

In *Seemabaddha*, Tutul's wordlessness, her desire not to pass judgements without adequate observation, her intelligence and her quiet determination to stick to what she believes and the choices that she makes in both the onscreen spaces and the offscreen ones (her boyfriend or fiancé is an idealist, who perhaps reminds her of the Shyamalendu of the past), make her a distinctive woman character in Ray's oeuvre, perhaps in tune with the times when 'political commitment' was demanded of the artist in Bengal. If one were to compare Shyamalendu to her, we might say that he has taken the path that the radicalism of the times frowned upon while she has stuck sternly to moral choices.

Tutul is delicately placed in the story in relation to the male protagonist, in that she is an object of allure for him but also an intellectual rival. When she says that she has studied psychology and a whole lot of other things and her remarks imply reading and education, Shyamalendu quickly retorts, 'Fortunately, it will be difficult for anybody to decipher that.' Since she returns his feelings (as least as he was), his fall in her eyes is more than 'moral judgement'. If Aditi felt nothing for Arindam but had an impact upon him in *Nayak*, Tutul feels something for Shyamalendu – if not for what he has become. Since her idealistic fiancé is not mentioned, it is Shyamalendu (as he was) that she might have chosen, if she could have still made that choice. In this film again Ray uses the same tropes from *Nayak* – a weak man meeting an intelligent and independent woman who makes him come to face with his own moral weakness at the height of his success. As in the other film there is alcohol in attendance and a contrasting, shallow feminine character to the one played by Sharmila.

Aparna's appearance in *Aranyer Din Ratri* belies the confidence in her character – she is stylish, speaks very little, a characteristic people might associate with shyness or arrogance. Although Aparna is attractive, she seems deliberately asexual and one could see her as a contrast to the sensuous Jaya, who fails in the exercise of seducing Sanjay and is left humiliated. Aparna is distant and aloof and although her position is similar to that of those in the other two films, she has a romantic side denied to the others when she signals her acceptance of a visibly chastened Ashim.

But in all three films the women played by Sharmila act as moral agents, rather than as flesh and blood characters with failings of their own. Although the male protagonists are attracted to the respective women and pairing off does take place in one's mind, the films are not potential romances. It is almost as if Ray primarily wanted to make a statement with the woman character as pretext – about the underlying vulnerability of successful men who have been unable to handle success. The woman steps in here as someone who, without admitting change to herself, chastens the man and offers him hope of a righteous, moral and/or caring existence. Another characteristic that the films have in common, apart from the portrayal of the ideal woman, is the trope of alcohol – and hormonal responses to the other sex – to connote moral weakness. The issue here is: since the woman played by Sharmila Tagore does not admit change to herself, what are they doing in the three films just described?

This brings us to the inevitable question of masculinity: the men, all being achievers, may be taken to be very masculine and it is significant that one of them is a matinee idol who has women throwing themselves at him. Sharmila Tagore, in her role of Aditi, is deliberately made asexual and almost 'masculine' in her unemotional and analytical way of approaching things, and she plays virtually the same role in the other two films. The men are actually more emotional than she is. My interpretation of the relationship is that Sharmila Tagore in the roles is deliberately introduced to play down the masculinity of the men by exhibiting seemingly masculine qualities herself. To explain this in the context of masculinity studies, masculinity and femininity exist only as socio-cultural constructions and not as innate qualities of persons.[14] Gender, it has been posited, is ideological and the terms masculinity and femininity are used to create differences between people, and demands are made socially to act out one's gender. Ray, arguably, uses Sharmila Tagore in this way, with responses identifiable socially as 'masculine' even while in appearance she is feminine and sexually attractive. In each of the films Ray seems to set up a possible relationship only for the woman to show up her masculinity to the man and undermine his sense of achievement. We cannot but equate 'achievement' with 'masculinity' here since the achievers look for feminine approval.

Conclusion: Judging Success in Difficult Times

Nayak is slightly different from the other two films in that it does not use English like they do, for in the other two films, the characters are virtually reinventing India by rewriting it in English.[15] But in all three films, at the centre of the narrative is a complacent achiever who regards nothing as being as important as his own advancement. However, it does not stop with that, and all three men are revealed to have moral failings of some sort. They are weak and take recourse to alcohol to suppress their qualms. In all three films a moral agent in the form of a woman appears and it is she who brings out their flaws and helps them reconcile with their true but lost selves. While the protagonist becomes more human each time, the same cannot be said of the 'moral agent'. The sense of the woman being 'inhuman' – i.e. exhibiting none of the uncertainties and weaknesses that human beings have – comes from the way Ray problematises her gender by giving her responses socially associated with the male, as a way of undermining the masculinity of the men even while making the women attractive.

Interestingly, it is only in these films of Ray's that such a feminine character appears entirely as a correcting device. The men are curiously poised in as much as they appear strong but are made inherently weak, but still able to see their errors. While two of them – Shyamalendu and Arindam – have risen from the middle-class to higher stature, all three show a sense of entitlement; although overly polite they are arrogant and smug to a fault. So much so that they fail to take into account the feelings of others and are insensitive to their immediate surroundings, except when they make optimum use of its imperfections as in *Aranyer Din Ratri*. Yet, for all this they do not defend themselves against the woman played by Sharmila Tagore.

All three of these films study the fruits of Independence that Indranath Chowdhury once commented about in *Kanchenjunga*, and one comes away from them with the sense that the country did not go along the path that it should have taken. This brings us to another question - why Ray uses the woman-as-moral agent as a strategy as commentary on the smugness of a nationally ascendant class around 1970. One of the premises of this book was that in a patriarchal society like India, the burden of achievement falls upon the men and they, indirectly, become the measure of where the nation stands at any particular moment. But if the 'national subject' is male, an issue would be from where that subject should be studied/viewed. The answer seems to be that it is only the woman who can then become arbiter. In all three films, complacent and callous[16] men chance upon women strangers who bring to them abruptly a sense of what they are. As we examine Ray's men in the course of this book, we find that women have a large part to play in their development, but that was only anticipated. Ray's three films use a strategy that could be interrogated, but they are nonetheless deep engagements with the nation at a critical juncture in its history.

Notes

1. For instance, Immanuel Wallerstein, *World Systems Analysis, World Systems Analysis: An Introduction* (Durham, NC: Duke University Press, 2006), 84–85.

2. This finds correspondence in one of the purposes attributed to drama by the *Natyashastra*, that it 'should be a diversion for people weighed down by sorrow or fatigue or grief or ill-luck; it should be a rest (for the body and the mind)'. Lothar Lutze, 'From Bharata to Bombay: Change and Continuity in Hindi Film Aesthetics', in Beatrix Pfleiderer and Lothar Lutze (eds), *The Hindi Film: Agent and Reagent for Cultural Change* (New Delhi: Manohar, 1985), 113–14.
3. M. K. Raghavendra, *Seduced by the Familiar: Narration and Meaning in Indian Popular Cinema* (New Delhi: Oxford University Press, 2008), 152–6.
4. The IIMs have become synonymous with material success in the field of education today, but their appeal had just begun in the late 1960s.
5. Satyajit Ray as quoted in Andrew Robinson's book *The Inner Eye: The Biography of a Master Film-Maker* (New Delhi: Oxford University Press, 2004), 177.
6. Robinson (2004), 177–8.
7. Here is an interview with Amitabh Bachchan reproduced from the magazine *Stardust*. There no question in the interview that presumes dissatisfaction with his life on the part of the actor as Aditi's questions do: <http://www.sugandh.com/seema/amitabhji/stardust.html> (last accessed 9 January 2022).
8. The motif of a successful man journeying to another city to receive an award and parts of his life appearing before him in reminiscences is also seen in Ingmar Bergman's *Wild Strawberries* (1957). In that film as well is a nightmare about death dreamed by the protagonist Isaak Borg. Ray admired Bergman and his film may have been inspired by *Wild Strawberries*.
9. 'New Indian Cinema' was launched through the Film Finance Corporation as an interventionist measure by the state under Mrs Indira Gandhi, with a view to making cinema more socially responsive. The earliest films financed were Mrinal Sen's *Bhuvan Shome* (1969), Basu Chatterjee's *Sara Akash* (1969) and Kantilal Rathod's *Kanku* (1969). Ashish Rajadhyaksha and Paul Willemen, *Encyclopaedia of Indian Cinema* (New Delhi: Oxford University Press, 1995), 154.
10. A 'character' is an agent capable of performing an intentional action, but in the process of performing that intentional action that character himself/herself must undergo transformation. In the instant case Aditi is a 'human agent' but not a character, in the sense that she remains unchanged. A pertinent examination of characterisation is Paisley Livingston, 'Characterization and Fictional Truth', in David Bordwell and Noel Carroll, *Post Theory: Reconstructing Film Studies* (Madison: The University of Wisconsin Press, 1996), 149–74.
11. Robinson (2004), 196.
12. Mrinal Sen's *Calcutta '71* appeared in the same year as *Seemabaddha* and Mahasweta Devi's novel *Hazar Churashir Ma* appeared in 1974. Both are romantic portrayals of Naxalism.

13. She is witness to his meeting a fixer in a café, which she later discovers is part of a plot to engineer a strike so that the non-despatch of a shipment finds justification as per the terms of a contract. Aditi's role in *Nayak* is much more passive since she hears only what Arindam tells her, which may or may not be true. It should be mentioned here that Tutul coming from small-town Bihar to Calcutta – and absorbing the goings on – does not transform and gain confidence. As played by Sharmila Tagore, she seems much too knowing from the very beginning.
14. John Beynon, *Masculinities and Culture* (Philadelphia: Open University Press, 2002), 8.
15. Suranjan Ganguly, 'In Search of India: Rewriting Self and Nation in Satyajit Ray's Days and Nights in the Forest', *Journal of South Asian Literature* 30/1/2, Miscellany (Winter, Spring, Summer, Fall 1995), 163.
16. Being uncaring about those less fortunate in trying times is something all three can be accused of.

CHAPTER 6

Trying Times: Aspiration and Failure in *Kanchenjunga, Mahanagar, Pratidwandi* and *Jana Aranya*

This chapter, like the previous one, deals with the decades of the 1960s and 70s through the aspirations and failures of the male characters in *Kanchenjunga, Mahanagar, Pratidwandi* and *Jana Aranya*. Success in the previous chapter was only for the few because of the limited opportunities in the decades, leading them to appear self-satisfied; thwarted aspiration was the rule. A characteristic of the films examined in this chapter is that the women are more successful, although the discourse would need interpretation – since it is not a straightforward representation of a prevalent state of affairs.

Hindi cinema recorded the milieu in the 1970s through the 'Angry Young Man', the figure made popular by Amitabh Bachchan. The failure of the state to provide solutions at the time was undeniable and several different kinds of crises erupted while Indira Gandhi was in office, but her era also propagated self-reliance as Nehru's had done. The agricultural sector did well later in her regime due to the Green Revolution of the previous decade[1] and there were also populist measures, with party cadres as conduits. But overall, few of the benefits were reaped by the salaried classes. Employment was only in public sector financial institutions like banks and insurance; manufacturing sector employment levels were low.

Unemployment and inflation were high in the 1960s and 70s, and with the death of Nehru in 1964 realpolitik took over. When Indira Gandhi took charge in the mid-1960s India was at its most vulnerable, both economically and politically. The wars of 1962 and 1965, two successive monsoon failures of 1965 and 1966, a fall in agricultural output by 20 per cent and food stocks so low as to threaten famine-like conditions had placed India in an unenviable situation, unprecedented after 1947.[2]

Indira Gandhi was quick to realise that India would not be able to maintain a sovereign independent stance vis-a-vis the advanced countries if her economy remained weak and depended on those countries for food. She pushed the 'Green Revolution' strategy vigorously and it yielded results. But while the economic conditions improved on account of these measures, there was dissatisfaction among the middle-classes since the economic boom – in which it could fruitfully participate – was to come only decades later. We could say that Ray's films examined in this chapter represent the flip side to those in the previous one, in that they deal with disaffection.

The 70s were a decade that heralded significant changes in the Indian political scenario. In 1975, Indira Gandhi declared the 'Emergency', a twenty-one-month long period from 1975 to 1977 in which elections were suspended and civil liberties curbed. Most of Mrs Gandhi's political opponents were also imprisoned and the press was censored. It was one of the most contentious and controversial periods in Indian political history, appropriately reflected in mainstream films. An examination of Ray's films made during this time gives a sense of the nation's ethos when Ray was making them.

Representing the Times

Through a substantial part of the 70s and 80s, Amitabh Bachchan's prodigious act as the Angry Young Man held centre stage. His career, which began in 1969 with *Saat Hindustani*, was exceptionally admired. He came into his own with *Zanjeer* (Prakash Mehra, 1973), in which he plays a tough cop reminiscent of *Dirty Harry*. The key motif here is the policeman's friendship with a petty criminal, the two coming together to fight a much bigger villain. The motif of petty criminals being enlisted by the law to fight bigger evil (also present in *Sholay* (1975)) has been interpreted as the marginalised being mobilised by the state.[3] This has been associated with Mrs Gandhi's populist stand, her notion of 'committed judges' with the judiciary aiding in social uplift through the right kind of verdicts.[4] She used her power to supersede the three senior-most judges in the Supreme Court to make a favoured 'left-leaning' judge the Chief Justice of India. One can infer from this that there was a great deal of pro-poor rhetoric in the public space, to the extent that even the law was seen as standing in the way of ushering in social change.

In the Amitabh Bachchan blockbuster *Deewar* (Yash Chopra, 1975), the film to actually inaugurate the motif of the Angry Young Man, the protagonist is the son of a union leader – unfairly accused of betraying his colleagues – who becomes a criminal (smuggler). He helps educate his younger brother, who joins the police, turns against the protagonist and eventually guns him down – with their mother's blessings. The motif is reminiscent of *Mother India* and here too the mother figure is equated with the nation. *Deewar* is a film that speaks with a 'forked tongue', as it were, in mobilising our emotions against social injustice, making us sympathise with upward mobility at any price but then punishing the upwardly-mobile individual for being anti-national. The discourse is confusing but so were the times – since alongside the valorisation of labour, Mrs Gandhi brutally crushed a railway strike in 1974 with Communist support.[5] Mrs Gandhi's brand of radicalism, it was later noted, was largely gestural but at that time she even inducted well-known Communists (like Mohan Kumaramangalam) into her ministry, who were convinced of her politics. Kumaramangalam had also had a hand in developing the notion of the 'committed judiciary', who would strive to further 'social causes'.

Another key film of the period, *Bobby* (1973), is ostensibly a romance between socially unequal categories – a capitalist's son and the granddaughter of their domestic employee. Significant here is the fact that the girl's father is a (small) businessman himself who demonstrates his wherewithal to the boy's capitalist father. Interpreting the motif, one could associate it with Mrs Gandhi courting smaller businesses against monopoly capital[6] through the nationalised banks, which were exhorted to help the needy and the poor.[7] This was a period in which many in the salaried middle-classes got into business with mixed results, although some did become wealthy in the next decade. But it is important to note that the small businesses were largely dependent on major industries as vendors, and the relationship between the two was hardly hostile, the way it is portrayed in *Bobby*.

When we come to art cinema, films like Shyam Benegal's *Ankur* (1974) and *Nishant* (1975) seem radical at first glance, but their anti-feudal stand was in line with Mrs Gandhi's left-leaning rhetoric. Shyam Benegal's films lost their political edge when Mrs Gandhi's political rhetoric changed, but others like M. S. Sathyu (*Garam Hawa*, 1974) tried to continue in the same vein. Ray himself made the polemical *Sadgati* (1981) much closer to the art cinema of the times than to his own work. Other works making bold social statements were in the regional languages, like B. V. Karanth's *Chomana Dudi* (1975), but focused on the subject of caste discrimination. One forgets, while watching the film, that Karanth is dealing with the past because the conditions were apparently pertinent to the present as well. The important thing to note is that the 1970s represent a watershed for art cinema in India. Mrs Gandhi was engaging in rhetoric, and if her gestures did not lead to an improvement in the condition of the poor, they nevertheless encouraged (political) radicalism in cinema that cannot be willed away.

A distinction must however be made at this juncture between art cinema in the rest of Indian and Bengali cinema. Ray's contemporaries in his own state treated the tumultuous times in a very different way. Mrinal Sen, especially, was responding to the times through films such as *Interview*, *Calcutta 71* and *Padatik*. These films are stringently political, more so than those outside Bengal. But if they were more radical, they were hostage to local politics – just as other Indian art films were hostage to Mrs Gandhi's rhetoric. The Communist Party of India (Marxist) was a constituent of the United Front, then in power, and Mrinal Sen's polemics found acceptance in the corridors of power.

The same year that Ray produced *Pratidwandi*, Sen produced his own version of the times in *Interview* (1971), and we see in it a kind of challenge to Satyajit Ray's cinema. In *Interview*, for instance, Sen uses agit-prop methods, and has a 'Brechtian' sequence in which the *actor* playing the protagonist (Ranjit Mallick) is recognised in a tram and the shooting of the film is itself part of the film; glamorous advertisements are also cut to documentary footage of the poor to underline the stark economic differences in India. The film is difficult to watch today but it put a lot of pressure on Ray – especially from students – to take a more radical stand in his films.[8] These are factors that must be kept in mind while dealing with Ray's films of the 1970s. Ray's portrayals of male aspiration and failure, however, began earlier in the 1960s when Nehru was still Prime Minister.

Ashok in *Kanchenjungha* (1962)

Kanchenjungha presents a peculiar situation in that it contains remnants of both the old as well as the new in India, and in conflict. On one hand, it is peopled by characters like Indranath Chaudhury, who (as brought out earlier) is a relic of the colonial times, an unpromising present represented by his wastrel son, and most importantly, the aspiring Ashok who has been set up to approach Indranath.

As reiterated, the Indian state had failed on many counts by the early 1960s, most importantly in being unable to make India a self-reliant nation on the food front, and in being unable to repair social differences, which had become more glaring. Already, Nehru's Hindu reform bills had suffered a defeat in parliament, and with Patel as Home Minister after 1947 and sympathetic to the entrenched classes, agrarian socialism made no progress. It was only with Patel's death in 1950 that Nehru's dreams might have seen some sort of realisation, but the strength of traditional interests can hardly be attributed to Sardar Patel alone. *Mother India* (1957) and *Ganga Jumna* (1961), in which the rebel against social injustice is punished (albeit reluctantly), can be regarded as popular cinema's warning against potential rebellion. Specifically, the films may be referring to the agrarian insurrection in Telangana in the 1950s.

In *Kanchenjunga* Ashok is a young graduate but unemployed. He makes ends meet by giving private tuitions to students. It seems to well-wishers that he might find employment if a person of some influence exerted himself to that end; his uncle therefore makes a request to Indranath, introduces Ashok to him, and implies to the latter that he should ingratiate himself with the old man. This was the time in India when the country was not self-reliant in most things and foreign companies were the best places in which to find employment. Banerjee, whom Indranath wants his daughter to marry, has a British degree and has such a position. It was only the public sector industries that began to provide steady jobs to educated people – going a long way to create a strong middle-class – but they were only established in the mid-to-late 1950s. Ashok therefore can only look to the Indranaths of the time in the film, since they seemed to hold all the cards.

It would be useful to compare Ashok with Indranath's unnamed wastrel son, who spends his time flirting with young women by taking their pictures. Whereas Ashok is earnest and anxious about his future, the latter seems to be without anxieties, implying that he can expect the support from Indranath that Ashok desperately needs. The differences between the two in a sense embodied the India that was around 1960 (before the debacle of the Sino-Indian War hurt sentiments) and the hope in its future that Ray had. Ashok's capacity for industry and his hope in his own future therefore embody Ray's own visions for India, then beginning to find its feet. For all the difficulties the frail Ashok faces, he is still a symbol of hope that appears to decrease conspicuously in *Mahanagar*.

Subrata in *Mahanagar* (1963)

Mahanagar is the first Ray film to examine contemporary Calcutta with a focus on the struggles of the lower middle-class. It is set in a joint family with Arati the protagonist (who is married to Subrata) as its eventual anchor. The film is about clashing social values: those of an older generation who would keep the married women at home against those of a younger generation who see the necessity for change, but also need the money that a wife's employment might bring. Arati's problem is however a perennial one – whether she should take up a job or try to please her in-laws, husband and child by staying at home – but it is a problem that eases. As her husband tells her – affectionately but tinted by Ray's irony – 'a woman's place is in her home', it is part of a value system that was entrenched in certain orthodox Bengali/Indian households, but with the aspirations of the men rarely yielding success, orthodoxy has no option but to surrender social ground.

Subrata is the only earning member of the Mazumdar household and finds it difficult to run his family – comprising his parents, a younger school-going sister, his wife Arati and a young son – on the salary he takes home as an employee in a small private bank. He also gives private tuitions to make ends meet but finds himself still falling short of being able to lead a comfortable, trouble-free life. But his wife comes to the rescue when she decides to herself work. While he goes along with Arati at first because he needs her financial support, he later begins to resent her success at work.

Narendranath Mitra, whose short story 'Abataranika' Ray adapted in *Mahanagar*, exhibited a familiarity with the milieu, and so Ray's film is natural in showcasing it. While Ray was familiar with working women in his family, he also said that resentment against working women was rampant. This was a time when women were beginning to make inroads in professions other than teaching, which Andrew Robinson sees as an attitude present from the early years of the century.[9] Subrata is a mild-mannered

Figure 6.1 After a few tense scenes between the couple Subrata asks Arati to resign.

man of average intelligence and talents, but is essentially of a conservative disposition. Arati, his wife, is however a person of great charm and sensitivity with a strength of purpose and character that emerges as the narrative progresses. Subrata's financial worries accost him the moment he returns to his home: his father wants to know what he has done to procure the glasses he has been requesting for; he has forgotten to bring his mother a key ingredient for her *paan* (betel-nut preparation) and the money for household expenditures will last only for another three days.

Initially Subrata is happy with the extra money coming in through Arati, although not for long. He takes the initiative and cites a couple they know whose wife has gone out to work as an example worth following. But it was Subrata who found her the job through the newspaper, making the necessary arrangements for her to apply and appear for the interview. At her job she settles in quickly and begins to earn, but the atmosphere at home changes. Her decision to take up a job has already provoked a 'cold war' between the father and son, and Subrata's pride is also hurt by the presents she brings home; she seems to be holding up her newly found wherewithal to the others.[10]

After a few tense scenes between the couple, Subrata asks Arati to resign – based on a friend's promise to get him a part-time additional job. He forces her into writing the letter and makes her promise to hand it over. But that is the moment when he learns that his bank has shut down and he calls her desperately to hold the letter. Arati therefore continues to work, now as the sole breadwinner, efficient and loyal as ever, while her husband sinks into gloom scanning the newspapers for a job every day.

Ray does something in this latter part of the film that Indian filmmakers – however radical – rarely try, which is to be ambivalent about the woman's sexuality. He tries to see through the viewpoint of a jealous husband without reassuring us that the woman is 'virtuous at heart', that she is not attracted to other men. There is an enormous difference between Madhabi Mukherjee in this film and Sharmila Tagore in *Aranyer Din Ratri* or *Nayak*, in that the latter is put across as attractive but asexual while Madhabi oozes sexual charm, which she does not hide as a saleswoman. Aparna's heart is more assured to her suitor Ashim than Arati's is to her husband Subrata. There is nothing in the film to say that Arati is not loyal, but her portrayal is still ambivalent.

Arati is efficient as a saleswoman, but success at her job is partly based on her allure and, in no time at all, this comes to Subrata's jealous attention. The publicity poster for *Mahanagar* (designed by Ray) is in black and white and shows Madhabi Mukherjee as Arati, submitting to the lipstick being applied to her lips, and the lipstick alone is in colour (red).

It emphasises the social transformation of the woman by circumstances that are central to the film. The lipstick is gifted to her in the film by an Anglo-Indian colleague, Edith, who is ill-treated and loses her job when she reports sick, but it is Edith who teaches her about the benefits of lipstick as a saleswoman. Anglo-Indians to the Indian middle-classes at the time were emblematic of licentiousness, and Arati's friendship with her makes the family suspicious. The emotional low point for the unemployed Subrata is when he follows Arati to a café and sees her in conversation with a strange man. The conversation is innocent – the man is a friend's husband – but the inaudibility of the conversation is still threatening.

At the conclusion of the film, Arati gives up her job in sympathy with Edith, who has been terminated and Subrata is unemployed too, but both are hopeful of finding employment. The hopefulness does not look plausible, especially for Subrata. That Subrata has learned from the past does not seem convincing – although one is not in doubt that Arati will soon be employed again. It is difficult to make out a case for such surmising, but the film was made at a low point in Indian history after 1947. Nehru lost popularity because of his handling of the Sino-Indian War and he died a year later. The fact that Arati has stamped her superiority over Subrata by this time by being employable – as he is not – is especially significant because he was the one with the respectable bhadralok job. She has the job of a saleswoman that would certainly have invited gossip among their kin. But given the approach in this book – seeing the men rather than the women as the archetypal national subjects – Subrata's feeble optimism may point to Ray's own pessimism in 1963.

Mahanagar is actually Arati's film and not Subrata's, and Ray is apparently dealing with the woman's position in contemporary society. Indian cinema has dealt with the subject many times – that of the woman as breadwinner – and the attitude is generally of the woman being exploited by her family, as in Ghatak's *Meghe Dhaka Tara* (1960) and Mrinal Sen's *Ek Din Pratidin* (1980), which came much later and may not bear comparison. In Ghatak's film, the family eventually moves into some affluence through the man, although the woman is too sick to partake of it. But Ray is focusing on the man's failure as provoking the woman into success. The employment that Arati finds is not 'respectable' – by bhadralok standards – but it will keep the household going. To reiterate an earlier observation, while there is little doubt that Arati will find employment – since being employed relies on her natural propensities – Subrata's chances of re-employment seem bleak. The kind of job he held (clerk in a private bank) was obtained in the 1960s through connections, the kind that Ashok was required to approach Indranath for in *Kanchenjungha*. Ray could only have been deliberate in this, since Subrata is not only far from being re-employed, but he has also conducted himself that way – as someone with little hope, which is different from Arati. The feebleness of his optimism at the conclusion suggests that it is gestural.

Siddhartha in *Pratidwandi* (1970)

Pratidwandi is the first film of the Calcutta Trilogy made in the early 1970s. It is about the twenty-five-year-old, sensitive and intelligent Siddhartha, who is educated but jobless. He feels trapped and frustrated in his situation, obliged to support his widowed mother and family but unable to find a job worthy of his class. Adapted from Sunil Ganguli's novel by the same name, Ray's Siddhartha is however older, more mature and intellectual. When the film opens, he has just lost his father and the family is left without much means. Siddhartha must give up his medical studies and look for employment. Much like *Seemabaddha*, which was Shyamalendu's story, *Pratidwandi* too is a story that belongs to Siddhartha. It pertains to his struggle in search of a job, the fulcrum around which the other characters as well as the episodes revolve. The moment at which this story is located was a particularly critical one – socio-politically as well as economically.

As an exhibited newsreel shows in the course of the film, the words 'growth', 'export drive' and 'import substitution' make appearances along with photos of the then Prime Minister Mrs Indira Gandhi, while West Bengal is associated with 'Naxalism'. In a nutshell it represents the two spaces Ray is engaging with – the larger space of India and the smaller space, Calcutta. Although a local problem, Naxalism bears direct link to the national in that a bomb is shown to go off in the auditorium while a newsreel praising national achievements is being screened. In this complex and contradictory milieu Sutapa, Siddhartha's younger sister, has employment, and has also got a promotion and a raise. But the family is horribly convinced that her boss is also sexually using her. Family honour is at stake even though Sutapa is apparently unconcerned. She is more preoccupied with her clothes, make-up and modelling than with the family's standing. Her mother is harsh in her criticism of Sutapa's ways – even though it is she who earns the money, which is much needed.

Also in the family is Tunu, the youngest brother, giving up his studies to focus on politics and applying his talents to bomb-making. He is a reckless young man who has embraced wholeheartedly the political ideology that has drawn him, with none of the doubts that beset the reflective Siddhartha. The interactions between the three in their

Figure 6.2 Siddhartha is unhappy with the whiff of scandal in Sutapa's conduct but stands up for her.

respective situations creates the tension in the film and Siddhartha keeps having visions or dreams about the other two. Like Shyamalendu in *Seemabaddha*, Siddhartha too is implicated in the socio-political conditions linked to Calcutta of the 70s – although he is not close to being an achiever.

The film traces Siddhartha's life over a few days as the story unfolds. His sense of failure is given emphasis by his sister's success, or so it seems. He tells his friend that it is Sutapa's allure that has got her a job. If this is interesting because it is indicative of what men thought of working women at the time, Sutapa is not only a 'working woman' like Arati. The film came seven years after *Mahanagar* and Sutapa is actually involved sexually with her boss, since the man's wife comes complaining. Siddhartha is only brother to her and not in Subrata's position vis-à-vis Arati in *Mahanagar*, but the notion of the independent woman had evidently travelled by 1970, since Sutapa is unrepentant.

Siddhartha is unhappy with the whiff of scandal in Sutapa's conduct, but stands up for her in the family with the following words: 'So what if she is late? It doesn't mean she is doing something with her boss. It may mean that she has a lot of pressure at work'; however he clearly believes that something is wrong. Much like his mother, Siddhartha too feels discomfiture but has taken a moral position.

Adinath, Siddhartha's friend, is a contrast to him. While Siddhartha left his studies when his father passed away, Adinath is a medical student with few moral qualms. At the time that Siddhartha visits him in his hostel room, he is busy extracting coins from the Red Cross fund box. Though he comes from a rich family, his father being a doctor, when Siddhartha chides him for stooping so low Adinath retorts, 'The whole country is going down, brother. What am I supposed to do? If I don't keep pace with it, I will soon be suspended in limbo.' This justification by Adinath of his moral stance is matter-of-fact. He also visits a nurse who is a prostitute in the evening to supplement her income. Adinath can afford to behave in this particular manner because he has the means, but Siddhartha is someone who actually has moral qualms that he cannot quite afford.

In his Calcutta Trilogy, beginning with *Pratidwandi* and concluding with *Jana Aranya*, Siddhartha was perhaps the protagonist who Ray felt closest to. Siddhartha is too sensible to commit himself to a course of political action, though he knows right from wrong at the personal level. What makes him 'weak' is perhaps his incapacity to act on the basis of partial knowledge, his tendency to see the other side, as it were. In Sen's *Interview*, often mentioned alongside *Pratidwandi*, the protagonist has none of Siddhartha's doubts because he has identified himself as a victim of the 'system' with no political responsibility. But Siddhartha, like Ray's other male protagonists, has responsibilities – although without power or authority. Ray was perhaps in Siddhartha's position because he felt responsible for the 'system' that the Marxist utopianism of the time had abjured, but saw 'idealists' like Tunu as more driven by the glamour of 'class violence' than as people with solutions. But if Siddhartha finds no hope in India's 'achievements' of the period or in the Marxist call to revolution – because of his intelligence and capacity to think – Suttappa nonetheless finds a way out.

Somnath in *Jana Aranya* (1976)

Jana Aranya is a more intricately plotted film than the others in this section and begins with rampant cheating in an exam hall plastered with Naxalite slogans. Somnath the protagonist and some others try to remain honest during this episode, representing a sort of systemic failure during the 1970s in Calcutta. Somnath misses an honours degree because of an overworked, underpaid examiner's irritation at his microscopic handwriting – and a borrowed pair of glasses. Somnath's father, who is an old-fashioned, upright man is aghast at his son's showing and wants to get his papers rechecked, but Bhombol his elder son points out the chaos reigning in the university, the Vice Chancellor being 'gheraoed' by protesting students and examination copies going missing. The chaos is rampant not only in the education sector but infects the civic amenities as well. Somnath's girlfriend walks out on him because of his situation, and his desire to settle down is dashed.

Ray includes shots of postal workers being overwhelmed by millions of applications for advertised jobs. After several futile interviews in which he is asked questions with no bearing on the nature of work to be done, Somnath decides to take up 'business'. His friend Sukumar assesses the chances of someone with a 'pass degree' getting salaried employment as negligible, and business is the only way out. Somnath is therefore among the enormous number of people trying to be self-employed at the time – though what 'business' entails is not clear. After a harrowing interview in which he is asked the 'weight of the moon', Somnath strolling towards home slips on a (metaphorical) banana skin. It is then that he finds himself face to face with Bishu da, who insists on introducing him to the world of business, the man being an older acquaintance (Utpal Dutt) from previously watched football matches at the Maidan. His father, although sceptical, accorded him due permission.

It is now that Somnath has his first brush with the conditions of business. Somnath joins Bishu da's office as an order supplier – someone who buys cheap and sells dear, a middleman or as Bishu da exclaims, a 'dalal' (a term used to also denote pimp in everyday parlance) with which Somnath is uncomfortable. But the times are such that he has to take the chances he gets. With the bespectacled innocence of his appearance (that endears him to many) and a clear conscience accompanied by lots of leg work, Somnath at least sees some real money. He is jubilant and lands up at the house of his friend Sukumar, who he finds is ready to 'compromise' as well. We get a brief sense of the latter's family and its disarray, with Sukumar struggling with a recalcitrant younger sister Kauna.

Given his lack of financial means, Sukumar has decided to drive a taxi. But unlike Sukumar, who caves in under the pressure of joblessness, Somnath still has bigger ambitions. He wishes to crack a bigger deal in business and it seems that Goenka, the head of the purchase department in a company, will give him an opportunity. However, Somnath on his own is unable to crack the deal and he decides to enlist the help of the PR expert Natabar Mitter (comedian Robi Ghosh in his darkest role).

Mitter is a character who can only belong to this particular era in India, when the middle-man wielded enormous power. Functionaries had to be approached by people they trusted and the middleman was trustworthy. One of the achievements of the liberal era after 1991–1992 was to curtail the influence of the category. 'Corruption' is normally associated with governmental agencies, but in a mixed economy like India's it infects everything. There is nothing that Mitter will not do in order to achieve his ends – including immersing himself in piety. But for all that he is prepared to do to satisfy his clientele, he still has a clear conscience. He decides to help Somnath and quickly identifies Goenka's weakness – women. Somnath, burdened by middle-class qualms, hesitates at first but he is soon overcome by Mitter's hard stance that given his proclivities, Somnath's options are limited. Somnath submits and is dragged by Mitter to several establishments where women can be procured. These sequences are darkly comic since none of the usual women are available. Mitter leads Somnath to a typing school that doubles as a brothel in the evenings. This time a girl, Juthika, is available, but Juthika is Sukumar's younger sister Kauna. This is a humiliating encounter for both of them but it concludes with Somnath dropping Kauna off at Goenka's place.

Figure 6.3 Somnath, burdened by middle-class qualms, hesitates at first but he is soon overcome by Mitter's hard stance.

Jana Aranya is a stringent and ironic commentary on the chaotic 1970s. Since Ray had always restricted his field of vision to Bengal, he adapted Shankar's novel of the times. But the tone is far darker in the film than in the novel; it is sour, tough but ultimately a mordant piece of social commentary. In both *Pratidwandi* and *Jana Aranya*, the socio-politico-economic conditions are intrinsically linked to the Calcutta of the 70s. This afflicts the protagonists Siddhartha and Somnath and cripples them. However, not only are the women not overwhelmed, but they cope with the situation. In both films, Bengali women are seen to go out of the precincts defined by their men folk, to support their families as the men cannot. They are bringing in money but are still in an uneasy relationship with their respective kin. Kauna is stabilising Sukumar's family financially, but there is also Somnath's sister-in-law Kamala, whose support to him cannot be underestimated in the film.

It is Kamala, Somnath's sister-in-law, who provides him with the much needed monetary and moral support that he needs when his life is at the crossroads. Kamala is an affectionate sister-in-law who holds the family together since Somnath's mother is dead. Kamala is constantly by his side as well as her father-in-law's, an old man given to brooding over his family's fortunes. Kamala, at once, acts as Somnath's mother, older sister, friend and confidante. She acts as the perfect foil to Somnath's father since she softens his dominating presence through her comforting touch. She is more encouraging in her attitude towards Somnath than his father is and mediates between the two. Even though Kamala is only a housewife she has more worldly wisdom than the men.

Ray also gives us much information about Sukumar, a seemingly peripheral character. Sukumar's father is, as he tells Somnath, unable to provide for his family in the absence of a suitable job, apart from tending to some people as a homeopath. While Sukumar takes to selling forms for various jobs to earn a living, Kauna, being less educated, has fewer openings. The sons are seen to study but the girls in Sukumar's family are discouraged from doing so. Somnath encounters Sukumar's younger brother Aju studying, while his sister Shikha, almost his age, is seen helping her mother with household chores. Here again, there is the sense of women having fewer options. Kauna comes across as more practical in the brothel scene and serves as an antithesis to Somnath. As a woman belonging to the middle-class, where marriage means everything, Kauna has had to take tough decisions. Interestingly, Ray provides insights into the family lives of the other amateur prostitutes as well – those that Mitter and Somnath encounter before engaging Kauna/Jyothika – and the women are all coping with family crises, often created by the husbands.

Jana Aranya came four years after *Pratidwandi* and the world inhabited by Somnath is a much harder place. Ray's particular portrayal of the women is a critique of the milieu and the moral crisis that surrounds it. It also acts as a response to what Cowie says about such a society: 'patriarchy controls the image of woman, assigning it a function and value determined by and for men, and in the service of the construction of definitions of the male and more specially of masculine desire'.[11]

The Lessons of Two Decades

The 1970s was an especially turbulent decade, not only for women but for men as well. In the two films dealt with from the Calcutta Trilogy as well as Arati in *Mahanagar*, women deal with it in by using the advantage they have – their allure – although in Arati's case she is not overtly conscious of it. This difference may even be read as reflective of the differences between the times in which the films are set – *Mahanagar* having been made in the last years of the Nehruvian era. This leaves us with the question of why it is the women who are made 'amoral' in the later films (Arati is not amoral) and not the men, and an answer could be that Ray is conscious of it being a patriarchal society; the women, in a sense, only respond to a world ruined by men, on whom social ambitions ride. The failure of the man as a national subject gets emphasis through the trajectory of the women. If the women had, been equally 'national subjects' as the men, the chosen strategy might have failed.

On considering the various portrayals of men and women discussed in this chapter, one detects a trajectory in the deemed 'respectability' of the women, a comparison justified by all four films being commentaries on contemporary times and not period reconstructions. While unemployment is either the fate of the male protagonists or the threat hanging over their heads, Monisha in *Kanchenjungha* (1962) is a marriageable young woman who yearns for the independence she risks losing because of her father's domineering ways. Financial problems are distant from her family. In *Mahanagar* (1964), Arati is a married woman with a child who takes up employment as a saleswoman, required to travel door-to-door and having to meet strange men. It is the kind of job that an Anglo-Indian woman might have done in normal times, but she is solidly 'bhadralok'. If her husband being unemployed means that she has no option, she does her job well and even likes it.

Arati in *Mahanagar*, although her husband is jealous, does not consort with men but Sutapa, Siddhartha's sister in *Pratidwandi* (1970), who is virtually running the family through her earnings, is in a relationship with her boss and is making her way upwards deliberately and with few regrets. In *Jana Aranya* (1974), Kauna, Sukumar's sister, works as a prostitute to support her family. The burden of running the household is gradually shifting to the women and Ray is making the conditions of the women more and more deplorable – since it is difficult to believe that Ray has no moral take on the kind of society which is gradually pushing women into selling themselves to keep the kitchen fire burning. That the women are not complaining does not mean that Ray does not see their plight in such terms and the men required to shoulder their burden are singularly incapable of doing so. The notion of masculinity in crisis has been studied in relation to the 1990s[12] in the West and one of the causes has been given as unemployment issues, leading men into psychological problems that they are unwilling to admit. I am not proposing that Ray's film is dealing with the same issues since the men are not exhibiting 'psychiatric symptoms', but there can never be such one-to-one correspondence between different cultures. The crisis in their masculinity in the films is therefore projected onto the condition of the women in each of the films – which transgresses the traditional boundaries laid by patriarchy itself. By implication it impacts on the trajectory of the nation by the second and third decades of independent India.

Conclusion: Morality and Personal Conduct

Satyajit Ray's films, because they are realistic/mimetic, observe the nation as mainstream cinema – which allegorises its 'meaning' – does not, and his films, nearly always, have something original to say about the changing social landscape. As already discussed, Ray had a place as a national filmmaker in the Nehruvian era and we see Mrs Indira Gandhi's era later scrutinised in his films – though not politically but in social terms, in that the national ethos is commented upon. It will be out of place to examine India under Mrs Indira Gandhi here, but it was a darker and more cynical period, as was portrayed in Ray's films of the 1970s, notably his Calcutta trilogy. In the same period Bollywood came up with an anti-hero – the 'Angry Young Man' – who is nominally the product of social injustice but rather than move to set right that injustice, he goes about trying to find a solution for himself largely through illegalities, which in a way reflects the same cynicism – albeit differently – and which even found popularity. One could propose that finding 'personal solutions' for social ills has also been the traditional way in India, but the Angry Young Man is duly punished.

One can therefore surmise that what is merely registered in mainstream Hindi cinema can be said to be commented upon or critiqued in Ray's films and this necessitates raising the issue of 'morality' that mainstream cinema does not raise. To elaborate, we do not need the notion of 'morality' to judge Gabbar in *Sholay*, since good and bad are Manichean divisions in the film. In popular films like *Sholay* people are 'good' or 'evil' intrinsically and that dictates their actions a priori instead. But in *Jana Aranya* Somnath is caught in a moral dilemma that necessitates a choice. The solution Ray opts for (Somnath's choice) is indicative of citizens forced into ways by social conditions.

At this point we need to address another question, which is: why did Ray use the peripheral figure of the woman in this fashion only in his 1970s films, seeing as they disappeared thereafter? Arati in *Mahanagar* is the central figure in the film. It is a fact that the women appear as part of his Calcutta trilogy when Ray himself was under pressure for not being radical enough by the emergence of Mrinal Sen as a potent force, with greater acceptance among students than Ray. In an interview Ray was asked by the interviewer to respond to a point often made about his work: that Ray, in his films, had stayed away from major political statements. Here is a segment from Ray's reply which brings this out:

> I have made political statements more clearly than anyone else, including Mrinal Sen. In 'The Middleman' I included a long conversation in which a Congressite discusses the tasks ahead. He talks nonsense, he tells lies, but his very presence is significant.[13]

Ray obviously felt he was being political in his films and the term 'political' is not so well-defined that we can say with certainty that he was less 'political' than a filmmaker like Mrinal Sen. My proposition here is that Ray, in being 'political', was more concerned with the collective responsibility of Indians in having made the nation what it had become in the 1970s after the expectations of the 1950s, and both Siddhartha and Somnath are hence ineffective. Ray does not take refuge in the notion of the 'system', that Marxist filmmakers like Mrinal Sen who located themselves outside it generally took. The idea of 'destroying the system' puts its weight on a future utopia, although those who advocate it (like Tunu in *Pratidwandi*) have no idea of how it will come about. Ray, in contrast, is talking about the here and now even when it is about politics.

Siddhartha and Somnath are both 'moral' in that they have qualms but that morality is directed inward, without any viable solution for even their own situations. The increasingly 'amoral' women (if they can be described as that) have fewer dilemmas, but they are nonetheless effective as the men are not. In his other portrayals of women Ray shows them as dependent on the dispensations of patriarchy, but the tumult of the 1970s, Ray suggests, led to the creation of the ineffectual Indian man and the amoral woman only responds to that. It is a reversal that connects the women of *Pratidwandi* and *Jana Aranya* to the other women in Ray's oeuvre. There is a critique of *Jana Aranya* that Somnath emerges 'unscathed'[14] from the experience of pimping to further his business because he is still the identifiable subject. But I would argue that the fact that we identify with him enlarges the scope of *his* horror to include *us* – as also fellow-citizens.

In Ray's films the women are not merely victims but are actively resisting the circumstances imposed on them through ways frowned upon by traditional patriarchy. The woman negotiates her way into a new position instead of simply breaking with an unacceptable one; Ray goes much beyond a lament, which would have been the case if the woman had merely been a victim. These women's images stay on with their audiences because they are 'positive images, both to challenge existing, negative definitions and as progressive figures for identification.'[15] They imply the need for a correction in patriarchal Indian society but they also comment upon the trajectory of the nation as a community.

Notes

1. Technological solutions for the country's problems like the Green Revolution were envisaged in the fading years of the Nehru era and the Shastri interregnum, but the resuts became impressive under Mrs Gandhi. Sunil Khilnani, *The Idea of India* (New Delhi, Penguin, 1997), 90–1.
2. Khilnani (1997), 44–6.
3. The marginalized and the dispossessed have been seen to be represented in *Zanjeer* by the female knife-sharpener played by Jaya Bhaduri and the owner of the gambling den, a Pathan named Sher Khan described as the 'criminalized but essentially honest proletariat'. M. Madhava Prasad, *The Ideology of the Hindi Film: A Historical Construction* (New Delhi: Oxford University Press, 1998), 142–4.
4. M. K. Raghavendra, *Seduced by the Familiar: Narration and Meaning in Indian Popular Cinema* (New Delhi: Oxford University Press, 2008), 183.
5. Ibid., 193.
6. Meghnad Desai, 'India: Contradictions of Slow Capitalist Development', in Robin Blackburn (ed.), *Explosion in a Subcontinent* (London: Penguin, 1975), 19. Also see Prabhat Patnaik, 'Imperialism and the Growth of Indian Capitalism', 73, in Robin Blackburn (ed.), *Explosion in a Subcontinent*, 73. Patnaik argues that the nationalisation of the banks initiated by Mrs Gandhi in 1969 was a move forced by the smaller bourgeoisie against the growing strength of the monopoly houses.

7. There were poverty alleviation schemes made compulsory for banks to implement with party cadres as conduits, as a way of electorally mobilising the masses through her party.
8. Here is a segment from a memoir of the times: 'Since Ray's films did not outwardly call for revolution, my radical friends saw him as an aristocrat who was for the status quo. Political, but wrong politics. Some probably saw him as a class enemy in Marxist terms. I saw such arguments as facile, caricaturing Ray. To see Ray as a chronicler, the depicter of humanity, a lyrical artist, a poet on celluloid who shows us our inadequacies but then does not want to overthrow the system, seemed good enough, but not for them.' Salil Tripathi, 'Was Satyajit Ray a Political Film-maker?', in *Mint* (3 October 2021), <https://www.livemint.com/mint-lounge/features/was-satyajit-ray-a-political-film-maker-11591960773599.html> (last accessed 29 August 2022).
9. Andrew Robinson, *The Inner Eye: The Biography of a Master Film-Maker* (New Delhi: Oxford University Press, 2004), 149.
10. The parents feel shame that Arati should work, and the essence of the shame is in the implication that women, being frail and helpless, should be at home. The only thing necessitating the woman's working is financial destitution, the son being unable to earn a living. Paul Glushanok, 'Mahanagar-Ray on Revolution', *Cineaste*, 1/2 (Fall 1967), 21.
11. Elizabeth Cowie, *Representing the Woman: Psychoanalysis and Cinema* (London: Macmillan, 1997), 12.
12. John Beynon, 'Masculinities and the Notion of Crisis', in John Beynon, *Masculinities and Culture* (Philadelphia: Open University Press, 2002), 76–7.
13. Udayan Gupta, 'The Politics of Humanism: An Interview with Satyajit Ray', *Cineaste*, 12/1 (1982), 24.
14. Amaresh Misra, 'Satyajit Ray's Films: Precarious Social-Individual Balance', *Economic and Political Weekly*, 27/20/21 (May 16–23, 1992), 1053.
15. Elizabeth Cowie, *Representing the Woman: Psychoanalysis and Cinema* (London: Macmillan, 1997), 12.

CHAPTER 7

At Odds with the Nation: *Joy Baba Felunath, Hirak Rajar Deshe* and *Sadgati*

Shatranj Ke Khiladi was well-received in the West, but in India itself there was grumbling that Ray had destroyed the patriotic essence of Premchand's story.[1] Although this may be contested, Shyam Benegal's *Junoon* (1978) may have been intended as an antidote to Ray's film – it has an English girl falling in love with a leader of the 1857 Mutiny. Ray, as already indicated, was particular that history should be respected and there are no indications that the 'nationalist' spirit even existed in 1857 – although the Mutiny has been officially renamed the First War of Indian Independence. Ray had been critical of the Congress Party in his Calcutta Trilogy; this was a much more bitter pill to swallow for the regime than the radical cinema of the 1970s, which often employed the same rhetoric as Mrs Gandhi – railing against the West, the colonial mindset and feudalism and being pro-worker and pro-peasant. Mrs Gandhi had aligned with the Communists in the 1970s and had brought left-wingers into her government, among them intellectuals like Mohan Kumaramangalam, who became Minister for Steel and Mines and Ashok Mitra, who was Chief Economic Advisor to the Government of India. Ray was considered 'conservative' in relation to radical filmmakers like Mrinal Sen, but the radical polemic of these latter filmmakers was actually more aligned with political power. Ray, it can be surmised, found himself marginalised with Mrs Gandhi at the helm when he became critical of her party/government, and the films dealt with in this chapter examine the effect of the cultural marginalisation of the filmmaker on his films. Ray had made *Pather Panchali* in 1955 and had been internationally renowned for decades, but he received the Dada Saheb Phalke Award, the highest recognition for a film personality, only in 1985 after Mrs Gandhi's death – when much less important people associated with films had been honoured earlier. The films dealt with here were made in a five-year period at the turn of the decade.

  A strategy employed in the course of this book is to examine Bollywood in the same period to which Ray's films dealt with in this chapter pertain, and Bollywood has always been deeply sensitive to the political currents at any time. In the timespan covered by the films in this chapter, Mrs Gandhi lost power (1977) after having imposed a very unpopular 'Emergency' during which press freedom was curtailed. The alliance that came to power in 1977 was driven apart by internal disagreement and fresh elections were held in 1980, in which Mrs Gandhi swept back into power. This time, however, she was faced with a different kind of opposition, mainly Sikh separatism and militancy, which led to her assassination in 1984. Bollywood in this period seems to have been at a loss, since there was little discernible rhetoric in the public space corresponding to the 'mood of the nation' which had been evident earlier with left-wing rhetoric ruling.

In this politically indeterminate period, therefore, Bollywood was noncommittal socially and among the most important Bollywood directors was Manmohan Desai, who was famous for 'masala films', a euphemism for frivolous formula films. *Amar Akbar Anthony* (1977), for instance, is about three brothers who are separated in childhood and brought up separately as a Hindu, a Muslim and a Christian. The film parodies many of the devices of popular Hindi cinema by grossly overdoing them: the fragile mother, sick with tuberculosis and then being struck blind by lightning; identical twins, one a scientist and the other a smuggler; and devotion affecting miracles. In one sequence the villains in pursuit of the blind woman as she enters a prayer hall are thwarted by a poisonous cobra. Desai's next film, *Naseeb* (1981), continues in the same way, although less successfully. However, alongside this were also art films like *Ardh Satya* (1983) and *Aakrosh* (1980), which restated truths about Indian society after 1947 – such as state corruption and the exploitation of tribals. The actual political concerns of the day, however, did not find much of a representation in either Hindi or Bengali films, perhaps because politics itself had become clouded. Mrinal Sen's films of the period, for instance, are more about pre-1947 India.

Coming to Satyajit Ray's films, unlike the earlier 1970s, which found a representation in his Calcutta Trilogy that also included a view on the Naxalite uprising and the refugee crisis of 1971, these later films by Ray seem evasive; there is studied retreat from his commitment to documenting the state of the nation. Two of the three films dealt with here are children's films, and *Sadgati* (1981) – which was made for state television – even adopts the polemical tone of a Mrinal Sen film of the 1970s.

Joy Baba Felunath (1979)

Satyajit Ray's detective fiction, as many critics have noted,[2] has more the quality of a fairy tale, with few of the situations or stock characters of the whodunnit finding a place. Although a borrowed genre, albeit a colonial one, Ray's detective fiction and his subsequent adaptation of them brought distinctively Indian concerns into the genre, at the same time advocating cultural cosmopolitanism since the films go outside Bengal into other parts of India, where other kinds of characters are featured.

In 1978, after filming *Shatranj Ke Khilari*, Ray turned to one of his own stories featuring the trio already made famous in *Sonar Kella* – the detective Feluda, his assistant Topshe and their writer friend Jatayu. Perhaps he felt the need to compensate his Bengali audience with a Bengali film after *Shatranj Ke Khiladi*, or perhaps it was Ray's own need to revisit Varanasi after *Aparajito*, the city that had 'intoxicated' him as Ray had once confessed to Marie Seton.[3] It could also have been an urge to make a commercial success for his faithful producers after the poor showing by *Shatranj Ke Khilari* at the box office.

Ray had written the story 'Joi Baba Felunath' before 1976 and it found an onscreen expression in 1980. The world had altered but not unrecognisably so, and Ray stuck to his original story, with a few additions or alterations. Ray establishes a Varanasi different from the pristine one that we saw in *Aparajito*. In *Joi Baba Felunath*, Varanasi houses the ills plaguing modern India – greed, corruption and criminal enterprise – all still rampant in India and which make the film as pertinent today. In a way, such universality is a good thing until we recollect that the earlier films were valued for their timeliness. *Jana Aranya* is specific to the 1970s and cannot be placed at either an earlier date or later.

Joy Baba Felunath's title suggests a godman and, by implication, religion, and so Ray goes about laying the foundation for his crime thriller among holy men. It begins with young Ruku avidly listening to old Shoshi Babu narrating the mythological story of the Hindu goddess Durga's creation, only to be interrupted by an arriving car that he goes to investigate. It is Maganlal Meghraj, an old college mate of his father Umanath Ghoshal and now a shady criminal in the guise of a businessman who has come to their house to acquire a golden Ganpati figurine, an integral part of the Ghosal family which he threatens to acquire by force when his demands to buy it at 30,000 rupees fails. But a thief does indeed come calling later and the threat turns real.

The next scene is a lighter one as we see Feluda, Topshe and Jatayu make their way to the Calcutta Lodge, their accommodation as they holiday in

Varanasi. In Ray's settings the urban centers usually pose as hubs of corruption but in this case, it is the holy town of Varanasi, famous for its temples, ghats and its godmen. Egged on by this challenge as well as his suspicions of Macchli Baba, on whose arm he spots a tattoo – that of an airplane – on his first visit to him, Feluda is drawn into the happenings. The feebly lit and murky atmosphere of Holmes's London here gives way to narrow, dark alleyways, with tall houses with hardly any sunlight reaching them, which is a feature of this ancient city. In fact, much of Ray's film concentrates on the architecture, the ghats and wide open spaces. The Ghosal residence rooftop, which features in the film, offers a splendid view of the Ganges, only to be contrasted with the dark room in which the arch villain Maganlal Meghraj holds his private circus to intimidate Feluda and company. This in turn contributes to the idea of an enclosed and separate sub-space that truly breeds evil. The film could well be a Sherlock Holmes story with Moriarty replaced by Maganlal, but it is nonetheless a children's film.

Another interesting addition to the film text is the character of a fellow Bengali guest in the hotel who constantly expresses his ire by passing comments like, 'You'll not change the towels in the guest's rooms? or, 'What is the cooking medium in your hotel?' whenever the hotel manager sees to the trio's comfort or chats with them. The man seems upset that Feluda and his friends get special treatment. This may be Ray's commentary on the malicious tendencies of the Bengali community, which he may have found irksome at times. Most of the criticism for his films stemmed from the Bengali community and there were apparently attempts to hurt his career by his own people.

But with all its Holmesian characteristics there is a marked difference between the film and the earlier Feluda mystery *Sonar Kella* (1974). The difference is that Ray is putting in 'social criticism' by introducing corruption, superstition and, most importantly, the trafficker in antiques. The smuggler was a figure in mainstream cinema of the period and the government had enacted a law (The Conservation of Foreign Exchange and Prevention of Smuggling Activities Act, 1974 also known as COFEPOSA). But the smuggler is also associated with western behaviour since the smuggler crosses boundaries between east and west.[4] Mrs Indira Gandhi, in the 1970s, was stridently anti-West because of her left-wing affiliations and Bollywood had the figure of the Western smuggler of antiques dealing with the principal villain, as in films like *Yaadon Ki Baraat* (1973). Alongside was the discourse on Western decadence in films like *Johny Mera Naam* (1970) and *Purab aur Paschim* (1970). Also, antique idols are not made of gold and are usually of bronze. Mainstream cinema, however, makes them in gold to lend them glamour, but Ray follows this representation.

From the above we could surmise that Ray is deliberately engaging with popular representations. One recollects the fake godman in films of the 1970s, including in regional languages, and Ray makes Macchli Baba an agent of Maganlal. It is difficult to say much more but even while withdrawing from the project of documenting the nation's trajectory through his subjects, he is still drawn to the nation's ills. The device of the whodunnit is universal but the motif of rational enquiry into religious activity and that of smuggling antiques is topical. But *Joy Baba Felunath* is a compromise; Ray seems to be making peace with popular culture in his motifs. Perhaps the commercial failure of *Shatranj Ke Khiladi* also pushed him in that direction and the film suggests a subdued period for Ray.

Like Holmes, Feluda is cerebral and calls upon his vast knowledge, superior intelligence and quick observation to solve cases. Feluda also meets his quarry face to face, confident of his intellect, which he refers to as 'Magajastro'. Still, Feluda, unlike Sherlock Holmes,[5] is children's fare – with instructions for them. The fact that Ray places child characters – with whom the detective has rapport – unfailingly in the narratives implies that the Feluda films primarily address children. Topshe is an adolescent and not yet fully adult in his appearance, and both *Sonar Kella* and *Joi Baba Felunath* have key child characters who participate in the unravelling of the mystery.

In the book, Ray, through the voice of Feluda, actually pronounces godmen as charlatans. This could be associated with his reformist Brahmo background, but Ray's excursion into addressing children also needs

Figure 7.1 The heady concoction of religion mixed with corruption and business.

comment since it is curious that something as dark as *Jana Aranya* is followed by children's stories. It should be noted that Feluda, unlike Holmes, has no character eccentricities (like playing the violin, taking cocaine) and is apparently a stand-in for Ray himself.[6] *Joy Baba Felunath* also includes a bodybuilder who personifies the adulation of the body at the expense of intelligence and courage. Ray's urge in the film is apparently instructive and one catches the sense that he is counselling a younger generation, perhaps because of his sense of being sidelined in the present. Arguably, his compromise with popular cinema – using its motifs – was also to make himself heard. The sequel to *Goopy Gyne Bagha Byne*, *Hirak Rajar Deshe*, is also didactic as the earlier film was not.

Hirak Rajar Deshe (1980)

Made more than ten years after *Goopy Gyne Bagha Byne*, *Hirak Rajar Deshe* is serious-minded and a much more somber and instructive film than *Goopy Gyne Bagha Byne*, which was the first of what may be called the Goopy-Bagha trilogy; the last of which was made by Sandip Ray. Both *Goopy Gyne Bagha Byne* and *Hirak Rajar Deshe* had long runs, the longest ever for a Bengali film in the case of *Goopy Gyne Bagha Byne*. Surprised at this reaction, Ray wrote to Marie Seton about it: 'It is extraordinary how quickly it has become part of popular culture. Really there isn't a single child in the city who doesn't know and sing the songs.'[7] Robinson talks of the dialogues and lyrics of singular wit that make both these films stand out. Ray was rather proud of his lyrics: 'They are my songs if you come to think of it. I have definitely set a style of singing which doesn't come from Tagore, doesn't come from Western music, but which is essentially me.'[8]

Goopy Gyne Bagha Byne was adapted from Ray's grandfather's writings. Fantasy which was given free rein in both his father's and grandfather's writings found expression in these two films.[9] Goopy and Bagha first made their appearance in 1915, in the magazine *Sandesh*, accompanied by Upendrakishore's (Ray's grandfather) illustrations and Satyajit first read it as a child. Despite his aversion for labels and political commitment, Ray did not demur from accepting his films as being political. 'In a fantasy one can be forthright,' he said, 'but if you're dealing with contemporary characters, you can be articulate only up to a point because of censorship. You simply cannot attack the party in power.'[10] This remark again provides evidence of his experience of political hostility.

The two protagonists of *Hirak Rajar Deshe* are now older. In a lively duet, as the title credits roll, they introduce themselves through song to those who have not yet met them. They have now been residing in comfort for the past ten years as the favoured sons-in-law of the King of Shundi and blessed with a child apiece, but they are still dissatisfied. It is Bagha who expresses his dissatisfaction at the boredom gnawing away at their lives. It has been ten years since they solved the problem between the two brothers – the kings of Shundi and Halla – and prevented war from breaking out. When Bagha expresses a desire to travel, even their magic shoes seem to have cobwebs on them.

The evil king of the Land of Diamonds now invites Goopy and Bagha to a festival of sorts, in which they are required to give a musical performance and the king will have a giant statue of himself unveiled. But before that, he intends to bring some order into this kingdom. To that end he has the court poet produce rhyming couplets for each class of his subjects. To the farmers he orders: To keep my taxes pending/mean trouble unending; for the miners: Miners must be underfed/miners fat are miners dead. His scientist wizard has developed a brainwashing machine with which each of these sayings can be ingrained into the minds of people. This is perhaps Ray being 'forthright' about Mrs Gandhi's Emergency with its sloganmongering over her 20-Point-Programme, and her son Sanjay Gandhi's additional five points.

The king now proceeds to stop education being imparted to young minds and orders all books to be burnt. He then orders that the teacher Udayan (meaning 'Sunrise') be arrested so that he can duly undergo brainwashing, leaving him incapable of imparting knowledge to his future subjects. However, Udayan (Soumitra Chatterjee) escapes, determined to oppose the evil king and hopefully reopen his beloved *pathshala* (school) once again. In this, he is assisted by a band of dedicated and loyal students who remain true to him. Soon enough, he is joined by Goopy and Bagha, who accidentally encounter him in hiding. They promise him help before they go to meet the king in his palace. Udayan is utterly unselfish and he declares: 'The good of the country and the good of my countrymen are all that I fight for. Education encourages questioning, which is why the king has ensured that no education should be imparted.'

The tone of this film has only to be compared with *Goopy Gyne Bagha Byne* to understand how preachy it is. In that film two young men without musical talent but with ambitions were driven out of their respective villages. But they came upon a ghostly occurrence when they were granted boons by the king of the ghosts – which enabled them to intervene in a fight between kings who were brothers, and bring about peace. As a reward they married the daughters of the King of Shundi.

Goopy Gyne Bagha Byne is a much truer children's film than *Hirak Rajar Deshe*. The didactic urge in children's fiction can be associated with the parenting impulse, because true children's fiction respects what children have not yet lost, which is their imagination. Robinson notes about *Hirak Rajar Deshe*'s music: 'Ray constructs an important plot motif out of rhymes.'[11] Ray himself points out: 'The king and his courtier's speeches are formal, rhymed kind of speech and very artificial and there is another kind of speech that ordinary people like the miners or the peasants use, which is naturalistic.'[12] This suggests that the ordinary people and workers are in the position of citizens suffering under the burden of an artificial construct – the dictatorial regime with its rhetoric – which had been deafening in the 1970s. These two kinds of spoken language then set up the world of Hirak Rajyo (Kingdom of Diamonds), in which political intrigue and greed for power abound. But if it is a more difficult world that Goopy and Bagha traverse and hope to set right, it is also one deliberately created as an allegory of the actual political world of the 1970s.

Hirak Rajar Deshe (as already noted) has a particular frame of reference – that of India after the suspension of democracy by Indira Gandhi in 1975. There are several markers in Ray's film, not the least of which is an oblique reference to Indira Gandhi's use of censorship of the media. There is an implicit warning in the film about language being used to propagate evil. The recognition of evil through the various pronouncements and actions by the evil king, the kind of violence – as in the destruction of the poor people's slum so that no ugliness greets his majesty's favoured guests – or the allusions to the inhuman conditions under which the miners work, are consonant with Ray's vision of what he saw in

Figure 7.2 The evil king who is ultimately vanquished by the power of the good.

the India of the 1970s. Of importance is the fact that Soumitra Chatterjee plays the teacher Udayan and articulates what Ray wants to say. Soumitra may have been to Ray what Marcello Mastroianni was to Federico Fellini in *8½*, a kind of alter-ego,[13] although he also played other kinds of roles, and he virtually pushes the messages of the two children's films.

Sadgati (1981)

Sadgati, made in 1981, is one of the two Hindi films made by Ray, the other being *Shatranj Ke Khilari*. It was made for Doordarshan (National Television). *Sadgati* is focused on caste exploitation in the feudal system, and is set around the early 1930s when Premchand wrote the story. *Sadgati* is a distinct film in Ray's oeuvre in that it uses stereotypes in the service of its political message. Ray described it thus: '*Deliverance* is a deeply angry film but it is not the anger of an exploding bomb, but of a bow stretched taut', but Ray's *Sadgati* in many ways follows the methods of the art cinema movement in India. Such ranting against social injustice and oppression were the strategies of films of the Parallel Cinema movement which, as already indicated, began in 1969 with state intervention. It follows films like B. V. Karanth's *Chomana Dudi* (1975), which talks about the past while documenting contemporary issues. These films echoed Mrs Gandhi's own polemic of the 1970s. 'Anger' was a cherished emotion in left-wing films,[14] but it was ineffectual; what was being targeted was the practices of centuries that Mrs Gandhi's radical posturing did little to eradicate.

The plot of *Sadgati* deals with the harsh exploitation of one class by another, with societal sanction based on caste. In this case, it is of the lowest caste under Brahmin domination in a village in central India. Dukhi, the protagonist, is a chamar (the caste of leather workers) and someone particularly 'unclean' to a Brahmin. When the film opens, Dukhi (Om Puri) is cutting grass in a field near his hut. He needs it as part of a gift to the local Brahmin priest Ghasiram, so that he will come to their hut and fix an auspicious date for his daughter's wedding. Without Ghasiram's intervention, Dukhi's daughter getting married is inconceivable. In order to get the priest to come over, Dukhi must meet his demands.

Dukhi feels unwell as he is recovering from a fever. He refuses to eat whatever his wife Jhuria (Smita Patil) gives him as he is afraid of being late for his appointment at the Brahmin's house. Dukhi sets off for the brahmin quarter of the village watched by Jhuria. The Brahmin Ghasiram (Mohan Agashe) is someone for whom Dukhi must labour without payment. But Ghashiram seeks to wring out every ounce of sweat and tears in exchange for his ritual expertise. Accordingly, Ghasiram sets

Dukhi one task after another, beginning with the sweeping of his veranda. Before Dukhi begins his work, Ghasiram asks his wife to give him some food – a stronger Dukhi will do more work – but when she is reluctant, he sets the starving Dukhi to work without feeding him. Dukhi does everything assigned to him since his daughter needs to be married and the Brahmin's intervention is necessary. As Dukhi performs these tasks on an empty stomach, his exhaustion becomes alarming. But Ghasiram still directs him to chop up a large log of wood, an impossible task with the equipment provided.

Ray establishes the cruelty that Dukhi is subjected to. He also establishes the contrast – created by caste – in the lives of the two men. Dukhi toils on with the log, but some tobacco might help alleviate his hunger and his struggle with the blunt axe. He goes to the Brahmin's house to ask for some coals for the clay pipe supplied by some Gond tribals. This angers Ghasiram's wife so much that she flings the coals at Dukhi with the intention of hurting him. Apologetic, and with feet burnt by the hot coals, Dukhi then proceeds to move out of the house and return to his impossible task.

While Ghasiram is inside, Dukhi is ineffectually trying to chop up the log of wood. When he tries hacking at the wood, clearly demonstrating his lack of expertise, a Gond tribal appears.[15] It is he who asks Dukhi whether he is up to the task of chopping wood and whether he has ever done the task before. The Gond then tells Dukhi about his rights – viz. that he should not chop wood if he is unable to, and to ask for food before he undertakes the task. The Gond assumes something of a political purpose as a commentator. However, Dukhi, conscious of his own lowly status, desists from asking the Brahmins for food, preferring to sweat over the unyielding log on an empty stomach until he falls down dead out of exhaustion. Tradition dictates that the Brahmin is forbidden to touch or be touched by a Dalit; Ghasiram refuses to remove the dead body. The Dalits, stirred by the Gond standing with Dukhi, and in a bid to punish Ghasiram, also refuse to remove Dukhi's body.

Sadgati has none of Ray's characteristically subtle touches and, to worsen matters, he casts Hindi art film actors to play the same kinds of roles that they normally played in the 1970s. Om Puri and Smita Patil had played an exploited tribal couple a year earlier in Govind Nihalani's *Aakrosh* (1980) and Mohan Agashe had been typecast in villainous roles, as in *Ghashiram Kotwal* (1976) where he played Nana Phadnavis; Ray even gives him a name here that recalls that role. The film repeats the anti-caste/anti-feudal polemic of 1970s art cinema,[16] which itself was in tune with Mrs Gandhi's rhetoric. If we consider when the film was made,

Figure 7.3 The unwieldy log which refuses to yield to Dukhi's blunt axe and empty stomach.

it was after Mrs Gandhi came back to power, while the other two films dealt with in this chapter were apparently made when she was out of it. It may appear that Ray was being critical of Mrs Gandhi (albeit allegorically) in *Hirak Rajar Deshe* when she had been unseated, but echoed her familiar polemic when she returned to power.

Sadgati may be an angry film, but there is a sad familiarity about the 'anger' – that so many directors, from Shyam Benegal to Mrinal Sen, had already voiced in the art film. A characteristic of Ray's films is that he did not make films about the marginalised classes whose lives he had no personal knowledge of – something that art cinema did routinely – but he broke that rule for *Sadgati*. It is also interesting that Ray places a witness to the action (the Gond) as the other art films also do (like the lawyer in *Aakrosh* and the boy in *Ankur*), who goes through an emotional trajectory that the audience is required to follow. They follow a model intended as instruction for the general public, and instructing is what Ray consistently does in all the three films covered in this chapter.

Making the Brahmin the heartless villain of the film is also in tune with the political compulsions of the times, since the uppermost caste virtually represented 'caste oppression' in Indian cinema, although it is more regional cinema where this is seen, as in the Kannada film *Bhootayyana Maga Ayyu* (1974). A much more nuanced picture of the Brahmin was presented by Ray in an earlier period in *Ashani Sanket* (1973), a film set in the Bengal famine of 1943. In that film the Brahmin enjoys privileges because of his caste, but he has to negotiate his way leveraging that benefit since he is not rich or powerful. The strong man in the village in that film is actually a peasant from a lower caste.

Conclusion: Political Choices and Compulsions

This chapter, which analyses Ray's cinema in the turn of the decade, yields some significant results. There are several important points that emerge: for one, Ray's earlier concerns about the nation and the creation of the national subject are absent. This book is primarily about the masculinity of Ray's male characters, but there are none in any of the films – i.e. individuals fleshed out as national subjects occupying a place in the social fabric that is recognisable to us. The closest in masculinity is Feluda in *Joy Baba Felunath*, and I have tried to argue that he is not a fleshed-out character so much as a substitute for Ray's own rational, instructive voice. Soumitra performs the same function in *Hirak Rajar Deshe*, Udayan representing Ray's own political perspective. In *Sadgati* there is no identification with anyone by Ray, and he places a witness as in many other art films – alongside whom we witness the happenings in the story. All this suggests Ray's disconnect with the nation at that particular juncture – when he had been earlier celebrated as a national filmmaker. I propose that this was due to his perceived position, as an adversary of the regime.

Ghare Baire was another film he made in 1984, and although it has been seen from one perspective, looking at it in this context may also be useful. *Ghare Baire* came out against the Hindu nationalism of an earlier period and Mrs Gandhi also saw the nationalists as among her primary enemies.[17] The film is awkward, with Soumitra overplaying the 'villain' Sandeep to make him seem despicable. Ray was also recovering from a heart surgery and was restricted to the studio environs, which meant that he could not attend to the film as he might have. But of the other films dealt with here – made before *Ghare Baire* and before Ray suffered his first heart attack – all of them are politically vocal as Ray had not been. If Ray had been displaced from his standing in the 1970s, his political messages in *Hirak Rajar Deshe* and the subsequent two films – *Sadgati* and *Ghare Baire* – suggest that he was trying to regain that position by directing their discourses appropriately.

In the earlier chapters we saw how the woman was positioned almost in opposition to the man – as a corrective – and the absence of women in the children's stories needs comment. This absence is not only in these two films but also in *Goopy Gyne Bagha Byne* and *Sonar Kella*. Ray himself explained the absence of women in the children's stories as a way of avoiding sexual intrigue,[18] since a strong woman's presence might do that – the detective not having a love interest – but even a strong woman in the milieu where the crime happens is absent. One cannot go along with the proposition that a woman's presence would necessarily introduce a sexual element into the story, since there could be all kinds of women – like the Queen of Hearts in *Alice's Adventures in Wonderland* or the Lady Jingly Jones in Edward Lear's poem *The Courtship of the Yonghy-Bonghy Bo*.

But the issue here is also what happens when the films are didactic, how that affects the absence of the woman, and we recollect that Mrinal Sen's polemical films like *Interview* (1980) also have a weak feminine presence, although there is a mother in that film who has a role. It can be argued that when Ray has such a deliberate socio-political message to offer as in these films, delivering it to a world entirely of men is a miscalculation. We must note that a message is normally delivered only to those who are capable of learning and acting on it, and this is a tacit admission on Ray's part that only men (of Ray's generation or the next) can be the primary recipients, in a sense reinforcing patriarchy.

One of the premises of this book was that because of patriarchy dominating Indian society, it was the men who were 'national subjects' in Ray's films; but the failure of the men in so many of the films implied that this supposition was improper and strong women were hence placed in the narrative as correctives. The absence of the feminine presence in *Goopy Gyne Bagha Byne* or *Sonar Kella* was suitable, since there was neither a strong male presence nor a message in them; Goopy and Bagha are children in male guise. The two children's films dealt with in this chapter are different in that Soumitra/Ray's instructive voice is male in each of these films, and it instructs a male world. Bertolt Brecht and George Bernard Shaw wrote didactic plays and they put female characters in all of them.

In *Sadgati*, the wife's presence is weak and does not rescue the film from being about conflicts in a male world. The Brahmin has a wife but she does not take a position markedly different from her husband's, and this again is different from *Ashani Sanket* where the Brahmin's wife influences her husband. The couples may be taken to represent family units rather than man and woman as individuals. Ray's films, as indicated, deal with individuals rather than social types and the feminine presence emphasised this point – that the woman from the same social circumstances would see the world differently. In *Sadgati* he uses stereotypes as in the art film. He could have made the film differently, but he perhaps saw himself as driven into a corner from which only fulfilling political demands would extricate him.

Notes

1. After Ray became a national celebrity, this was an issue that was not raised about the film in India, but a Pakistani newspaper recollects the controversy. Raza Ali Sayeed, 'Weekly Classics: *Shatranj Ke Khilari*,' *Dawn* (8 February 2013), <https://www.dawn.com/news/784520/weekly-classics-shatranj-ke-khilari> (last accessed 3 December 2021).
2. See Anindita Dey, *Sherlock Holmes, Byomkesh Bakshi, and Feluda: Negotiating the Center and the Periphery* (London: Lexington Books, 2021), 121–46, for a discussion on Feluda and Holmes.
3. Marie Seton, *Portrait of Director: Satyajit Ray* (New Delhi: Penguin, 1988), 93.
4. Beatrix Pfleiderer, 'An Empirical Study of Urban and Semi-Urban Audience Reactions to Indian Films', in Beatrix Pfleiderer and Lothar Lutze (eds), *The Hindi Film: Agent and Reagent of Cultural Change* (New Delhi: Manohar, 1985), 127.
5. In the Holmes stories there is adult material including adultery, violence and brutality, as in *The Cardboard Box*. Ray's stories, in contrast, hardly contain adult material of this kind.
6. Feluda shares some of Ray's own likes; for example word games, something that Ray was fond of. The memory game in *Aranyar Din Ratri* is actually a similar kind of game that assumes some reading.
7. Andrew Robinson, *The Inner Eye: The Biography of a Master Film-Maker* (New Delhi: Oxford University Press, 2004), 182.
8. Ibid., 183.
9. Both Sukumar Ray and Upendrakishore's writings mostly catered to children. In fact, Upendrakishore came up with the novel concept of a magazine devoted exclusively to children, which he named *Sandesh*. All the Ray children and Upendrakishore himself contributed extensively to it.
10. Robinson (2004), 189.
11. Ibid., 189.
12. Ibid., 190.
13. When Soumitra Chatterjee, the actor who played Feluda onscreen, met Ray after he had written his first Feluda novel, he asked Ray: 'Manikda, I think you have modelled Feluda on yourself? The illustrations look a bit like you.' Ray had replied laughingly, 'But no, many people have come to me and said it looks like you!' In due course Ray had admitted to the strong resemblances

between the detective and himself: 'I'm sure there's a lot of me in him but I can't tell you to what extent.'
14. M. K. Raghavendra, 'Beyond Anger and Empathy: The Failings of Social Realism in Indian Cinema', *Cinema in India*, 4/2 (April–June 1990), 6–12.
15. The Gonds are a Dravidian ethno-linguistic group. They are one of the largest groups in India. They are spread over the states of Madhya Pradesh, Maharashtra, Chattisgarh, Uttar Pradesh, Andhra Pradesh, Bihar and Odisha. They are listed as a Scheduled Tribe for the purpose of India's system of reservation. They are also associated with Maoism.
16. Shyam Benegal's *Ankur* (1974) dealt with the sexual exploitation of Dalit by caste Hindus. In 1977 Mrinal Sen had made the Telugu *Oka Oorie Katha*, based on a novel by Munshi Premchand like *Sadgati*, dealing with the lowest caste and their misery, along with the issue of the disposal of a corpse. Govind Nihalani's *Aakrosh* (1980) is about the rape and murder of a tribal woman by the leading citizens of the town, for which the husband is blamed.
17. With the Forty-second Amendment of the Constitution of India enacted in 1976 during Mrs Gandhi's rule, the Preamble to the Constitution asserted that India is a secular nation. This may be interpreted as a deliberate move against the Hindu right-wing.
18. Robinson (2004), 299.

CHAPTER 8

'An Essay on Man': The Wise Person in *Ganashatru, Shakha Prosakha* and *Agantuk*

The films covered in this chapter are the very last that Satyajit Ray made before he passed away in 1992 and they differ on many counts from the ones which he made earlier in his career. The last few years of his life saw Ray being given the highest accolades in cinema and in India as a citizen – the Honorary Oscar for Lifetime Achievement and the Bharat Ratna. In 1987 he was awarded the Legion of Honour by the French President Mitterrand, who himself travelled to Calcutta to confer the award on Ray as he was too unwell to travel outside the country. Ray's health was precarious and had already started breaking down before he began filming *Ghare Baire* in 1984. However, as he told his biographers, it was the thought of making more films that kept him alive and hopeful.

As noted in the previous chapter, Ray had found himself on the wrong side of the Indira Gandhi administration, which prevented him from being recognised for what he truly was – the 'gold standard' in cinema that India had to offer to the world – and acknowledged through the Honorary Oscar before getting the Bharat Ratna in India. Ray, as a Bengali, knew that Tagore suffered the same fate – recognition outside India before he was accepted by his compatriots. In 1913 Tagore had won the Nobel Prize in Literature – the first Asian and the only Indian to have won in this category. He received his knighthood only later in 1915 after winning the Nobel Prize, although he repudiated the knighthood in 1919 in protest against the massacre at Jallianwala Bagh in Amritsar.

His health having broken down in 1984, Ray was now restricted to his bed, but thoughts of filming kept him going. When the doctors sensed an improvement in his health, they allowed him to shoot, but movement was restricted and so location shooting was limited and mostly relegated to the studio. The last three films are thus more verbose, relying more on the spoken word than on the moving image, always a hallmark of a Satyajit Ray film, but they are also more polemical.

The period of rest was perhaps a period of introspection for Ray, but one cannot say that he was at the height of his powers when he recovered enough to make films. Many critics have considered *Agantuk* his swan song and one of his best works, but that is debatable at the very least. The last three films seem more like a testament founded on a lifetime of accumulated wisdom than a response to the filmmaker's immediate reality, which is the way I characterised his films set in contemporary times. One may perhaps draw a comparison with Tagore's last testament on the state of the world around him – 'The Crisis in Civilization' since an analysis of the last trilogy bears it out.

Ray and Tagore

There are several bonds linking Tagore and Ray, not the least of which are the films based on Tagore's novella and short stories – *Charulata* and *Teen Kanya*. Tagore was both his grandfather's (Upendrakishore Ray Chaudhury) and father's (Sukumar Ray) friend and the two families, which were Brahmos, were extremely close. It was at Tagore's behest that Sukumar Ray's widow Suprabha Ray sent Satyajit Ray to the art school at Vishwabharati University in Santiniketan. It was this contact and the fact that he had acquired a familiarity with several of Tagore's works of fiction and ideas that led to the documentary on Tagore when Nehru commissioned it.[1] But there was also a lasting impression created by Tagore on the way Ray thought – although that was only discernible later – since several times during Ray's lifetime he iterated that Tagore was a larger-than-life influence on the way Bengalis regarded life and culture.[2]

In 1982 Ray wrote of Tagore:

> As a poet, dramatist, novelist, short story writer, essayist, painter, song composer, philosopher, and educationist Tagore is obviously more versatile than Shakespeare. As a Bengali I know that as a composer of songs, he has no equal, not even in the West – and I know Schubert and Hugo Wolf; as a poet, he shows incredible facility, range and development; some of his short stories are among the best ever written; his essays show an amazing clarity of thought and breadth of vision; in his novels he tackled some major themes and created some memorable characters; as painter starting at the age of nearly seventy he remains among the most original and interesting that India has produced.[3]

It is interesting that Ray noted Tagore's versatility, because it was Ray's versatility as filmmaker, writer, illustrator and composer that marked him out even among the filmmakers of the world, let alone India.

Ritwik Ghatak, too, echoed similar sentiments when he wrote:

> 'I cannot speak without Tagore. That man has culled all my feelings long before my birth. He has understood what I am, and he has put in all the words. I read him and I find that all has been said and I have nothing new to say. I think all artists in Bengal at least, find themselves in the same difficulty.'[4]

Here, significantly, Ghatak is describing Tagore in a completely different way, but we can still take his words to mean that Tagore had a towering, sage-like presence in Bengali culture, that he even anticipated what Bengalis thought. It would seem from Ray's last three films that, towards the end of his life, Ray had begun to see himself as taking Tagore's place and the evidence presented here is his last trilogy of films – *Ganashatru*, *Shakha Prosakha* and *Agantuk*. The latter two films, based on original screenplays, show Ray even trying to don Tagore's sage-like cultural persona through the chosen central character around whom the action in the film revolves.[5]

His testament, 'The Crisis in Civilization', was written in 1941 when Britain was at war, and it is an anti-British diatribe. But more important here is the sense that India had gained a lot through the British, who had opened up the world to India. Here is a well-known passage from this celebrated essay:

> Our direct contact with the larger world of men was linked up with the contemporary history of the English people whom we came to know in those earlier days. It was mainly through their mighty literature that we formed our ideas with regard to these newcomers to our Indian shores. In those days the type of learning that was served out to us was neither plentiful nor diverse, nor was the spirit of scientific enquiry very much in evidence. Thus, their scope being strictly limited, the educated of those days had recourse to English language and literature. Their days and nights were eloquent with the stately declamations of Burke, with Macaulay's long-rolling sentences; discussions centered upon Shakespeare's drama and Byron's poetry and above all upon the large-hearted liberalism of the nineteenth-century English politics.[6]

Let us now examine Ray's last three films for discourses, to see if a comparison with Tagore is legitimate.

Ganashatru (1989)

In 1988, Ray's doctors, who sensed an improvement in his health, decided to let him continue filmmaking with the sole stricture that he would do so in studio settings, and under strict medical supervision. This meant that there would be greater emphasis on dialogues and that the film would have to be set indoors. Given Ray's state of mind, Ibsen's *An Enemy of the People* may have seemed the ideal work to adapt. With the rising Hindu nationalism, India could perhaps do with a Dr Stockmann, an individual who stands up for what he thinks is right. It is interesting to note the many parallels between the two creators, Ray and Ibsen, despite their difference in time and space, since Ray is faithful to Ibsen's moral vision despite it seeming rather uncomplicated today.[7]

This particular play by Ibsen appeared in 1882, only a year after the publication of 'Ghosts', and Weigand argues[8] that the doctor's ideas about society, as well as the vehement and paradoxical form of their utterance, are Ibsen's own. Some of Doctor Stockmann's programmatic ideas are stoutly championed by Ibsen in his letters a decade before the play was written. Ibsen was fairly aching to tell the world, and his Norwegian countrymen more specifically, what he thought of their governing classes, their political party life, their press, the catch words of the multitude and the march of progress in general.

There is hence solemnity in the very theme of *Ganashatru*, and one notices that in all the last three films Ray was to have made, before his demise in 1992. The film deals with corruption, something with which Ray had dealt with several times, especially in the dark *Jana Aranya* (1975) and *Joi Baba Felunath* (1979). Only this time, one notices an emphasis on the defiant individual with whom Ray apparently identifies more than any character he had created before. One would also notice a directness of language and tone, hitherto unnoticed in any of his films, as well as a lack of adornment, and these factors combined with the fact that he placed it in 1989, which was a contemporaneous date, and which may have caused some unease since he was evidently critiquing the present.

And so much like Ibsen in his time, Ray too came to identify himself with the outspoken and honest protagonist of the story, but contemporised the play to suit his times, setting it in Chandipur, a fictional town in Bengal. But this time it is religion that causes both the political crises portrayed in the film. If here again, as in *Devi* (1962) – set in the dark days of nineteenth-century Bengal – Ray critiques religious superstition, *Ganashatru* differs from the earlier film in dealing with its own times, since Hindu nationalism was making headway in India with Ayodhya as the epicentre.[9]

Dr Ashok Gupta, the protagonist in Ray's film, is the chief medical officer of a hospital trust in the town built by Bhargava, a Marwari businessman based in Chandipur. A sudden rise in the number of patients suffering from hepatitis and typhoid, both water-borne diseases, rattles him and being both a doctor and a good citizen, he alerts the press of the town. The doctor makes a shrewd guess as to the cause of this epidemic, since most of his patients live in and around the temple area or visit the temple on a regular basis. In the beginning, his advice is welcomed and honoured, especially by the newspaper owner and the editor of *Janabarta*, and they even propose to felicitate him for his timely warning.

The offending water sample is from the most populous part of the town, in the vicinity of which is also the holy temple of the town and the economic mainstay of most of the populace because of the pilgrims who visit Chandipur. More specifically, the *charanamrita* or the sanctified water served to the devotees is the cause of the looming epidemic. However, vested interests are loath to have this declared openly as the economic implications are too many to forget. Therefore, both Nitish Gupta – Dr Ashok Gupta's brother and chairman of the municipal corporation whose duty it is to ensure a clean supply of water to the town – and Bhargava, the architect of the temple, refuse to heed the protagonist.

As in Ibsen's play, it becomes very clear on whose side Ray's sympathy lies and the audience too is steered towards that. However, the doctor from Ibsen's play – egoistical, jovial and fun loving – is replaced here by the quiet, mild-mannered Dr Gupta. The doctor humbly requests his townsmen to listen to his scientific views on health and hygiene, at the same time assuring them earnestly that he respects their religious beliefs. While the character of Dr Stockmann of *An Enemy of the People* openly declares his rivalry with his elder brother, the mayor of the small spa town in Norway, here in Ray's film the good doctor is reluctant to even discuss his younger brother's flaws with his wife – to direct the narrative away from the personal. Evidently Ray's protagonist is less a 'character' than Dr Stockman, and much more the embodied viewpoint of his creator.

One is able to see that the clash between science and religion is at the forefront of Ray's *Ganashatru*, as it is not in Ibsen's play. The serious tone maintained by Ray does not allow him to make use of any comic or distracting elements and it remains a solemn effort despite the risk of becoming too polemical. In Ibsen's play, it should be noted, the seriousness is at times undercut by comedy, which is integral to the spirit of that play, while Ray's film is single-minded in its purpose.

Very soon the doctor is declared an 'enemy of the people' by some graffiti on the outer wall of his house: 'Let it be known that Dr Ashok Gupta is an enemy of the people', with stones being hurled at his windows by a mob on the rampage. But Dr Gupta continues to think about his patients, about the infected water that is only turning deadlier by the day. 'I can't leave them behind and run away', he declares and Ramen, his daughter's friend,

Figure 8.1 The two brothers, one representing corruption and greed and the other a selfless attitude to save humanity.

and Biresh, an honest reporter at *Janabarta*, also join him. Biresh supports the doctor by telling him that he wishes to send his piece to newspapers in Calcutta. Ramen informs the doctor that there are young, educated people of Chandipur who are gathering to support the doctor in his fight against vested interests.

Simple as it is, the story which Ray chose to tell almost at the end of his career reasserted the need to think wisely and rationally, as had always been a way of life with the Rays. While Ibsen's Dr Stockmann declares 'The strongest man in the world is the man who stands alone', Ray changes it to include a group of like-minded people, even if it is miniscule. Ray once told Andrew Robinson 'Democracy is very much like that ... I think democracy is an admirable thing in practice but on occasions the situation in *An Enemy of the People* does occur in actual life. And that justifies Dr Stockmann's reaction to it.'[10] **(10)**

But if Dr Stockmann is a possibility in a Western democracy, why did Ray make his equivalent Dr Gupta so much more incredible in *Ganashatru*? Since pilgrims come to Chandipur from outside, the local authority would naturally be superseded at a higher level – say the state government – which would then take safety measures. The position of a small town in

Scandinavia or the US would be very different from India, where local authority does not carry the same weight and the local press – if there is any – is hardly influential. One could propose that ill health and surgery had made such a difference to Ray that he could not adapt the original text plausibly, making it pertinent to local conditions in India, and simply took a universal dilemma out of it for his statement.

Shakha Prasakha (1990)

The central figure in *Shakha Prasakha* is Anandamohan, an unflinching idealist, a philanthropic businessman who literally rose from rags to riches through mica mining. He lived and worked by the twin gospels of 'Work is worship' and 'Honesty is the best policy'. Before he retired, he did so much for the welfare of his employees and for the development of the locality, that the beneficiaries and townspeople gratefully named the town after him. He lives his retired life with his second son, Prashanta, a prodigy reduced to a mental condition by an accident in London. Of his other three sons, Probodh, the eldest, is the general manager of a big company, Prabir, the third, is a businessman, and Pratap, the fourth, holds a high position in a corporate house. They live in Calcutta and away from their parental home. The old father nurses the fond belief that his successful sons follow his ideals – although the issue of inheriting his business is not brought up.

Anandamohan's sudden critical illness brings together his scattered family into the house – in which also lives his senile nonagenarian father. As the narrative advances, we see that the four brothers occupy different positions in the moral spectrum. Probodh, himself a teetotaler, nevertheless treats his rich guests to expensive foreign liquor, and uses his apparently clean public image as a cover for corrupt practices. His younger brother Prabir is a known gambler and alcoholic but exposes Probodh at dinner. Probodh avoids rebutting the accusation but says 'The way father defined them [truth and honesty] there's no place for them', admitting his culpability before his startled wife.

As a psychiatric patient, the second oldest brother Prashanta is cut off from the world. Exempt from the pressure of social living, he is free from any taint. The motor accident in London has affected only his surface consciousness, but not his sensitivity to the deeper rhythms of life. In his own way, he is alive to the goings-on around him and dotes on music. Thus, when Probodh and Prabir engage in exposing each other's misdeeds, he bangs the table to express his anguish. His love for his father is as wholehearted and deep as his love for music. The irony is that this 'failed' son ultimately

Figure 8.2 The brothers at dinner with their families.

appears to his father as the only upholder of his spiritual legacy. In Ray's films Prashanta and Pratap, the youngest, are the two foils to Probodh and Prabir, one passive and the other active. Pratap gives up a lucrative corporate job that involves compromises to pursue theatre as an actor.

Ray's view of Indian womanhood is reflected in his portrayal of the principled wives of the ignoble Probodh and Prabir. The warm-hearted Uma is Probodh's opposite. Unlike her husband, she is caring about her senile grandfather-in-law and attends to him when she can. In contrast, Tapati, Prabir's wife, is a modern woman. She is as critical of Prabir's profligacy as she is appreciative of Pratap's career choice. Ray remarked in an interview that the duty-conscious Indian woman could triumph over all temptations. Uma and Tapati are meant to illustrate this, but where the position of the women was justified in the earlier films in terms of a well-defined social situation, the women here are simply 'moral beings'. The notion that women are somehow above temptation is also a dubious one, judging from how women politicians are known to have amassed wealth in India.

There are, arguably, some things amiss with *Shakha Proshakha* and the first is our reluctance to accept a wealthy businessman – in the mining industry – as a moral exemplar. Mining requires a number of governmental clearances, which means that businessmen engaged in it will come face to face with the worst side of the bureaucracy, exacerbated by mica mining being hazardous[11] and illegal mining of the mineral causing untold misery. I am not suggesting here that Anandamohan would necessarily be corrupt because of this, but that corruption within his own family could not drive him to despair since he would have experienced it at close quarters. Also, if a small town is named after him,[12] it would mean immense wealth created by his business and the issue of there being no inheritors of his wealth or claimants among his children is strange, especially because some of them are struggling with financial troubles. One is struck by the incongruity of the filmmaker who gave us a searing portrayal of 'business' in *Jana Aranya* also giving us *Shakha Proshakha*.[13] (13)

The fact that this is an original screenplay also merits comment. Ray's best films have adapted other people's writings although he made changes. Ray writing an original screenplay at the end of his career in his last two films suggests that he was conscious of an independent statement expected from him because of his stature and he felt that, being versatile like Tagore, he could 'go it alone' – when tempering other people's visions was where he excelled.

Lastly, the film, although set in contemporary times, has virtually nothing to say about a recognisable India except the abstraction of 'corruption' – when his earlier films had been sensitive to the actual ethos and 'corruption' had a definite meaning. The differences between *Mahanagar* and *Jana Aranya*, both of which comment on 'business', indicate that Ray had seen India transforming and it is this transformation that the present book has been charting. But suddenly, in *Shakha Proshakha*, Ray is offering a treatise that is not sensitive to contemporary currents – subordinated as they are to authorial discourse of a 'universal' nature not seen in Ray's films earlier.

Agantuk (1971)

In this film Anila Bose, who lives in Calcutta, receives a letter from someone claiming to be her long-lost uncle, Manomohan Mitra (Utpal Dutt). He writes that he is visiting India after thirty-five years abroad and, as Anila is his only surviving relative, wants to meet her before he sets off again. Anila looks forward to it, but her husband, Sudhindra, is suspicious that this uncle has come to claim his share of Anila's grandfather's property. The uncle arrives and stays for quite a while. He claims that he is an anthropologist who has been a globe-trotter, and immediately wins the friendship of their son, Satyaki. Gradually, it emerges that Manmohan Mitra is wise and selfless and Sudhindra's suspicions have been unjust. As in the other two films, Ray introduces, through Manmohan Mitra, a sage at odds with the 'civilised' world in which moral standards have fallen.

Ray constructs Manmohan Mitra in this way: a 'topper' all through, right from matriculation to graduation, he has every reason to look forward to fame and fortune. But a chance encounter with the picture of a bison, drawn by Alta Mira cavemen 30,000 years ago, releases in him a burning desire to explore the world. He lives the first five years of his wanderings with various Indian tribes and becomes, like them, an omnivore. Then he leaves for the West, and studies anthropology. Thus, theoretically equipped, he starts living with the Native Americans and his wisdom comes out of education that has been fortified by experience with 'primitive life'.

In this film, as in the last one, Ray makes the woman much more sympathetic and in tune with his message. The radical difference between Sudhindra and Anila is, at one level, the difference between masculine drives and feminine sensibility, at another between the reason-based modern civilisation and the instinct-based primitive civilisation which the woman is prepared to acknowledge. Ray's women are closer to their own instincts than the men, who are driven by considerations of personal advantage.

It is not a whim but a realisation of the limitations of reason and science that orientates Manmohan Mitra towards primitivism, but there are virtually no limits to what he knows or seeks to find out. Ray apparently made the film after reading two books by Claude Lévi-Strauss, but there is information from all kinds of sources, and particularly recognisable is a bit from Robert Flaherty's *Nanook of the North* (1922) – that Eskimos use transparent ice for the windows of their igloos and opaque ice for the walls.

As may be evident from this descriptionm Ray is trying to construct Manmohan Mitra as a cultural ideal. Here are some details that add up to the kind of ideal Manmohan Mitra represents:

1. Much before shedding their mutual distance, Manmohan and Anila engage in a conversation on the Hare-Krishna cult. This leads to a musical interlude and Manmohan Mitra later demonstrates his love of tribal culture through his appreciation of dancing with Santhal tribals in Tagore's Santiniketan. Anila's whole-hearted participation in it brings the two of them closer. A mutual acquaintance, Sheetalbabu, confirms their blood relationship, finally putting all doubts to rest.

2. Manmohan has travelled extensively, but far from being rootless, he remains – in his unshaken command of the mother tongue and in his food and dress preferences – a Bengali at heart. That he can identify and appreciate the artworks in his host's drawing room shows his cultivated taste, in which the local is not ignored. Normally mild and modest, he is provoked to assert that he has absorbed 'Shakespeare, Bankim, Freud, Rabindranath'.
3. The film works out the theme of civilisation in terms of three successive generations represented. Sheetalbabu and Manmohan represent the past generation and Indian receptivity at its best, Sudhindra and his circle (including the lawyer Pritwish) the present generation and cultural hybridity at its rootless worst, Satyaki and his peers the future generation in whom Ray expresses hope.
4. There is also in the film a critique of the nuclear family. The spirit of solidarity which informs the extended family also inspires the Indian custom of hospitality, even to those unknown.
5. As regards the dubious aspects of India's tradition, Manmohan Mitra hardly falters. In reply to the lawyer Prithwish's sceptical questioning, Manmohan declares that he hates casteism and any organised, divisive religion.
6. Modern science might have robbed him of faith in an all-loving, all-powerful personal God, but not in a cosmic controller, whose existence is outlined in the Tagore song sung by Anila. To lend weight to his contention, he says that he was once successfully treated by a very accomplished witch doctor. But he confesses that he cannot rid himself of his acquired culture to become a true tribal in spirit: '... I myself am not a tribal. It's something I lament about. That I'm not a tribal, that I can't draw a bison like the caveman of Alta Mira.'
7. He distrusts the civilised world for having created weapons capable of destroying the world.
8. Before he disappears, Manmohan leaves behind a cheque, gifting away the whole of his inherited fortune to his niece not only to honour the bond of blood, but also as recognition of a kindred spirit. Once his stay in India is over, Manmohan Mitra heads off to Australia for more cerebral pursuits.

Ray paints Manmohan Mitra as a sage less mindful of material wants (like Anandamohan in *Shakha Proshakha*) than to spiritual questions. Still, 'globe-trotting' is an expensive business and one wonders where his resources come from. Ray demonstrated acute awareness of economic considerations in everyday life and there are any number of his characters

Figure 8.3 The figure of the sage framed in a particular way that looms large, perhaps to showcase his moral stature.

(e.g. *Pather Panchali, Kanchenjungha Mahanagar, Jalsaghar, Pratidwandi, Janaranya*) to whom becoming financially stable is a principal preoccupation. The protagonists of *Shakha Proshakha* and *Agantuk* are too 'otherworldly' even though their actions would not have been possible without money being an issue in their lives. Manmohan gives a perfunctory account of having worked his way up, but it would be a difficult task to gain so much knowledge, travel so extensively, without the wherewithal to acquire them.

Agantuk came ten years after the story on which it is based[14] appeared in the Bengali language, and it would be helpful to compare the two. In the story the husband and wife are notified of the uncle's arrival, the husband harbouring suspicions as in the film, but the uncle leaves after five days of an intended ten-day stay, saying nothing much about himself but leaving three foreign coins for the child Satyaki. He was initially a sadhu but moved on to other things, and he has been around the world. His achievements are related to them by a common relative, Sheetalbabu, who describes the man's life as 'stranger than fiction'. The uncle is also a writer and has written a book under the name Pulin Ray, when they have only known him as 'Choto Mama,' her mother's younger brother. The story is slight;

the actual achievements of the uncle are filtered through Sheetalbabu – who could be unreliable since we are not told much about him. Here is Sheetalbabu's description:

> I do believe our country has never seen a globe-trotter like Pulin Ray. And he did it all with his own money. He worked as a ship-mate, a coolie, a labourer in the timber trade, sold newspapers, ran a small shop, drove lorries – no work was too small for him. His experiences are stranger than fiction. He's been attacked by a tiger, bitten by a snake, escaped from a violent nomadic tribe in the Sahara, swum to the shore of Madagascar after a shipwreck. He left India in 1939 and made his way through Afghanistan. He says if you can come out of the confines of your house, then the whole world becomes your home. There is no difference then, between whites and blacks and great and small or the civilized and the barbaric.[15]

There is little in this story to make the uncle a sage with the kind of 'wisdom' he displays in the film, and Chotu Mama is a more credible character than Manmohan Mitra, as are the husband and wife in whose house he stays – who behave as people would do when required to accommodate a stranger. The husband is more suspicious but there is some justification in it, considering that they are required to put up an unknown person in their house. I would like to add that the wisdom Manmohan Mitra articulates is not different from the kind voiced by public figures on formal occasions, usually well-worn truisms.

Conclusion: Surfeit of Truisms

Ray had once said:

> 'Looking around me I feel that the old values of personal integrity, loyalty, liberalism, rationalism, and fair play are all completely gone. People accept corruption as a way of life, as a method of getting along, as a necessary evil. In acquiring material comforts, you grow numb with placid acceptance. Maybe you resist it in the beginning. But the internal and external pressures crowd to a point where you learn to overlook the moral decline they spell.[16]'

But more interesting is the theme of the lone crusader that pervades all the three films coming at the end of his career – whether it be the character of Dr Ashok Gupta of *Gana Shatru*, or Prashanto and his father Anandamohan Majumder in *Shakha Prasakha*, or Manmohan Mitra of *Agantuk*. It is significant that music becomes important in his last two films with Prashanto listening to Bach – music which his philistine younger brother denigrates as 'rubbish' – and music becoming a point of contact between Manmohan Mitra and his niece. In 1980, as Robinson notes,[17]

Ray wrote to Alex Aronson, a friend from his days in Shantiniketan, that ever since his music-loving professor friend David McCutchion had died seven years before, he had sorely needed someone he could talk to about the things that interested and involved him. To another long-time friend, Norman Clare,[18] he wrote about the deaths of his two best friends, David McCutchion and Bansi Chandragupta, and how there was no one of his age who he could call a friend, and music plays a part here as well: 'Much of the time I'm sitting alone in my favourite armchair in a large room overflowing with books and containing an upright piano and a modern Neupert spinet.' One can almost say that the character of Prashanto in *Shakha Prasakha* – who almost lives Bach, Beethoven and the Gregorian chants – was modelled on this aspect of Ray's life, namely in his devotion to music.

To make an intervention at this point, firstly I see Ray progressively losing interest in India's trajectory in his last films. In *Ganashatru* he is still dealing with issues first seen in *Devi*, while in *Shakha Proshakha* contemporary India is seen only in terms of the 'corruption' endemic to it. Corruption is not an issue new to Ray's films, but never did it take up the entire space of the film as here. *Agantuk*, while duly acknowledging aspects of Indian culture like tribal music and dance and Bengali literature, is essentially internationalist, with Bengal rather than India representing the indigenous component. This loss of interest in the *Indian nation* goes along with music rising to the fore and I posit a connection. Music is almost pure form and it is difficult to locate ethical/social/political concerns in it – especially in orchestral music. Art tending towards music is arguably tantamount to it losing its ethical/social/political thrust, which is something that could be said about Ray as well. Ray is more vocal about ethics but he is also being less observant and more vaguely rhetorical.

I had wondered earlier if there was any similarity between Tagore and Ray in their last testaments, but while Tagore saw the West as floundering (in 1941) and was hopeful that the East (presumably India) would show the way, Ray (in 1991) has apparently seen India as having floundered so badly that only the most primitive and morally untainted in India (the Santhal tribals) possessed anything that Manmohan Mitra values. His defense of primitivism actually leads to the culminating moment in which Anila dances with Santhals in the film. Also significant is that the setting is Santiniketan, where Tagore located his Viswabharati University. With the nation retreating in significance, Ray had apparently begun to see himself as the lone crusader that he portrays, someone who, like Tagore, was more preoccupied with the world than with the trajectory of his own country. If we were to judge by what was said in the last chapter, we may also surmise that Ray – perhaps unlike Tagore – arrived at the position because the world gave him more respect than his own country's leaders gave him.

This brings us to the use of women as the moral voices in the bleak universes portrayed in the last two films. In the first place both Anandamohan and Manmohan Mitra are men, and Ray apparently identifies with them since he makes them articulate his moral viewpoint; still, they are more embodied voices than 'men'. There was recognisably Ray's sense of mischief and irony in Feluda in *Joi Baba Felunath*, but little of Ray as a person in these films. The masculine attitude is therefore carried forward by Anila's husband in *Agantuk* and by the unworthy sons Probir and Probodh. It is significant that both Protap and Prashanto, the morally upright sons, are unmarried, while Probir and Probodh have wives who disapprove of their ways. I had earlier seen male weakness in Ray's films as owing to their being unable to bear the burden placed upon them as 'national subjects', but with the nation retreating from the narratives of these two films, one wonders what 'male weakness' might mean. The only meaning I can attach to it in the context of Ray's internationalism is that he now sees patriarchy not as 'Indian' but as a universal phenomenon, and squarely blamed for the ills of civilisation. The question of how primitive cultures measure up in this department – since Manmohan Mitra is so much in favour of primitivism – is perhaps something Ray did not consider. Based on what has been said about the three films examined in this chapter, one could say that they represent the replacement of observation by rhetoric, which can be regarded as a perceptible decline for Ray as a filmmaker sensitive to the world. He was at his best when charting the nation's trajectory, not as a universal sage with abstract wisdom to offer humankind.

Notes

1. When commissioned by Nehru to make a documentary film on Tagore, Ray tried incorporating some of the most salient points about Tagore in his fifty-one-minute work. Most importantly, Ray traced the life of the poet in his last days, during which Tagore tried to leave a message to the world at large. By the time the poet died in 1941 the Second World War had already begun and the world was witness to an enormous amount of atrocities and violence. Tagore's plea to the Western nations was to put an end to the warfare – that not only led to the destruction of man but also to all that stood for Western civilisation.
2. Robinson records statements from two larger-than-life cultural figures in Bengali cinema who expressed how indebted they are to Tagore. Andrew

Robinson, *The Inner Eye: The Biography of a Master Film-Maker* (New Delhi: Oxford University Press, 2004), 47.
3. Ibid., 47.
4. Ibid., 47.
5. On 14 April 1941, the Bengali New Year, Tagore delivered his eightieth birthday message, 'Sabhayatar Sankat', translated henceforth as 'Crisis in Civilization', which Ray used in his documentary to highlight Tagore's internationalism and his reluctance to stick to Indian problems and nationalism in particular.
6. Rabindranath Tagore, 'Crisis in Civilization: A Message on Completing his Eighty Years', *Indian Culture*, <https://indianculture.gov.in/reports-proceedings/crisis-civilization-message-completing-his-eighty-years> (last accessed 25 December 2021).
7. It is an interesting fact that Ibsen's moral viewpoint is so simple today that it has been used as a plot device in a Hollywood blockbuster. Steven Spielberg's *Jaws* (1975) is also about a small town dependent on tourism that is threatened by something that could dry up the money trickling in – a great white shark in the waters killing swimmers and holidaymakers. As in Ibsen's play and Ray's film, the protagonist is the lone person trying to take precautions – by shutting down the beaches – while the mayor tries to dismiss the threat for economic reasons. William Baer, *Classic American Films: Conversations with the Screenwriters* (Westport, CT: Praeger 2007), 208.
8. Hermann Weigand, *The Modern Ibsen: A Reconsideration* (Boston: E. P. Dutton, 1960), 101.
9. Rajiv Gandhi played the 'Muslim card' in the Shah Bano case, which was a controversial maintenance lawsuit in India, in which the Supreme Court delivered a judgement favouring maintenance given to an aggrieved divorced Muslim woman. Then the Congress government under Rajiv Gandhi enacted a law in 1986 that denied right to basic maintenance available to Muslim women under secular law. As a counterbalance to appease Hindus, he did not take concerted action when the District and Sessions Judge of Faizabad ordered the locks of the Babri mosque in Ayodhya, which had remained padlocked for decades, to be opened for Hindu worshippers on 1 February 1986. The unlocking of the gates was 'manipulated through a judicial order' with the aid of the Uttar Pradesh government, but the Congress party acquiesced in it. Zoya Hasan, *Congress after Indira: Policy, Power, Political Change (1984–2009)* (New Delhi: Oxford University Press, 2012). Excerpt in Scroll.in (21 October 2019), <https://scroll.in/article/941140/ayodhya-how-rajiv-gandhis-plan-to-use-the-ram-temple-for-the-congress-party-came-undone> (last accessed 25 December 2021).
10. Robinson (2004), 340.
11. 'All that Glitters: Safety Concerns in India's Mica Industry', *IEMA: Transforming the World to Sustainability*, <https://www.iema.net/articles/all-that-glitters-safety-concerns-in-indias-mica-industry> (last accessed 25 December 2021).

12. This bears comparison with the representation in the crime novel *Red Harvest* by Dashiell Hammett, which offers a dark portrayal of a small town dominated by a single financial interest – an industry. The observation here (and it is a truism) is that if a town is named after a living businessperson, the typical case is that it is because he or she dominates it financially.
13. It has been noted about *Shakha Proshakha* that the 'aging patriarch's education in the fact of corruption leaves us incredulous and betrays a loss of contact with the real dimensions of societal change'. M. Madhava Prasad, 'Satyajit Ray: A Revaluation', *Economic and Political Weekly*, 43/3 (19–25 January 2008), 31.
14. Satyajit Ray, 'Stranger' (trans. Gopa Majumdar), in *The Collected Stories of Satyajit Ray* (New Delhi: Penguin, 2015), 303–14.
15. Ibid., 313.
16. Robinson (2004), 340.
17. Ibid., 341.
18. Ibid., 341.

Conclusion
Moving Away from the Nation

The two aspects of Satyajit Ray's films covered in this book pertain to his position as a filmmaker vis-à-vis the nation and his portrayal of male characters as national subjects. Masculinity is a key notion with regard to which the British, and those they colonised, had entirely different civilisational perspectives, and with the stabilising of British control over India there was a grading of masculinities in the colonial space. By the late nineteenth century, the politics of colonial masculinity was organised along a descending scale: senior British officials associated with the administration and military establishment, and elite non officials, those not directly related to the colonial administration, occupied positions at the top of the scale.[1] Other groups and classes that made up colonial society supposedly shared some, though not all, of the attributes associated with the figure of the 'manly Englishman'. In this colonial ordering of masculinity, the politically self-conscious Indian intellectuals occupied a different place; they represented an 'unnatural' or perverted form of masculinity.[2] Hence this group of Indians, the most typical representatives of which at the time were the middle-class Bengali Hindus, became the quintessential referents designated as 'effeminate babus'.[3] A thread in this book has been how colonial masculinity, in the context of the changes in the imperial social formation in the late nineteenth century, produced and furthered such categories.

The portrayal of the English in *Shatranj Ke Khiladi*, who are pitched against the Indians, is a particularly significant one in this context through the characters of General Outram and Nawab Wajid Ali Shah. While Premchand, from whose short story Ray adapted his film, holds the Nawab culpable on this account, Ray, aware of the complexities of colonisation, and himself being the product of a postcolonial society, takes a different stance. Wajid Ali Shah's is an androgynous presence, but only due to the civilisational contrasts between British and Indian societies noted by Ashis Nandy. To reiterate whatever has been said already, bisexuality in India has been taken to be an indicator of saintliness and spiritual accomplishment, which is also associated with singing and dancing.[4] The person close to godliness is expected to show a little less concern for the worldly division between the sexes and more ability to transcend the barriers imposed by his own sexual selfhood. He subscribes to values that are unfettered by society's prevalent sexual identities.[5] Wajid Ali Shah's public conduct, in not exuding masculine power, is simply going along with this. It may also be significant that Wajid Ali Shah was a Shia Muslim of Persian ancestry, known for cultural attainments, and not a Sunni of the martial stock that invaded India.

While the film carries information about Wajid Ali Shah's daily activities, the emphasis is on the above aspects just noted, which do not impress the British since their idea of kingship revolves around exercising earthly power – while the royalty in India spent its time in 'otherworldly' pursuits. This proposition would demand more substantiation than is possible here, but the more martial among the kings in medieval India tended to be either Sunni Muslim (like Tipu Sultan and the Mughals up to Aurangzeb) or saw themselves as Kshatriyas (like Shivaji), i.e. the warrior caste among Hindus.[6] Nandy notes that many nineteenth-century movements tried to make Kshatriyahood the 'true' interface between the rulers and the ruled and an indicator of authentic Indianness,[7] because of the natural gap between the colonial mindset and the qualities valorised in India. These factors are not problematised by Ray, but noting them helps us understand Ray's ambivalence. Rather than take Premchand's uncomplicated political viewpoint, he tries to see a clash of civilisational perspectives. Both the General and the Nawab have their own cultural perspectives but, as may be anticipated, it was earthly power that eventually triumphed historically.

But there is another aspect here – with a bearing on 'masculinity' – which is the notion of 'dharma', interpretable as worldly duty here, which Wajid Ali Shah should have also fulfilled as king but does not. Ray (wittingly or unwittingly) may have been drawn to the notion that informs much of Indian thought, because so many of his protagonists fail at it. Perhaps the most incontrovertibly 'masculine' of Ray's protagonists – in the sense of attending to his dharmic responsibilities as householder – is the adult Apu, who realises late in *Apur Sansar* that being father to his child is key to self-fulfilment rather than having his writing published, because of memories of his own father's irresponsibility. Apu can be contrasted with the weak husbands and fathers in Ray's oeuvre, like Charu's husband Bhupati in *Charulata* and Nikhil in *Ghare Baire*, although these men are good citizens, and even nationalists and patriots. Since parenthood is what confers 'masculinity' upon Apu, we may glance briefly at the fathers in Ray's oeuvre, who are not so many in number.

If 'masculinity' is the exercise of authority alongside the shouldering of responsibility, we could cite the patriarchs in *Jalsaghar*, *Kanchenjunga* and *Devi*. The weakest of the three is the one in *Jalsaghar* who has also lost his son in an accident, and is consequently immersed in himself. Two of these three patriarchs exercise authority which has been handed down to them by a system instituted by the British (the Zamindari system), which suggests colonial origins in this masculinity as portrayed by Ray. We should, however, note that this 'masculinity' is not eulogised since it leads those who possess it to self-righteous and/or morally incorrect positions, often inflicting hardships. The patriarch in *Kanchenjungha* is not a landowner but an elite non-official, also regarded as masculine by the British.

An interesting contrast in this context is *Abhijan* since its protagonist is unmarried. In *Abhijan*, although the protagonist Narsingh's self-image is that of a martial Rajput, a kshatriya respected for valour, his masculinity is significantly associated with his imported car, a sturdy old Chrysler. Throughout the narrative he is made aware of his difference from other characters by the fact that he owns and drives it. The society he inhabits is an amalgam of various denominations – Marwaris, Sikhs, Christians, among whom he emerges as the most 'masculine'. But on scrutiny he stands apart entirely by virtue of his car, which gives him authority – since it is instrumental in him being acknowledged and looked up to. Again, much like the protagonists Indranath Chaudhury (*Kanchenjungha*) and the music-loving zamindar of *Jalsaghar*, Narsingh's personal sense of masculinity is, in effect, conferred upon him by a foreign agency from the colonial period.

As counterpoint to this 'colonially-constructed' masculinity is the Indian male as a product of nationalism or nationhood, those who might be termed an 'effeminate babu'. It is significant that in the films from the category there are usually stronger women in attendance – whose primary function is conspicuously to show up the inadequacies in the men. Some of these men are dharmic failures and the women try to assume their responsibilities the way Sarbajaya took on Harihar's role in *Pather Panchali*; but even when the men are ostensibly successful, there is an intelligent woman showing them up for what they are. The woman taking on the responsibilities of the failed men can once again also be associated with the notion of dharma, but what about the relationships in Chapter 5 where the men are successful but 'complacent'? The men try to be authoritative – or are able to show authority in their other relationships – but Ray deliberately places the woman in a vantage position to undermine it. The women in these films (all played by the adult Sharmila Tagore) are less flesh and blood than most of Ray's female characters and do not open up their own vulnerabilities to the same scrutiny. Even in *Aranyer Din Ratri*, where Aparna has 'suffered' in the past, her suffering becomes ammunition against the male protagonist who has 'lived a sheltered life'. An interpretation of Ray's use of women in all these films is that they are deliberately placed there in order to play down or subvert the 'masculinity' that the men might have otherwise exhibited. The 'masculinity' of the other men noted earlier was associated with colonialism or its legacy, and that 'masculinity' – whether that of General Outram or Indranath Chowdhury (*Kanchenjungha*) – generally had authoritarian implications. To Ray, colonial or postcolonial 'masculinity' reeks of authoritarianism, which is why the men in post-Independence India need to be 'shown their place' by women, in order not to get ahead of themselves.

Ray is acutely aware that India's is a patriarchal society but, overall, the thrust of his films is not on patriarchy but on the 'national subject' – who is male. The ill-treatment of women in society, for instance, is not a key occurrence in his films and the women, by and large, are treated courteously by the men in their lives. One could even propose about *Nayak* that in such a real-life situation, a small-time woman journalist like Aditi would be so upstaged and at such a personal disadvantage with a celebrity film star that being candid and critical would be impossible; but she does just that, and is tolerated. As long as Ray was confident of his position as a national filmmaker, his placement of the woman as a corrective continues. If he identifies with the men as representative Indians – which is not unlikely – the women are there to bring down their self-importance in this role. This concern with the kind of subjects produced by the independent nation can be attributed to Ray's unquestioned position as 'national filmmaker', but I have tried to produce evidence that Ray lost this favoured position around 1980. His films thereafter undergo an enormous transformation, suggesting a weakened attachment to the independent nation, as it were.

Ray's films beginning with *Joi Baba Felunath* (1979) and right up to *Ghare Baire* (1984) – when he took ill on the sets – are different from the earlier films. In the individual chapters I dealt with *Charulata* alongside *Ghare Baire*, but that was more in terms of the political periods they dealt with and *Charulata* fits the perspective outlined in the last paragraph much more clearly. *Ghare Baire* is problematic in terms of characterisation and Sandeep is virtually painted black as a 'communalist'. India after 1977 was an uncertain space politically because of the wavering Janata Party experiment, which lasted only until 1979. I have argued that in the few years before 1984, Ray felt himself marginalised as a public figure by the government in power because of what he had said about the Congress Party and the veiled criticism of its tyranny present in *Hirak Rajar Deshe*. Both *Ghare Baire* and *Sadgati* can hence be seen as efforts to mollify the ruling party by echoing its ideology. *Ghare Baire* is anti-communalist and *Sadgati* is anti-caste, which were both central to Mrs Gandhi's earlier rhetoric.

Ray made his last three films under the shadow of ill health and with a number of restrictions working on him, which affected both the style and the content of these films. Also, two of these three films are original screenplays in which he perhaps felt pressured to deliver a 'universal' message like Tagore, whom he admired. However, they also show up the fact that Ray had lost touch with the India contemporaneous to him at the time and the attention to context is missing. Beyond the abstract notion of 'corruption' they have nothing much to offer about an India recognisable to his audience. In these films the protagonists seem less the products of India's social life after Independence, and more ideals unattached to national issues. Indeed, Manmohan Mitra, the protagonist of *Agantuk*, is arguably Ray as the cultural ideal that he saw himself as at the end of his life – fully in line with Tagore. *Agantuk* is essentially internationalist in its concerns, as Tagore's views were, and it is aspects of Bengali culture that are invoked rather than India as a whole. Local/regional culture in India after Independence has demanded less loyalty, and Ray, by turning from India to Bengal, should be seen in this context as surrendering the status of 'national' filmmaker.

By the end of his career Satyajit Ray arguably began to see himself as a lone crusader, more preoccupied with his own philosophical vision than with the India he once had faith in. As a result, one notices the absence of the keen observations of its socio-political and economic life, once a hallmark of his films, being replaced by well-meaning but vague rhetoric. Ray is widely celebrated as 'universal' and a 'humanist', but he became most broadly 'humanist' only when he gave up his attachment to the independent nation, which is what had preoccupied him in his best films.

Notes

1. Mrinalini Sinha, *Colonial Masculinity: The 'Manly Englishman' and the 'Effeminate Bengali' in the Late Nineteenth Century* (Manchester: Manchester University Press, 1995), 3.
2. Ibid, 2.

3. An acknowledgement of this can be found in Rudyard Kipling's story 'The Man Who Would be King', which also finds a due place in John Huston's film adaptation of 1975.
4. Sri Ramakrishna, one of India's most revered mystics, was known to lose himself in song and dance.
5. Asis Nandy, 'Woman versus Womanliness in India', in Ashis Nandy, *At the Edge of Psychology* (New Delhi: Oxford University Press, 1980), 38.
6. The position of a king's jati (local caste group) in the four varnas (abstract caste identity in terms of priest, warrior, merchant and farmer) is not easy to determine exactly and many kings, through the connivance of brahmins, got themselves kshatriya or warrior status; Shivaji was one of them.
7. Ashis Nandy, *The Intimate Enemy: Loss and Recovery of Self under Colonialism* (New Delhi: Oxford University Press, 1983), 7.

Bibliography

Anderson, Benedict (1983), *Imagined Communities: Reflections on the Origin and Spread of Nationalism* (London: Verso).
Armes, Roy (1987), *Third World Filmmaking and the West* (Berkeley: University of California Press).
Baer, William (2008), *Classic American Films: Conversations with the Screenwriters* (Westport: Praeger).
Bandopadhyay, Bibhutibhushan (1968), *The Song of the Road* tr. T. W. Clark (London: Allen and Unwin).
Banerjee, Sikata (2005), *Make Me a Man! Masculinity, Hinduism, and Nationalism in India* (Albany: SUNY Press).
Bayly, C. A. (2012), *Recovering Liberties: Indian Thought in the Age of Liberalism and Empire* (Cambridge and New York: University of Cambridge Press).
Bertocci, Peter L. (1984), 'Bengali Cultural Themes in Satyajit Ray's "The World of Apu"', *Journal of South Asian Literature* 19/1, Miscellany.
Beynon, John (2002), *Masculinities and Culture* (Philadelphia: Open University Press).
Bhabha, Homi K. (1985), 'Signs Taken for Wonders: Questions of Ambivalence and Authority under a Tree outside Delhi, May 1817', '"Race," Writing, and Difference', 144–65.
Blackburn, Robin (ed.) (1975), *Explosion in a Subcontinent* (London: Penguin).
Bordwell, David (1999), 'The Art Cinema as a Mode of Film Practice', in Leo Braudy and Marshall Cohen (eds), *Film Theory and Criticism: Introductory Readings*, 5th ed. (New York: Oxford University Press), 716–24.
Brooks, Peter (1985), *The Melodramatic Imagination: Balzac, Henry James, Melodrama and the Mode of Excess* (New York: Columbia University Press).
Cardullo, Bert (2007), *Satyajit Ray: Interviews* (Jackson: University Press of Mississippi).
Carroll, Noel (1996), 'Prospects for Film Theory: A Personal Assessment', in David Bordwell and Noel Carroll (eds), *Post Theory: Reconstructing Film Studies* (Madison: The University of Wisconsin Press).
Chakraborty, Dipesh (2007), 'Introduction', in Dipesh Chakraborty, Rochona Majumdar and Andrew Sartori (eds), *From the Colonial to the Postcolonial: India and Pakistan in Transition* (New Delhi: Oxford University Press).
Chopra-Gant, Mike (2006), *Hollywood Genres and Post-War America: Masculinity, Family and Nation in Popular Movies and Film Noir* (New York: I. B. Tauris).

Cohen, Bernard S. and Nicholas Dirks (1988), 'Beyond the Fringe: The Nation State, Colonialism, and the Technologies of Power', *Journal of Historical Sociology* 1/2, 224–9.

Cooper, Darius (1993), 'The White Man's Burdens and the Whims of the Chess-besotted Aristocrats: Colonialism in Satyajit Ray's *The Chess Players*', *Journal of South Asian Literature* 28/1, 205–25.

Cowie, Elizabeth (1997), *Representing the Woman: Psychoanalysis and Cinema* (London: Macmillan, and Minneapolis: University of Minnesota Press).

Dasgupta, Chidananda (2001), *The Cinema of Satyajit Ray* (New Delhi: National Book Trust).

Dey, Anindita (2021), *Sherlock Holmes, Byomkesh Bakshi, and Feluda: Negotiating the Center and the Periphery* (London: Lexington Books).

Dyer, Richard (2001), 'Rock – The Last Guy You'd Have Figured', in *The Culture of Queers* (London: Routledge), 159–74.

Ferguson, Niall (2003), *Empire: How Britain made the Modern World* (New York: Basic Books).

Fuller, C. J. and Haripriya Narasimhan (2008), 'From Landlords to Software Engineers: Migration and Urbanization among Tamil Brahmins', *Comparative Studies in Society and History* 50/1, 170–96.

Ganguly, Keya (2010), *Cinema, Emergence and the Films of Satyajit Ray* (Berkeley: University of California Press).

Ganguly, Suranian (1995), 'In Search of India: Rewriting Self and Nation in Satyajit Ray's Days and Nights in the Forest', *Journal of South Asian Literature* Vol. 30, No. 1/2, Miscellany (Winter, Spring, Summer, Fall 1995).

Ganguly, Suranjan (2000), *Satyajit Ray: In Search of the Modern* (New Delhi: Penguin).

Ghosh, Shohini (2000), '*Hum Aapke Hain Koun* ...! Pluralizing Pleasures of Viewership', *Social Scientist* 28/3/4, 83–90.

Gjurgian, Ljiljana Ina (2011), 'The (Im)possibilty of Women's Bildungsroman', *SRAZ-LVI*, 107–21.

Guha-Thakurta, Tapati (2009), *Art and Visual Culture in India 1857–2007* (Mumbai: Marg Publications).

Kael, Pauline (1966), *I Lost it at the Movies* (New York: Bantam).

Kael, Pauline (1976), *Reeling* (Boston: Little, Brown and Company).

Kakar, Sudhir (1989), *Intimate Relations: Exploring Indian Sexuality* (New Delhi: Penguin).

Kemper, Steven (1991), *The Presence of the Past: Chronicles, Politics, and Culture in Sinhala Life* (Ithaca: Cornell University Press).

Khilnani, Sunil (1997), *The Idea of India* (New Delhi: Penguin).

Kapur, Geeta (2003), 'Sovereign Subject: Ray's Apu', in *When was Modernism: Essays on Contemporary Cultural Practice in India* (New Delhi: Manohar).

Livingston, Paisley (1996), 'Characterization and Fictional Truth', in David

Bordwell and Noel Carroll (eds), *Post Theory: Reconstructing Film Studies* (Madison: The University of Wisconsin Press), 149–74.

Lutze, Lothar (1985), 'From Bharata to Bombay: Change and Continuity in Hindi Film Aesthetics', in Beatrix Pfleiderer and Lothar Lutze (eds), *The Hindi Film: Agent and Reagent for Cultural Change* (New Delhi: Manohar).

McCull, Bruce (1935), 'The Origins of Indian Nationalism According to Native Writers', *The Journal of Modern History* 7/3, 295–314.

McNeill, William (1990), *The Rise of the West: A History of the Human Community* (Chicago: University of Chicago Press).

Majumdar, Neepa (2005), 'Pather Panchali: From Realism to Melodrama,' in R. L. Rutsky and Jeffrey Geiger (eds), *Film Analysis: A Norton Reader* (New York: Norton), 510–27.

Martin, Jay and Sumathy Ramaswamy (2014) (eds), *Empires of Vision: Objects/Histories* (Durham, NC: Duke University Press).

Misra, Amaresh (1992), 'Satyajit Ray's Films: Precarious Social-Individual Balance', *Economic and Political Weekly* 27/20/21, 1052–4.

Mohanty, Satya P. (2011), *Colonialism, Modernity and Literature: A View from India* (New York and London: Palgrave Macmillan).

Mukherjee, Meenakshi (2000), 'Nation, Novel, Language', in *The Perishable Empire: Essays on Indian writing in English* (New Delhi: Oxford University Press).

Nandy, Ashish (1980), *At the Edge of Psychology: Essays in Politics and Culture* (New Delhi: Oxford University Press).

Nandy, Ashish (1985), *The Intimate Enemy: Loss and Recovery of Self Under Colonialism* (New Delhi: Oxford University Press).

Nandy, Ashish (1994), *The Illegitimacy of Nationalism* (New Delhi: Oxford University Press).

Neher, Erick (2015), 'Satyajit Ray's Apu Trilogy Restored', *The Hudson Review* 68/2 (Summer 2015).

Nigam, Aditya (2020), *Decolonizing Theory: Thinking Across Traditions* (New Delhi: Bloomsbury).

Panikkar, K. M. (1920), *Indian Nationalism, its Origin, History, and Ideals* (London: Faith Press).

Pfleiderer, Beatrix (1985), 'An Empirical Study of Urban and Semi-Urban Audience Reactions to Indian Films', in Beatrix Pfleiderer and Lothar Lutze (eds), *The Hindi Film: Agent and Reagent of Cultural Change* (New Delhi: Manohar).

Pinney, Christopher (1997), *Camera Indica: The Social Life of Indian Photographs* (Chicago: University of Chicago Press).

Prasad, M. Madhava (1999), *Ideology of the Hindi Film: A Historical Construction* (New Delhi: Oxford University Press).

Prasad, M. Madhava (2008), 'Satyajit Ray: A Revaluation', *Economic and Political Weekly* 43/3, 38–42.

Pritchett, Frances W. (1986), 'The Chess Players: From Premchand to Satyajit

Ray', *Journal of South Asian Literature* 21/2, Essays on Premchand, 65–78.

Raghavendra, M. K. (1990), 'Beyond Anger and Empathy: The Failings of Social Realism in Indian Cinema', *Cinema in India* 4/2, 6–12.

Raghavendra, M. K. (2008), *Seduced by the Familiar: Narration and Meaning in Popular Indian Cinema* (New Delhi: Oxford Universty Press).

Raghavendra, M. K. (2009), *50 Indian Film Classics* (New Delhi: HarperCollins).

Raghavendra, M. K. (2016), *The Politics of Hindi Cinema in the New Millennium: Bollywood and the Anglophone Indian Nation* (New Delhi: Oxford University Press).

Rajadhyaksha, Ashish (1987), 'The Phalke Era: Conflict of Traditional Form and Modern Technology', *Journal of Arts and Ideas*, 14/15, 47–78.

Rajadhyaksha, Ashish and Paul Willemen (1995), *Encyclopaedia of Indian Cinema* (New Delhi: Oxford University Press).

Ray, Satyajit (1976), *Our Films Their Films* (New Delhi: Orient Blackswan).

Ray, Satayajit (1994), *My Years with Apu* (New Delhi: Penguin).

Ray, Satayajit (2005), *Speaking of Films* tr. Gopa Majumdar (New Delhi: Penguin).

Ray, Satayajit (2015), 'Stranger' tr. Gopa Majumdar, in *The Collected Stories of Satyajit Ray* (New Delhi: Penguin), 303–14.

Robinson, Andrew (2004), *The Inner Eye: The Biography of a Master Filmmaker* (New Delhi: Oxford University Press).

Roy, Anuradha (2003), *Nationalism as Poetic Discourse in Nineteenth-Century Bengal* (Calcutta: Papyrus).

Rudolph, Lloyd and Susanne Rudolph (1960), 'The Political Role of India's Caste ssociation,' *Pacific Affairs* XXXIII/I, 5–22.

Said, Edward (1979), *Orientalism: Western Conceptions of the Orient* (New York: Vintage).

Said, Edward (1996), *Representations of the Intellectual* (New York: Vintage Books).

Sarkar, Bhaskar (2008), *Mourning the Nation* (New Delhi: Orient Blackswan).

Sen, Amartya (2005), *The Argumentative Indian: Writings on Indian History, Culture and Identity* (New York: Farrar, Straus and Giroux).

Sengoopta, Chandak (2016), *The Rays before Satyajit* (New Delhi: Oxford University Press).

Seton, Marie (2003), *Portrait of a Director: Satyajit Ray* (New Delhi: Penguin).

Shohat, Ellie and Robert Stam (1994), *Unthinking Eurocentrism, Multiculturalism and the Media* (London: Routledge).

Singh, Nikki Guninder Kaur (1993), 'From Flesh to Stone: The Divine Metamorphosis in Satyajit Ray's Devi', *Journal of South Asian Literature* 28/1/2, Miscellany, 227–50.

Sinha, Mrinalini (1995), *Colonial Masculinity: The 'Manly Englishman' and the 'Effeminate Bengali' in the Late Nineteenth Century* (Manchester: Manchester University Press).

Som, Reba (1994), 'Jawaharlal Nehru and the Hindu Code: A Victory of Symbol over Substance?', *Modern Asian Studies* 28/1.

Thomas, Rosie (1989), 'Sanctity and Scandal: The Mythologization of Mother India', *Quarterly Review of Film and Video* 2/3, 11–30.

Todd, James (1920), *Annals and Antiquities of Rajasthan* (London: Humphrey Milford/Oxford University Press).

Turner, Graeme (1993), *National Fictions: Literature, Film and the Construction of the Australian Narrative* (London: Routledge).

Valck, Marijke de (2007), *Film Festivals: From European Geopolitics to Global Cinephilia* (Amsterdam: Amsterdam University Press).

Vasudevan, Ravi (ed.) (2000), *Making Meaning in Indian Cinema* (New Delhi: Oxford University Press).

Vasudevan, Ravi (2010), *The Melodramatic Public: Film Form and Spectatorship in Indian Cinema* (Ranikhet: Permanent Black).

Virdi, Jyotika (2003), *The Cinematic ImagiNation: Indian Popular Films and Social History* (Delhi: Permanent Black).

Viswanathan, Gauri (1998), *Masks of Conquest: Literary Study and British Rule in India* (New Delhi: Oxford University Press).

Wallerstein, Immanuel (2006), *World Systems Analysis, World Systems Analysis: An Introduction* (Durham, NC: Duke University Press).

Watts, Ian (1957), *The Rise of the Novel, Studies in Defoe, Richardson and Fielding* (Berkeley: University of California Press).

Weigand, Hermann (1960), *The Modern Ibsen: A Reconsideration* (Boston: E. P. Dutton).

Wood, Robin (1971), *The Apu Trilogy* (New York: Praeger).

Index

Note: 'n' indicates note.

Abbas, K. A.
  Dharti Ke Lal, 77, 88n
Acts
  The Conservation of Foreign Exchange and Prevention of Smuggling Activities Act, 1974 (COFEPOSA), 128
  Dowry Prohibition Act (1961), 82
  Hindu Adoption and Maintenance Act (1956), 82
  The Hindu Marriage Act (1955), 82
  Hindu Succession Act (1956), 82
Agashe, Mohan, 133–4
Alea, Tomas, 7
Alvi, Abrar
  Sahib Bibi Aur Ghulam, 27
Anandmath, 54
Anderson, Benedict, 3, 48
  acknowledge profound emotional legacy, 41
  Imagined Communities: Reflections on the Origin and Spread of Nationalism, 56n
  imagined political community, 41
  national community creation by, 4
  on non-Western nationalisms, 41
anglophile Indian, 75–6, 79, 82, 85–7
art cinema, 2, 10, 35, 107–8, 133–5
avant-garde filmmakers, 3

Bachchan, Amitabh, 15, 103n, 105–7, 120–1
  as Angry Young Man role in *Deewar, Saat Hindustani, Zanjeer* and *Sholay*, 15, 21n, 105–7, 120–1
Baer, William
  Classic American Films: Conversations with the Screenwriters, 156n

Bandopadhyay, Bibhutibhushan, 10–13, 60
  Pather Panchali novel, 61–3
Banerjea, Surendranath, 50, 54
  The Bengalee newspaper, 47
Banerjee, Sikata, 73
Barua, P. C.
  Devdas, 9, 72n
Benegal, Shyam
  Ankur, 107, 139n
  Junoon, 35, 125
Bengal Chemical Swadeshi Stores, 57n
Bengal cultural Renaissance, 23, 32, 36, 38n, 41, 44–9, 52, 55
Bengal School of Art, 42, 50, 57n, 81
Bergman, Ingmar, 2
  Wild Strawberries, 103n
Beynon, John
  Masculinities and Culture, 104n
Bhabha, Homi, 74
Bhadra, Gautam, 88n
bhadralok class, 7
Bhaduri, Jaya, 122n
Bhootayyana Maga Ayyu (Kannada film), 136
bildungsroman novel, 12, 22n
binary representation in Indian cinema, 37n
Birri, Fernando, 7
Biswas, Chhavi, 79
Bollywood/Hindi films, 13
  1942: A Love Story, 35
  of 1950s as symbols of postcoloniality, 76–7
  An Evening in Paris, 90
  Ankur, 135
  Aradhana, 90

Ardh Satya, 126
Aurat, 72n
Baazigar, 15
Bharat, 14
Bobby, 107
Deewar, 9, 15
Devdas, 15, 26, 35, 63
Ganga Jumna, 89, 108
Ghashiram Kotwal, 134
Hum Aapke Hain Koun ...!, 47
Humayun, 9
Hunterwali, 26
Insaaf Ka Tarazu, 15
Jaal, 15
Jewel Thief, 90
Johny Mera Naam, 128
Lagaan, 15
Love in Tokyo, 90
Mangal Pandey: The Rising, 35
Mughal-e-Azam, 9
Nayak, 90–3, 97, 99, 101, 104n, 111, 162
Purab aur Paschim, 128
Sholay, 2, 14
Teesri Manzil, 90
Upkaar, 90
Uri: The Surgical Strike, 14
Yaadon Ki Baraat, 128
Bordwell, David, 2
Bradman, Don, 95
Brecht, Bertolt, 137

Carroll, Noel, 15–16
Caxton, William
  printing press introduction in Britain by, 48
Cesaire, Aime, 5
Chahine, Youssef, 7
Chandragupta, Bansi, 154
charanamrita, 145
Chatterjee, Bankimchandra, 45, 47, 53–4, 58n
Chatterjee, Basu
  Sara Akash, 103n
Chatterjee, Partha, 42, 56–7n, 75
Chatterjee, Soumitra, 133, 137, 138n
Chopra-Gant, Mike
  Hollywood Genres and Post-War America: Masculinity, Family and Nation in Popular Movies and Film Noir, 22n
Choudhury, Indranath Roy, 85
  Kanchanjunga, 74–5, 77–82, 86, 94, 102, 105, 108–9, 112, 119
  representative of postcolonial class, 81
Clare, Norman, 154
colonial/coloniality/colonialism, 4–6, 9, 11, 16, 24–9, 32–6
  modernity, 16, 23, 30
committed judiciary, notion of, 107
Communist Party of India (Marxist), 108
Constitution of India
  Forty-second Amendment (1976), 139n
culture
  creation of national subject by, 4–6
  defined, 3
  functions of, 3
  made of art, 4

Dada Saheb Phalke Award, 18, 125
Dasgupta, Chidananda, 11
  The Cinema of Satyajit Ray, 21n
decoloniality, 4–5
decolonisation process in Asia and Africa, 74
Desai, Manmohan
  Amar Akbar Anthony, 126
  Naseeb, 126
Devi, Mahasweta
  Hazar Churashir Ma Seemabaddha, 103n
Dharmendra, 14–15
Dr Stockmann
  An Enemy of the People, 145–6
Dutt, Guru, 15
  Kaagaz ke Phool, 76–7
  Pyaasa, 60
Dutt, Gurusaday, 50
Dutt, Utpal, 149

Eugenio, Antonio, 7

Fanon, Frantz, 5, 74
Fellini, Federico, 133
Ferguson, Niall, 34
film festivals, 2

Flaherty, Robert
  Nanook of the North, 150
Fuller, C. J., 72n

Gandhi, Indira, 73, 113, 120, 122n, 125, 134–5, 141
  crushed railway strike in 1974, 107
  declared Emergency from 1975 to 1977, 106, 126, 132
  lost power in 1977 elections, 126
Gandhi, Rajiv
  played Muslim card in Shah Bano case, 156n
Ganguli, Sunil, 93
Garewal, Simi, 94
Gauguin, Paul, 63
Ghatak, Ritwik, 11, 78, 143
  Meghe Dhaka Tara, 77, 112
Ghosh, J., 43
Ghosh, Lalmohan, 43
Ghosh, Nemai
  Chinnamul, 88n
Ghosh, Robi, 93
Goethe
  Wilhelm Meister's Apprenticeship, 59
Gonds tribes, 134–5, 139n
Green Revolution, 89, 105, 122n
Guha, Ranajit, 88n
Guha-Thakurta, Tapati, 42
  Art and Visual Culture in India 1857–2007, 57n
Gupta, Ashok, 144–5, 153
Gupta, Bimal
  Kapurush, 74, 82–6

Hammett, Dashiell
  Red Harvest, 157n
Hartley, Sylvia, 13
Hasan, Zoya
  Congress after Indira: Policy, Power, Political Change, 156n
Hindu Code Bill, 82
Hindu nationalism, 58n, 136, 144
Hollywood cinema, 7
  Alice's Adventures in Wonderland, 137
  Anna Karenina, 59
  Dirty Harry, 106
  Pride and Prejudice, 59

The Seashell and the Clergyman (Germaine Dulac), 3
hybridity, 74, 87n

Indian National Congress, 43
Indian People's Theatre Association (IPTA), 77

jalsas, 27–8, 37n
James, C. L. R., 5
Jay, Martin and Ramaswamy, Sumathi
  Empires of Vision: Objects/Histories, 57n
journals/magazines/newspaper
  Janabarta, 145–6
  Sandesh, 130, 138n
  Sanjivani, 57n
  The Sentinel, 44–5
  Stardust, 103n

Kael, Pauline, 37n
  Aranyer Din Ratri, 13
Kalabhavan, 81
Kant, Immanuel, 34, 38n
Kapoor, Prithviraj, 76
Kapoor, Raj
  Awaara, 76–7
  Shree, 60
Kapur, Geeta, 13
  When was Modernism?, 11
Karanth, B. V.
  Chomana Dudi, 107, 133
Kemper, Steven, 48
Kennedy, Bobby, 95
Khan, Mehboob
  Aurat, 9
  Mother India, 6, 9, 72n, 106, 108
  Taqdeer, 35
Khanna, Rajesh, 90
Khan, Salman, 14
Khilnani, Sunil
  The Idea of India, 122n
Kipling, Rudyard, 164n
Kumaramangalam, Mohan, 107
Kumar, Uttam, 90
Kurosawa, Akira, 2

Landy, Marcia, 13
language problem in European film, 19n

Lear, Edward
　The Courtship of the Yonghy-Bonghy Bo (poem), 137

Macaulay's Education Minute Act of 1835, 43–5, 57n, 75
McCully, Bruce, 41–3
McCutchion, David, 154
McNeill, William, 34
Maitreya, Akshaya Kumar, 50
Marx, Karl, 34, 95
masculinity, 13–16, 56, 160
　colonial, 159, 161
　postcolonial, 73
Mastroianni, Marcello, 133
mimesis, 7, 20n
mimicry, 74, 87n
mindless escapism of Third World, 7
Mitra, Ashok, 125
Mitra, Krishan Kumar, 57n
Mitra, Narendranath, 110
modernity, 4, 10–11, 17, 23, 30–6
　in James Bond films, 90
　Nehruvian, 2, 12, 33–4
Modi, Sohrab
　Jailor, 63
Mukherjee, Madhabi, 111
Mukherjee, Prabhat Kumar, 31

Nandy, Ashis, 21n, 33–4, 38n, 54, 159–60, 164n
Narasimhan, Haripriya, 72n
Nargis, 21n
national cinema, 3–4
national identity, concept of, 3–4
nationalism, 48–9
　in cinema before 1947, 5
　as ideology, 43
　in India, 41–4
　Nehruvian, 89
nation, concept of, 3–4, 41
nationhood, notion of, 8, 42–3
Naxalism, 89, 98
Nehru, Jawaharlal, 73, 112, 155n
　concept of modern India, 8, 33
　foreign policy initiative, 8
　national morale during war of 1962, 6
　speech Tryst with destiny, 74

New Indian Cinema launched by Film Finance Corporation, 103n
Nihalani, Govind
　Aakrosh, 126, 134–5, 139n
Nillson, Leopoldo Torre, 7

O'Hanlon, Rosalind, 73

Patel, Sardar, 108
Patil, Smita, 134
Peries, Lester, 7, 79
Phalke era, 5
political hegemony, 42
political radicalism in cinema, 107
popular cinema in India, 14, 16, 27, 60
　depictions of writer, 60–1
　escapism of, 90
　and nation, 8–10
　postcolonial elite in, 75–7
　represent villages as national abstractions, 2
postcolonialism/postcoloniality, 4–5, 7, 15, 34, 73–4
Prasad, Madhava
　Ideology of the Hindi Film, 22n
pre-colonised world, 34
Premchand, Munshi, 10, 23, 26, 30, 36n
print capitalism, 42
Puri, Om, 133–4

Raghavendra, M. K., 35, 76–7
　50 Indian Film Classics, 21n
　Seduced by the Familiar: Narration and Meaning in Indian Popular Cinema, 21n, 38n, 71n, 88n, 103n, 122n
Rajadhyaksha, Ashish and Willemen, Paul
　Encyclopaedia of Indian Cinema, 103n
Ramaswamy, Sumathi
　Goddess and the Nation, 57n
Rathod, Kantilal
　Kanku, 103n
Ray, Acharya P. C., 57n
Ray, Harihar, 10
Ray, Satyajit, 36, 74–5, 77–8, 87, 141
　adaptations of literature, 10
　Agantuk, 142–3, 149–53, 163
　analysis of Bengal Renaissance and nation, 49, 73

Ray, Acharya P. C (*cont.*)
  Aparajito, 1, 6, 27, 63–6, 70, 127
  Apur Sansar, 6, 60, 66–9, 71, 160–1
  Apu Trilogy, 2–3, 6, 11, 13, 17, 21n, 59–61, 70–1, 88n
  Aranyer Din Ratri, 93–6, 100, 102, 111, 162
  Ashani Sanket, 136–7
  awarded Honorary Oscar for Lifetime Achievement and Bharat Ratna, 141
  Charulata, 5, 10, 41, 43–9, 54, 58n, 64, 71n, 83, 86, 142, 160, 162
  commitment towards liberal view, 2
  Devi, 30–3, 37n, 144, 154
  engagement with modernity, 2–3
  films focus on Naxalite uprising and refugee crisis of 1971, 126
  fraternity of artists in Nehru's India, 11
  Ganashatru, 143–7, 153
  Ghare Baire, 10, 17, 41, 44, 49–50, 52, 56, 58n, 71n, 136–7, 141, 160, 162–3
  Goopy Gyne Bagha Byne, 130–1, 137
  health deteriorates in 1984, 141
  Hirak Rajar Deshe, 130–3, 135–6, 163
  and India's literature, 12–13
  internationalism, 155
  Italian neo-realism, 8
  Jalsaghar, 10, 27–30, 71n, 152, 161
  Jana Aranya, 115–22, 144, 149, 152
  Joi Baba Felunath, 127–30, 136, 144, 155, 162
  Kanchenjungha, 77–9, 82, 85–6, 108–9, 112, 119, 152, 161–2
  locatedness, 73
  Mahanagar, 105, 109–15, 119, 121, 149, 152
  as a national filmmaker, 2, 6–8
  Pather Panchali, 1–3, 6–8, 10–12, 17, 20n, 27, 59, 61–3, 67, 69–71, 88n, 125, 152, 161
  political choices and compulsions, 136–8
  and popular cinema, 8–10
  portray of men and women, 16
  portray of sameness of rural Bengal, 19n
  Pratidwandi, 10, 105, 108, 113–15, 118–19, 121–2, 152
  product of postcolonial society, 5
  The River, 7
  Sadgati, 107, 126, 133–8, 139n, 163
  Seemabaddha, 86, 96–100, 103n, 113–14
  Shakha Proshakha, 47, 143, 147–9, 151, 153–4, 157n
  Shatranj Ke Khiladi, 10, 16, 23–8, 30, 32, 39n, 71n, 96, 125, 127, 129, 159–60
  Sonar Kella, 127–9, 137
  Teen Kanya, 142
  treatment of subject, 55
  views about Tagore, 142–3
  Western filmmaking practice adoption by, 5
  women in films of, 122
Ray, Sukumar, 6, 79, 81, 88n, 138n, 142
Ray, Suprabha, 142
Ray, Upendrakishore, 6, 50, 81, 88n, 130n, 138n
Renoir, Jean, 3
representative, 2, 11, 19n, 94, 159
revolutionary vernacularisation, 48–9
Robinson, Andrew, 79, 90, 110, 155n
  The Inner Eye: The Biography of a Master Film-Maker, 103n
Roy, Amitabh, 82–5
Roy, Anuradha, 54
Roy, Bimal, 63
Roy, Raja Ram Mohan, 44–5
  advocacy for sati abolition and widow remarriage, 30
  Brahmo Samaj, 30, 33, 43
Roy, Sir Baren, 86

Sadharon Brahmo Samaj, 54
Said, Edward, 32, 73, 87n
Sarkar, Bhaskar, 8
Sathyu, M. S.
  Garam Hawa, 107
Sen, Amartya, 7
  The Argumentative Indian: Writings on Indian History, Culture and Identity, 21n
Sengoopta, Chandak, 54
Sengupta, Aditi, 99
Sen, Keshabchandra, 45
Sen, Mrinal, 77, 121, 125–6
  Bhuvan Shome, 103n

Calcutta 71, 103n, 108
Ek Din Pratidin, 112
Interview, 36, 108, 137
Oka Oorie Katha, 139n
Padatik, 108
Seton, Marie, 130
  Portrait of a Director: Satyajit Ray, 38n
Shah, Naseeruddin, 35–6
Shakespeare, 10
Shantaram, V.
  Navrang, 60, 68–9
Shaw, George Bernard, 137
Sinha, Mrinalini, 73, 163n
Sinha, Suresh, 76
Solas, Humberto, 7
Spielberg, Steven
  Jaws, 156n
Sri Ramakrishna, 43, 164n
Srivasatava, Sanjay, 73
Strauss, Claude Levy, 4
subaltern studies, 78, 88n
Swadeshi movement, 6, 10, 42, 44, 49–55, 57n

Tagore, Abanindranath, 42, 57n
Tagore, Rabindranath, 42–3, 47, 52–3, 55, 79, 81, 142–3, 154–5, 155n
  idea of *atmashakti*, 50
  Nastanirh, 45
  Nationalism, 57n
  newsletters *(Bharati* and *Baalok)*, 56
  political dialogue with Bankim's nationalism idea, 58n
  Shapmochan, 83
  won Nobel Prize in Literature in 1913, 141
Tagore, Sharmila, 93–4, 96, 100–1, 111, 162
Tharoor, Shashi
  An Era of Darkness: The British Empire in India, 37n
Todd, James
  Annals and Antiquities of Rajasthan, 54
Tung, Mao Tse, 95
Turner, Graeme, 4

United Front government, 89

Varma, B. P., 76
Vasudevan, Ravi, 2, 7
  Making Meaning in Indian Cinema, 22n
Vidyasagar, Ishwarchandra, 45
Vishwabharati University, Santiniketan, 81, 142, 154
Viswanathan, Gauri
  Masks of Conquest: Literary Study and British Rule in India, 58n
Vivekananda, 43

Walker, Johnny, 76
Watts, Ian
  The Rise of the Novel, 72n
Western education, 33, 43–4, 63
Western liberalism, 44
Western naturalism, 50
Wieland, Christoph Martin
  Geschichte des Agathon, 59
World Revolution, 89

EU representative:
Easy Access System Europe
Mustamäe tee 50, 10621 Tallinn, Estonia
Gpsr.requests@easproject.com